DATE DUE

Social Influence and Social Change

European Monographs in Social Psychology

Series Editor HENRI TAJFEL

EUROPEAN MONOGRAPHS IN SOCIAL PSYCHOLOGY 10
Series editor: HENRI TAJFEL

Social Influence and Social Change

SERGE MOSCOVICI
École Pratique des Hautes Études
Paris, France

Translated by Carol Sherrard and Greta Heinz

1976

Published in cooperation with
EUROPEAN ASSOCIATION OF EXPERIMENTAL
SOCIAL PSYCHOLOGY
by
ACADEMIC PRESS *London, New York and San Francisco*

ACADEMIC PRESS INC. (LONDON) LTD.
24/28 Oval Road
London NW1

United States Edition published by
ACADEMIC PRESS INC.
111 Fifth Avenue
New York, New York 10003

Library of Congress Catalog Card Number: 75 19665

ISBN 0 12 508450 1

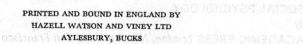

PRINTED AND BOUND IN ENGLAND BY
HAZELL WATSON AND VINEY LTD
AYLESBURY, BUCKS

Preface

A book is a result of the conjunction of many circumstances. This one is the outgrowth of a conference on the social influence of minorities, which met under the auspices of Dartmouth College (U.S.A.), at its Minary Center. The idea of holding that conference had been advanced by the Transnational Committee on Social Psychology of the Social Science Research Council, and sponsored by the National Science Foundation. The participants were: Jack Brehm (Duke University), Harold Kelley (U.C.L.A.), Charles Kiesler (Kansas State University), Helmuth Lamm (University of Mannheim), John Lanzetta (Dartmouth College), Robert Ziller (University of Florida), Ricardo Zuñiga (Catholic University, Santiago de Chile), and myself.

The beauty of the surroundings, the quality of the participants as well as the scientific level of the discussions which took place, all contributed to make the conference a most marvellous encounter for all of us. The warm reception and the sharp criticism I was then met with, encouraged me to pursue this work, which I had already set out beforehand. I feel particularly indebted to John Lanzetta—our perfect host on that occasion among so many others—for his kindness.

My collaboration with Claude Faucheux was crucial in starting the theoretical and experimental exploration of the phenomena exposed in this book. Later on, my work in co-operation with Mrs Elizabeth Lage, in Paris, and some exchanges of ideas with Charlan Nemeth (University of West Virginia)—who carried out independently some very interesting studies—led us to develop further the analysis of the social influence process.

But, so far, a book was not the portended outcome of all this. My intention was to write a very long chapter and to have it published separately. It was at the instigation of my friend and colleague Henri Tajfel that I gradually transformed the chapter into a book. If I bear the responsibility for the content of this book, Henri Tajfel is responsible for the form into which the content has been moulded.

Moreover, before shaping the matter, I benefited from the comments and constructive criticism of Hilde Himmelweit and by the incisive suggestions of Stanley Milgram, who were kind enough to devote their valuable time to reading and discussing the text with me. I also wish to acknowledge my intellectual and personal indebtedness to Leon Festinger whose early initiative and encouragement have been crucial in helping a small group of social psychologists in Europe to look afresh at old problems from their own perspectives.

Mrs Greta Heinz and Miss Carol Sherrard assumed the translation and gave the English version its definite shape. Let them find here the expression of my gratitude.

SERGE MOSCOVICI

Contents

**Part I   Consensus, control and conformity:
Social influence from the functionalist point of view**

Introduction

Some things seem to be so amazing to us that we are tempted to believe that they are completely outside the sphere of reason and that they work only by the intervention of supernatural powers. Among such phenomena, one that is very familiar to all of us, is the ease with which the ideas, language and behaviour of an individual or a group can be controlled; the readiness with which people will espouse, as though they were hypnotized, thoughts which were totally alien to them only yesterday. Phrases such as "the power of the press", "the tyranny of words", which express this idea, have become common sayings. They are the signposts of forces whose power seems to be beyond any one of us, a foreboding reminder of the ever-present threat of becoming, sooner or later, and against our will, the puppets of such forces. It is no less amazing when we realize that, in spite of the enormous pressure towards conformity in thought, taste and behaviour, individuals and groups are not only able to resist, but are even capable of generating new ways of perceiving, dressing, and living, new ideas in politics, philosophy, and art, and of inducing others to accept them. The struggle between the forces of conformity and the forces of innovation is a fascinating one, and one which, in many respects, is critical for the existence of each.

These forces can undoubtedly be explained by enumerating the economic, historical, and social circumstances which have given rise to and maintained them. But the fascination and amazement remain. Why? Because we feel certain that something more is involved, something other than the ordinary workings of human relationships.

In all of these phenomena, the type of human relationship involved is one of influence. Just as society is a machine that produces, consumes and distributes wealth and power, so, with its interest groups, churches and schools, society is a machine that creates, gathers and processes influence. To understand these relationships of influence is to have the privilege of understanding one very important aspect of the workings

of the social machine, and their psychology is very far from being eluci-
dated. The proposed contribution of this book is to place that psychology on a firmer foundation.

This will be done in two ways. Firstly, by adopting a new perspective.
The psychology of social influence has, until now, been based on a
psychology of conformity, of submission to the group and its norms. It
has been fashioned and considered from the point of view of the majority, authority, and social control. The time is ripe for a new orientation; an orientation towards a psychology of social influence which
will also be a psychology of innovation, of the possibilities of acting on,
and in relation to, the group; a psychology which will be thought out
and fashioned from the points of view of the minority, the deviant, and
of social change. Secondly, this reorientation can be considered as one
of those occasions which allow us to look again, with fresh and critical
eyes, at long established concepts, facts, and methods, and thereby to
renew the problems and solutions which we have been accustomed to
over several decades. In order to achieve this, I shall outline a new
framework or model of social behaviour, which will be more general
than previous ones. This may seem an ambitious, if not a peculiar
undertaking. Social psychologists are usually most reluctant to approach their problems in this way, or at this level. The reasons for this
reluctance are well known: it is feared that a speculative tendency will
become too strong, that abstract cogitations will fail to produce any
concrete research. This fear is not justified. In fact, social psychology is
greatly in need of a breath of fresh speculative air. This is today, as
always, a practical and urgent need. The proliferation of *ad hoc* experiments and concepts gives a thoroughly misleading impression of steady
development and enrichment of the field. The truth of the matter is
that there is a great deal of running on the spot, and much effort yielding diminishing returns in terms of scientific knowledge. Nothing more
need be said in defence of this enterprise.

For convenience in presentation and expression, I shall use the terms
"model" and "model substitution" in what follows. The nature and
role of models constitute a subject of continuing controversy in every
science. I shall not pay special attention to this issue here. In my view,
a model is at the same time a system of propositions and concepts, a
research programme, and a way of looking at reality. In substituting

one model for another, one is replacing systems of propositions and concepts, research programmes and ways of looking at the world. But at the same time one is replacing the realities looked at, just as much as the point of view which looks at them, or the point of view from which they are looked at.

The model which is now widely accepted, taught, and popularized by textbooks may be characterized as functionalist. Most social psychologists, irrespective of their psychological orientation, whether they are Gestaltists, behaviourists, Lewinians, or psychoanalytic, share this model. Its distinctive features are well known. Formal or informal social systems on the one hand, and environment on the other, are considered as given and predetermined with respect to the individual and the group. Social roles, statuses, and psychological resources are defined for each member before any interaction takes place at all, and behaviours are seen as merely translating and representing these roles, statuses and psychological resources. The function of behaviour on the part of the individual or group is to ensure adjustment to the system or the environment. Hence, since the conditions to which the individual or the group must adjust are given, reality is supposedly uniform, and the norms which are obeyed apply equally to everyone and appear as unequivocal. Therefore we have an almost absolute definition of what is deviant and what is normal. Deviance represents failure to adapt to the system, an interruption of its orderly progress, a lack of information or resources in relation to the environment. In consequence, normality represents a state of adaptation to the system, a neutrality towards the environment, and adequate coordination between the two. From this vantage point, the process of influence has as its object the reduction of deviance, the facilitation of a return to normal. Influence is a process of stabilization of the social system and its exchanges with the surrounding world. The implication is that the actions of those who go along with the norm are functional and adaptive for the group, while those who deviate from or go against the norm are seen as dysfunctional and maladaptive for the group. Thus conformity appears as a *sine qua non* of the social system and of human interaction with the environment. Social behaviours are rewarded in accord with this pressure towards conformity, the cornerstone of collective existence and of the overall adjustment to reality. There is a *necessary* relation between these behaviours and the bio-psychological characteristics of individuals. A person with a high need for social approval or low self-esteem, for example, would perforce submit to majority influence. On the other hand, a person with a low need for social approval, or high self-esteem, is led to exert this influence in the name of the majority. In general, all transactions, and all relationships, are evaluated in terms of whether or not they are conducive to consensus and equilibrium within the social system. Therefore nothing must change, or at least the only changes envisaged are those which make the system still more functional, more adaptive. Change in these circumstances must be directed by those who have resources or who are in positions of authority: leaders, majority, experts, etc. Their effectiveness is greatest when there is a high degree of social integration and control.

Such are, briefly stated, the broad features of the model in question. The *genetic* model, which I am proposing to put in its place, can also be described in a few words. The formal or informal social system and the environment are defined and produced by those who take part in them and confront them. Social roles, statuses and psychological resources are activated and given meaning only in and through social interaction. Hence, the behaviours of individuals and of groups have effect as behaviour *per se*, quite apart from the content and intention of the behaviour. Adaptation to the system and environment *by* individuals and groups is only the counterpart of adaptation *to* individuals and groups by the system and the environment. Therefore, since the circumstances in which adaptation occurs are contingent upon a variety of social and concrete situations, the norms which determine collective relationships are the outcome of past and present transactions between individuals and groups. They are not forced upon every individual or group in the same way, or to the same extent. Consequently, the normal and the deviant are defined relative to time, space, and individual situations. Deviance is not just an accident which happens to the social organization—it is also a product of that organization, the sign of an environment which is encroaching and evading control. If artists, the young, women, blacks, remain at the fringes of society, it is precisely because society defines itself in such a way as to keep them there, and this in turn determines the society's future direction. If talents remain unused, if the density of population is felt to be excessive, giving rise to contesting groups and counter-cultures, this is because the organization was not conceived in order to cater to all the needs which it creates, nor to deal with all the effects which it produces. Influence acts to modify this organization by being sensitive to the conditions of existence experienced by all, deviants included, and thereby in responding to their points of view, their conceptions, and their norms. Acts are functional or dysfunctional, adaptive or maladaptive, not because they conform to or oppose the norm, but because they allow the group to pursue its goals or transform itself according to the resources and values of its members. Innovation is as much an imperative of the social system and of a person's relation to the environment as is conformity. From this point of view, innovation is not to be seen as a form of deviance, non-conformity, or independence; it is to be seen for what it is: a fundamental process of social existence. The ordering and distribution of social rewards and positions are dynamic phenomena. They correspond to the evolution of this interaction, and depend as much on the forces of innovation and change as on those of conformity and control. Sinners or deviant minorities are not always punished, nor are the virtuous and law-abiding majority always rewarded, as everyone knows. The tension between those who must defend certain opinions, norms and values and those who must display certain social behaviours in order to *produce* certain effects, notably to change opinions, norms and values, is the result of contradictory pressures on which the *growth* of a group depends.

The relation between these behaviours and the bio-psychological characteristics of individuals is *arbitrary*. By this is meant that the mode of action in a situation in which one exerts influence takes on a form which is determined by the interests of the actor, his objectives, and the consensus he is seeking to obtain, and that this form of action is collectively standardized. The mode of action has no more relation to personality traits or psychological make-up than the meaning of a word has to its sound. It is of course possible that a person who is in a position to exert influence on a group happens to have a low need for social approval, or has high self-esteem. But a deviant person in the group cannot maintain his point of view or resist the pressures to which he is subjected unless he has a low need for social approval or has high self esteem, otherwise he could not assert himself. Conversely, in a group where there is a precarious balance of power, where there must be sensitivity to the contradictory demands of the members, a high need for social approval, or low self-esteem, can be conducive to a leadership position and to influence. The correspondence between bio-psychological characteristics and social roles and behaviours thus depends on the manner in which these roles and behaviours are acted out. When a deviant defines himself in relation to the group, he need not have the same qualities as a deviant who is against the group and who is also seeking to influence it.

To complete this outline, it should be added that interactions within the social system are evaluated in terms of whether or not they lead to stability and consensus. However, this stability and consensus are themselves only transitional states; stages in the process of change, of the creation of, and reduction of, divergences. The objectives that are sought, or that the group represent to themselves, are the product of transactions and controversies. The more widely these objectives are shared, the greater their hold on the group; interactions are more likely to be effective if they are geared towards an increasing recognition of existing differences, and towards a method of cooperation which takes account of these differences. If an existing social organization does not permit this, the need for and probability of its total overthrow must be envisaged as a healthy solution, a necessary outcome. Psychological theory, at least, must look at the situation in this way in order to grasp the total reality of it.

In order to highlight the differences between the functionalist and the genetic models, we could say that one views the social system and the environment as *givens*, while the other views them as *products*; one stresses the *dependence* of individuals on the group and their social *reaction* to it, while the other stresses the *interdependence* between individuals and the group and the social *interaction* in the group. Finally, for the one, the people and the group seek and tend to *adapt*, whereas for the other, their endeavour is to *grow*, that is, they seek and tend to develop the capacity to assimilate selectively and to create new ways of thinking and doing, to redefine and reconstitute their boundaries by combining old and new, internal and external, to modify the environment and expand the network of social relations, and to participate in the creation of new groups and subgroups.

It is legitimate at this point to ask what, apart from practical considerations, is the aim of replacing the functional model by a genetic model. The first aim is to stimulate a much needed discussion about the process of influence and the consequences it has for our conception of the group and of social relationships. It is my contention that influence is the central process of social psychology, upon which all the other processes depend. As such, it could serve as the principle which could integrate all the facts and all the theories of social psychologists. Without recognition of this, there can be no progress in theoretical and empirical knowledge. This will remain true at least as long as interaction is assumed to be the main concern of social psychology—something that has tended to be overlooked recently.

The second aim of replacing the functional with the genetic model is to make clear what stage we have reached. The first model had an undeniable usefulness in making social psychology possible. By virtue of its simplicity, and its agreement with actual experience and common sense, it gave social psychology the opportunity to extend the experimental method to a completely new field, to formulate a new set of questions, and to create its own terminology. Whatever its failures—naïveté, bias, imperfection—it allowed an irreversible movement to be launched towards the formation of an autonomous discipline amongst the sciences of behaviour by taking as its starting-point a conglomerate or largely established intuitions, assertions, and observations. To use a current expression: it was a first-stage rocket. Since then, the different areas—communication, attitude change, group decision, and so on—have tended to progress independently, each producing idiosyncratic concepts and techniques. Reciprocal borrowing has become less frequent, mutual enrichment more difficult. In addition, while theories relating to cognitive dissonance, attribution phenomena, psychological reactance, risky shift, polarization of group decision have brought about some change in our view of behaviour and social interaction, they have not had their full impact, it seems to me, because the frame of reference, the overall view of social behaviour and interaction, has remained relatively static. And yet, these theories conflict with the frame of reference at many points, prove its inadequacy, and render it somewhat obsolete. The search for a precise definition of the second model—the second-stage rocket—should help to consolidate social psychology, lead it to widen its scope, and to apprehend the less obvious and less ordinary aspects of social relations that are not so easily accessible, which means that they must be approached less conventionally, less commonsensically. In as much as the theories of the above-mentioned phenomena—cognitive dissonance, attribution, etc.—have actually modified our intellectual panorama, they must be a part of this renovation effort, which is, in fact, inconceivable without them.

Finally, I want to point out the main reasons which presently limit our understanding of psychosocial phenomena. Most social psychologists believe that these limitations stem from inadequacies in the psychological theories that support them. This is why some put forward explanations that are derived from reinforcement theory, while others advance explanations bordering on Gestalt or psychoanalytic theory. The only recognized disagreements and controversies appear to be on the order of the *psychological* mechanisms involved in behaviour and social relations, as if the definition and the content of these behaviours and relations were completely devoid of problems and called for no closer examination or criticism. But whatever we may do or think, we belong to a society at large, and with the changes in society we must look again and again at the definition and content of social behaviour and relations. What society is and how it works on different levels are important matters, and the answers we bring to these questions are as important as the answers each one of us gives to questions concerning our own mind and its mechanisms. There can be, and are, disagreements on these topics, in other words, on the *sociological* mechanisms that determine the daily life and the development of a group. We rarely touch upon or discuss such matters. What we would learn from such an inquiry, the answers we might discover, would certainly help us to remove the existing limitations on our understanding of psychosocial phenomena. It is at the societal level and viewpoint that the genetic model provides a new meaning to the existing notions and facts, introduces a critical perspective, and invites us to explore the reality concerning a broader spectrum of people, including the less privileged, the more invisible, those farther away from our usual life spaces. By providing a new point of departure for our understanding of social behaviour and increasing the range of social relations that we have to deal with, the researcher must swing the pendulum back from the individual to the social. Needless to say, the model is more intuitive and less rigorous than the functionalist model which has a long and venerable tradition and much spadework behind it. While this shortcoming may be a convenient alibi for sticking to the old path, it is not a sufficient reason for refusing the opportunity to find out where the new path will eventually lead.

Consensus, Control and Conformity:

Social influence from the functionalist point of view

> *To illustrate a principle you must exaggerate much and you must omit much*
>
> Walter Bagehot

Part One

Consensus, Control and Conformity:

Social influence from the functionalist point of view

1

Dependence and Social Control

To the best of my knowledge, most studies of social influence have concentrated on the reasons why people conform, and on the means successfully used to make them conform. There are two main questions motivating current thinking and research:

— Why and how does a group try to impose its view on an individual or subgroup?

— Why and how is an individual or a subgroup receptive to the views of a group or of those (leaders, experts, etc.) who represent it?

The following are the underlying assumptions that have been relied upon in answering these questions.

Proposition 1

Social influence in a group is unequally distributed and is exerted in a unilateral manner

The idea expressed in this proposition is clear enough, and appeals to common sense. Influence can occur when there is a *source* on one side and a *target* on the other. Using an analogy with the communication processes (Rommetweit, 1954) one might say that the source is a sender of norm information or influence, while the target is a receiver of norm information or influence. To this, an important qualification must be added: the exerting of influence, like the transmission of information, is an asymmetric affair. It proceeds from the source to the target of the interaction, but not in the reverse direction.

These concepts of source, target, and directionality will be found in all influence models. What differentiates the models are the rules followed in defining and combining these concepts. In the model I shall describe now—the functionalist model—the role of the influence source or sender and that of the influence target or receiver are strictly delimited and prescribed. Descriptions of the former are always in reference to the group, to its legitimate representatives (leaders, delegates, etc.) or to those persons who, in one way or another, possess power and resources (competence, for instance). Descriptions of the latter are limited to those individuals or subgroups that do not occupy any privileged position, who possess neither power nor resources, and who, for one reason or another, are inclined to deviate. With this attribution of roles as a starting-point, it follows that the *influence source is never seen as a potential target, nor the influence target as a potential source.*

As a consequence of this basic asymmetry, the majority point of view carries the prestige of truth and norm, and expresses the social system as a whole. Conversely, the minority point of view, or any opinion that reflects a different point of view, is branded as error or deviance. Hence the definition that every student is expected to know: "*Deviate* (noun). An individual who behaves in a manner other than that specified by the *group* or culture in which he is functioning. In research on communication and consensus in discussion groups, it refers to anyone whose views are distinctly different from the mode or majority" (Jones and Gerard, 1967, p. 711). The subtitle of a work by Freedman and Doob (1968) is equally revealing: *Deviancy: The Psychology of Being Different.* In this approach, the concepts of minority and difference are identified with the concepts of deviant and deviancy.

Why are individuals and subgroups viewed only as influence receivers? Essentially, because they are supposed to live in a closed social system. "Each social order", according to Asch, "confronts its members with a selected portion of physical and social data. The most decisive feature of this selectivity is that it presents conditions lacking in perceptual alternatives. There is no alternative to the language of one's group, to the kinship relations it practices, to the diet that nourishes it, to the art it supports. The field of the individual is, especially in a relatively closed society, in large measure circumscribed by what is included in the cultural setting" (1959, p. 380).

Everything is therefore concentrated around the pole of social relations where the determiners of the elements of this culture congregate. It is they who are entitled to decide what is true and good. Any diverging opinion, any different judgement, represents a deviation from what is real and true. This happens inevitably when the judgement emanates from the minority individual or subgroup.

It is clear, under these circumstances, that the group also emits information about where information is coming from. But it is equally clear that those members of the group who deviate have nothing of their own to emit, since they lack the means which would permit them to conceive of any valid alternatives. Hence the tacit conviction that the more common and less extreme opinions of the majority have a positive value, carry a greater psychological weight. Conversely, the less familiar and more extreme opinions of the minority, or of persons that have not been endowed with authority, have a negative value and a lesser psychological weight.

In ordinary language, as well as in experimental design, this is reflected in the assumption that an individual faced with the choice between two sets of opinions, one attributed to the majority or to a leader, and the other to a deviant or unspecified individual, will spontaneously opt for the former. In fact, there is no question of a genuine choice. As we observed earlier the point of view of the majority is the only full, normative choice; the minority point of view is simply not another point of view—it is a vacuum, a non-opinion, defined as nonmajority, anomic (and thus contrary to evidence, etc.). In other words, the relation is conceived as unidirectional: the group, the influence source, makes its own decision on the basis of the stimuli, code and judgements it has established; while the judgements, code and stimuli of the minority or of individuals, who are, of course, influence targets, are determined by the group.

Nor do matters rest there. Once this asymmetry has been posited one of the social partners is defined as active and open to change, the other as primarily passive and liable to change. Whatever is a right, or a positive act for the former becomes an obligation or a privation for the latter, and this complementarity in their roles precludes any possibility of real interaction. Locked into this situation, the minority individual or subgroup has only one escape route—deviance or independence—that is, withdrawal accompanied by the threat of isolation within and before the group. In such a context, conformist passivity acquires the positive connotation of being adaptive, whereas activity, innovation, private attitude, acquire the pejorative connotation of being maladaptive.

It is to be regretted that, along with this relatively sterile conformity, founded on submission and the suppression of genuine responses and attitudes, there has been no recognition of the existence of productive conformity, based on solidarity, the gratification of genuine responses and attitudes converging towards a common aim or framework. Essentially, it is regrettable that emphasis has been placed on passive acceptance of the group norm, rather than on active conformity to it. What is certain is that the underlying assumptions of this point of view could not have resulted in any other emphasis.

Independence, likewise, is seen above all as resistance to collective pressure, as a sort of active passivity, or obstinate refusal, rather than in terms of initiative or challenge to the attitudes and decisions of the group. According to a commonly accepted definition *"independence* reflects a lack of consistent movement towards or away from social expectancy" (Hollander, p. 423). Non-conformity, similarly, is seen as a protest, a withdrawal from the relationship, and not as an attitude which leads to the modification of this relationship: "Anti-conformity refers to consistent movement away from a social expectancy" (Hollander, p. 423).

This amounts to making a strict distinction between those who enforce conformity and those who give way to it; the former are able to wield the power of conformity against the latter. In fact, whether it is a matter of independence or of anti-conformity, a person defines the self with reference to the group and to social expectancy, and not with reference to one's expectations from the group or from society. This is the case, at least, according to the texts quoted from. They show that, apart from a few general observations, there has been little interest in the meaning of independence, in how independence is dealt with, or in how a person becomes independent. In other words, independence as a mode of self-assertion, and of collective or individual action, although present in many small group phenomena (sensitivity and training groups, for example) has been completely overlooked in this area of scientific research.

Some social psychologists have been aware of this. Asch, for instance, said that "we ought to treat with reserve the widespread assumption that there is a single form of social influence which is a prototype for all others . . . In particular, it is not justifiable to assume in advance that a theory of social influence should be a theory of submission to social pressures" (1956, p. 2). Some years ago, Kelley and Shapiro (1954) also emphasized that conformity may even constitute an obstacle to a group's adaptation to a changing reality; that non-conformers can be popular individuals who are liked by their peers, rather than seen as marginal or deviant. They deplored the neglect of independence in social psychology which, they felt, meant a disregard for the importance of independence in real life.

These and similar observations have had almost no impact. So it seems that, with due respect to some divergent opinions, the first proposition expresses a broad consensus. The following excerpt from a textbook summarizes the consensus very accurately: "Although there is mutual contingency, or independency, in all interaction, it is useful to distinguish between symmetric and asymmetric contingency. The latter may be analysed in terms of unilateral influence, of which imitation and compliance are examples; such influence is most readily accepted from persons who are liked and trusted, who are thought to 'have something' one wants, and who are thought to share one's norms and values that are immediately relevant" (Newcomb et al., 1964, p. 286). The lesson is well taken.

Proposition 2
The function of social influence is to maintain and reinforce social control

It is believed that "individuals can accomplish a concerted action or constitute a group only with the help of one form of social control or another" (Hare, 1965, p. 23). This assertion expresses an undeniable truth, if one keeps in mind the limits of its validity. The concept of group locomotion (Festinger, 1950), that is, the motion of a group towards an objective or goal defined and recognized as such by the group, clarifies the meaning of control in the field of social influence.

It must be postulated (and it is postulated by many authors) that in order for such a movement to take place, every person must have the same values, norms, and judgemental criteria; and that everyone accepts and refers to these. Moreover, the environment is assumed to be one and the same for everyone. In such a homogeneous context, it is easy to imagine that individuals and subgroups know what is expected of them, and that there are not several alternative interpretations of the meaning, the degree of truth or error attributed to their actions, perceptions, and judgements. Furthermore, when it comes to carrying out these goals, the existence of differences is viewed as an obstacle by members of the group: they tend to try and eliminate differences, to redraw the boundaries of the group so as to exclude those individuals who refuse to yield to change. But there can be no control without controllers. Since these controllers are expected to have superior wisdom and a noble unselfishness, it comes as no surprise that control is exerted to their advantage.

That influence which aims at inducing others to accept the point of view which is convenient for the controllers also has the greatest likelihood of succeeding. I have just paraphrased Secord and Backman; better yet, let them speak for themselves: "Normative controls arise in the area of behaviour in which members have become dependent upon the group for satisfaction of their needs. Attitudes and behaviours that are necessary to the satisfaction of the most powerful persons in the group are most likely to lead to norm formation" (1964, p. 351).

The so-called common norms are thus, inevitably, the norms of the majority or of authority. Consequently, any deviation from these norms implies two things about the individual. On the one hand, it implies resistance, a non-conformity which is threatening to group locomotion. On the other hand, it implies a deficiency: the individual does not know the proper response—he lacks the capacity to discover what the proper responses are. In both cases, deviation from the majority, the expert, the leader, for example, is symptomatic of inferiority, of marginality. It induces differential treatment of individuals within the group—in other words, it induces deviance.

Again and again, in hundreds of experiments, the individual who reacts is led to believe that he is in the wrong, that his behaviour is aberrant; he is made to feel anxious, and so on. It has also been demonstrated that such an individual has no claim to the esteem and affection of others; it was unthinkable that he might be chosen by them to take over any sort of function, regardless of his intelligence, the correctness of his opinions, or the effort made by him to understand his situation. Nothing could have been changed. "The statement by Hare", it has been said, "provides us with a set of abstract concepts based on small group research which does not allow for the negotiated and constructed character of interpersonal exchanges in daily life. In a laboratory setting we can easily lay down general and specific rules governing play in some game or simple task" (Cicourel, 1973, p. 15).

The moral of these rules is clear. If the demands of social control place legitimate authority at one pole, and the would-be deviant or dissenter at the other pole, they also determine the conditions for the ideal functioning of the group: reduction to a minimum of divergences between its members. In Festinger's theory, which I referred to above, the pressure towards uniformity in informal groups corresponds to the need to implement this ideal. The theory does not explicitly state that the pressure must inevitably be brought to bear on the minority individual or subgroup. It could just as well be brought to bear on the majority, or the person who exerts authority.

Nevertheless Festinger himself, his co-workers, and most social psychologists have understood and worked with the theory as though uniformity had to be established against the deviant. This orientation has affected authors who have attempted to demonstrate experimentally the existence of two kinds of social influence (Deutsch and Gerard, 1955; Thibaut and Strickland, 1956): the first, which is called "informational", or "task-centred", concerns the relation with the object. The second, called "normative" or "group-centred" influence, refers to the necessity of convergence towards identical opinions. This is determined by the relations between individuals, and not by the properties of the object. It is strengthened by cohesion of the group, and by other advantages attendant upon cohesion which serve to attract group members. Hence, cohesion and attraction operate to reduce any distance which may separate members of a group holding opposed viewpoints. They create an internal barrier to the tendency to move away from the group and be drawn into a different group, in seeking elsewhere the solution to one's problems and the satisfaction of one's needs.

It becomes clear that a whole set of concepts—group locomotion, cohesion, normative social influence, etc.—give concrete expression in various ways to the idea of external or internal group control over its members. These concepts, as is well known, have been studied extensively and in detail under a variety of experimental conditions. They also reveal what it is that constitutes the final goal, from this perspective, of influence processes: the reclamation of deviants. Their specific mechanism consists in making everybody alike, blurring the particularity and individuality of persons or subgroups. The further this process of identification and deindividuation is carried, the better each person's adaptation to others and to the environment.

How, for example, is group cohesion usually manipulated in experiments, or in real life? By telling naive subjects, or people, depending on what it is that you wish to manipulate, that on the basis of their intelligence, personality tests, votes, polls, etc., they are alike. The assumption behind this manipulation is familiar: cohesion or attraction of people is higher when they think of themselves as similar, and lower when they think of themselves as dissimilar. It is the compelling force of "we", the "group". The quantity of influence, in turn, is measured in most experiments by the movement towards group opinion of the deviant's opinion. It simultaneously reflects submission to others and loss of individuality.

The reverse movement has rarely been taken into account or investigated. Occasionally, *boomerang effects* have been recorded; they involve increased divergence between deviant and group. Curiously enough, these effects were never seriously interpreted as influence effects, nor subjected to any careful scrutiny. Why should one waste time on such incidental phenomena, after all, since they do not appear to relate to the essential features of sociability? It is hardly necessary to demonstrate here the extent to which these concepts have shaped the student's view of reality, his very concept of social psychology and its methods. In any case, it is clear to what extent the stress on non-differentiation, on cohesion, and on normative group pressure is a function of the interpretation of influence as a means of integrating the part into the whole, the individual into the collectivity.

Proposition 3

Dependence relations determine the direction and the amount of social influence exerted in a group

It is difficult to understand why social psychology has been so obsessed with dependence. The concept is neither clear nor self-evident. Moreover, where influence is operating, many attempts are made to change opinions and behaviour among equals. And this is not to mention the golden rule of advertising men and political propagandists which is to avoid anything which might give the impression that they represent powerful interests or might want to interfere with personal or group autonomy.

Nevertheless, the fact remains that dependence has achieved the status of a major independent variable in the study of influence processes. Or, one could say instead, it *explains* the effects of influence. Its action is postulated whenever a change of opinion or judgement is noticed. "Both congruence conformity and movement conformity", the student using Hollander's textbook is told, "involve an acceptance of influence which reveals dependence" (1967, p. 57). The French say "cherchez la femme"; social psychologists say "look for the dependence, and everything will be explained".

Let us take a closer look; details are always revealing. Two kinds of dependence are always considered: institutional and instrumental. The first kind changes influence into a facet of, and a means to, power. It may be individual (leadership, competence, etc.) or collective (majority, delegation, etc.). Power, or at least power status, is unequally distributed, and that faction of the group which has great power and status can do more than the rest of the group which does not.

It can actually be observed that, when one speaks of "minorities", one is not referring to their number (sometimes minorities are, from the demographic point of view, as important as the majority)—one is referring to the inequality of the distribution of power, to the logic of domination. The social hierarchy directly expresses this inequality. On the one hand, the assignment of "positions" (the clerk of the Middle Ages, the nineteenth-century senator, the secretary of the Communist party today, hold key positions) guarantees a certain authority over others who have not been given authority. On the other hand, the superiority conferred on the expert, the prince's counsellor, on whoever claims an area of knowledge in the division of labour, must in principle assure ascendance over others who lack such repute. It follows, in all cases, that those who are at the top of such a hierarchy have more influence than those at the bottom. At the same time, individuals or sub-groups with high status are subject to less influence than those with low status.

Several experimental observations demonstrate that subjects with high social status influence subjects with low social status (Harvey and Consalvi, 1960; Back and Davis, 1965). However, the work of Jones (1965) shows that the relationship between influence and social status is more complex: every individual, regardless of his status, submits to influence and tends to conform in order to gain the approval of others. Nevertheless, this conformist behaviour is not identical in individuals of opposite status.

Beyond all this, other factors, such as competence, assure the authority of the individual within the group and designate him as an agent of influence (Back and Davis, 1965; Hochbaum, 1954). Milgram's experiments on obedience (1956) are the most dramatic illustration of this aspect of reality. It is common knowledge that persons without the least monetary or moral incentive for carrying out instructions have been induced to obey the orders of an experimenter to inflict supposedly painful electric shocks upon people they did not know, and with whom they had no connection. The fact that they had been asked to do this by the experimenter, in the name of science, was apparently sufficient justification. Locked into the network of authority, represented in this case by the competence of the scientist, and overawed by the legitimacy of scientific research, one man blindly tortures another.

Other, less dramatic experiments have shown low-status individuals obeying high-status individuals, and incompetent individuals deferring to competent individuals. The convergence of these studies is so striking that they would have been more meaningful, it seems to me, if they had falsified, rather than confirmed, the maxim of politics and common sense—that might is right. In other words, the studies would have been more significant if, instead of setting out to show that the maxim was correct, they had concentrated on those circumstances—not so rare, after all—in which it does not apply. I am not making a value judgement, but trying to point out the existence of a bias.

Instrumental dependence has also been intensively investigated. Whereas institutional dependence shows the individual in the grip of the social system, this other form of dependence is more a matter of satisfying a certain "need for others". The questions raised here are practical ones: who submits to influence, and who resists it? In what situations is the need to adopt someone else's response intensified, and influence thus made easier? In short, we need to know who is conformist and who is independent; how one becomes a conformist, and how one stays independent.

It is always taken for granted that, in a group, persons who deviate are more inclined to change than persons who agree with each other and with the group norms (Festinger et al., 1952). The reasons for this tendency to change are related to the two sub-categories of dependence, which Jones and Gerard (1967) propose to distinguish:

Effect dependency—a subcategory of social dependency, in which one person relies on another for the direct satisfaction of needs. The other person is, then, in a position to provide gratifying needs (p. 711).

Information dependency—a subcategory of social dependency in which one person relies on another for information about the environment, its meaning, and the possibilities of action on it (p. 714).

(a) Effect dependence is observed in situations where deviants or other members of the group have personality problems. Need for affiliation, for social approval, for self-esteem, are the various guises in which the need for others is manifested. It seems to be closely interlinked with influence. Individuals who strongly experience these needs for affiliation, self-esteem and so on are more prone to conform than others who have less need. In a sense, they are less able to resist social pressure and are also prone to follow the majority and the leaders, hoping thereby to be accepted or even liked.

Empirical studies have confirmed expectations. Two studies in particular have brought out the fact that, the stronger an individual's need for approval, the greater his conformity (Moeller and Applezweig, 1951; Strickland and Crowne, 1962). Dittes (1959) in turn showed that subjects who were encouraged to believe that they were accepted by a group felt attracted to the group, and that, the weaker their self-esteem, the more likely they were to conform to group pressures. The role of anxiety has been shown in many other studies (Meunier and Rule, 1967; Smith and Richards, 1967; Millman, 1968). The importance of the need for affiliation has not been overlooked (Hardy, 1957).

In short, some individuals are destined to submission, others to independence, and others still to opposition (Linton and Graham, 1959; Smith, 1967; Hovland, Janis and Kelley, 1953; Abelson and Lesser, 1964; Back and Davis, 1965). Given this perspective, it is not surprising that attempts have been made to show the persistence of conformist behaviour in the same individuals when in different influence situations (Rosner, 1957; Back and Davis, 1965; Smith, 1967).

In a way, these experiments are redundant. They all tend to show that certain personality traits give rise to dependence or independence in accordance with a deeply-felt need—the need for others. In truth, and in spite of the large number of such studies, it cannot be claimed that the mechanism regulating this need is clearly understood; all that has been achieved so far is an inventory of the large variety of situations in which the mechanism comes into play.

(b) Informational dependence corresponds to the tendency of individuals to seek objective correctness in their judgements about phenomena, to seek validation of their judgements, and to seek adaptation to the environment in this manner. When they believe that they cannot achieve this by themselves, they are compelled to appeal to other individuals for judgement and validation of their own judgements. The unavoidable transition from individual to social adaptation, from direct dependence on the environment to dependence mediated by others opens the way to influence. The circumstances—and they are numerous—under which this social crutch becomes indispensable have also been studied experimentally. Among others, we could mention uncertainty about the reliability of one's senses, lack of confidence in one's abilities (Hochbaum, 1954; Di Vesta, 1959; Rosenberg, 1963), doubts about one's intelligence, lack of faith in one's own judgement (Allen and Levine, 1968). Degree of autonomy and heteronomy is in direct proportion to one's real or believed possession of these qualities.

From these studies have been derived robot-like portraits of the dependent personality who is willing to submit, and of the independent personality who refuses submission. "Conformers were said", Steiner writes "to be characterized by conventionality, conscientiousness, cooperativeness, patience, sincerity, and docile socialization. The self-ratings of such persons emphasized nurturance, affiliativeness, abasement, and denial of psychiatric symptoms. These interpretations are in close accord with the findings of Di Vesta and Cox who concluded that the conforming individual is restrained, cautious, submissive and oriented towards consideration of others. Vaughan found conformers to rank low on intelligence, assertiveness, neural reserves, extraversion, realism and theoretical value" (1960, p. 233).

At the opposite extreme are the characteristics which make individuals less liable to yield to influence: "Those individuals have a high degree of certainty of their own perception; they feel themselves more competent or powerful or of a higher status than others; they have one or more others in the group agreeing with them against the majority judgement; they find the others an unattractive source, possibly unlike themselves; and finally they see little to be gained by conformity in terms of any important personal goals" (Hollander, 1967, p. 558).

Obviously, these robot-portraits are not meant to be taken literally. The less dependent person has a "nicer" portrait than the more dependent person. This is not so much surprising as contradictory. If the conformist person is usually "weak", how does it come about that independent or deviant persons, who must be "strong", follow the majority, which is usually made up of conformists? The relationship between personality traits and conformity is far from being established. Situational factors are constantly at work (Goldberg and Rorer, 1966). At any rate it is doubtful whether the establishment of such a relationship would be of much interest. On the one hand, it would explain nothing—neither personality nor influence; it would reveal only co-variations of factors, not cause and effect relationships. On the other hand, if it did turn out that these various "needs" could explain any social phenomena, it would not be necessary to analyse further the phenomena from a psycho-sociological, or even sociological, viewpoint. It would be sufficient to know the basic personality types, and their distribution within a given group or within the society, in order to be able to predict events. If this were the case, differential psychology would advantageously replace social psychology.

However, these studies of "needs" establish nothing in social psychology, either in the domain of social influence, or in any other domain. I will therefore treat them here neither as proofs, nor as empirical studies, but as symptoms—symptoms of a belief according to which the pressure on deviants is always justified, because it answers to certain needs in them and is, to a certain extent, provoked by them. Deviants invite influence, just as others invite exploitation. The parallel is not accidental; what Bramel (1972) has written about the exploited applies equally well to deviants:

> The frequent observation, according to which exploitation is often associated with hostile attitudes towards the victims, could signify at first sight that weak and despised groups *attract* exploitation. This thesis could be supported with facts such as these: animals seem to attack and exploit the weakest members of their group; human groups reject and punish their deviant fellows just as much as animals do; the Nazis exploited and killed Jews because they considered them inferior, and dangerous; whites exploited black slaves because, to them (the whites), the blacks appeared as a savage and inferior race, fitted only for hard and painful work. Research in social psychology has recently provided an excellent body of evidence supporting a less obvious, but more interesting and more important explanation of the association between exploitation and hostility—which is that victims are despised *because they are victims*. In other words, contempt for victims is the result of their exploitation, and not the cause. Although this idea is not a new one, the social sciences have been astonishingly slow to take an interest in it (p. 220).

But, even to this day, social psychology has not begun to interest itself in the behaviour of deviants as the product of a group or system which obliges individuals or sub-groups to occupy an inferior or marginal social position. This idea would allow us, without too much difficulty, to describe the process of social influence in terms of the following patterns of compliance:

— compliance by individuals at the bottom of the status and power hierarchy towards persons at the top of the hierarchy;
— compliance by individuals who cannot autonomously adapt to their
environment towards individuals who are able to adapt autonomously;
— compliance by individuals whose psychological organization is oriented
in relation to others, and who are potentially deviant, towards individuals
who are not potentially deviant.

The chain reaction which leads one sub-group to submit to another can
be illustrated thus:

Increase in dependence→Increase in social or interpersonal pressure
                                              ↓
                         Increase in social control or uniformity
                                              ↓
                    Decrease in resistance, in tendency towards autonomy
                                              ↓
                              Increase in conformity

This diagram is self-explanatory: its meaning is immediately seen. How
are differences in hierarchy, personality, and psychological and intellectual capacities transformed into convergence of opinion and judgement?
The answer to this question is that the infusion of dependency into the
magic brew of human relations will miraculously transmute the base
metal of doubts, idiosyncrasies and disagreements into the gold of
certainties, similarities, and agreements. Of course, the secret of this
recipe consists in knowing where certainty and agreement are to be
found before the process begins. If all men are equal, some of them, like
the animals of Orwell's *Animal Farm,* are more so than others. Since the
decision was made, at some point, to concentrate on those who are more
equal, it is hardly surprising that dependence should have been the
catalyst chosen to aid the transmutations required by social influence.

2

The Pressures Towards Conformity

Proposition 4

States of uncertainty and the need to reduce uncertainty determine the forms taken by the influence processes

In his first studies on social influence, Sherif postulated that we generally live in an unstable, fluid environment. He went so far as to assert that this fluidity and instability are fundamental aspects of any stimulus in a social environment. Norms originate and change when individuals interact in these conditions of multiple alternatives, of many potential answers, and of ambiguity: "Under conditions lacking objective structure in some focal aspect", he states, "the individual becomes increasingly uncertain and suggestibility is increased. In other words, he is more prone to be influenced by the words, actions, or other communications of other individuals, groups, and mass media" (Sherif, 1969, p. 71). An increase in ambiguity or a blotting out of objective criteria results in a state of internal uncertainty in individuals. From that time on, they are ready to submit to the influence of others.

The following familiar propositions are formulated on the basis of this interpretation, and have been verified repeatedly:

(a) The less structured the stimulus, object or situation in relation to which influence is exerted, the greater the influence.

(b) Influence will be much greater when a complex social stimulus or a value judgement is at issue, than when a simple material stimulus or a factual judgement is involved.

But uncertainty may be aroused by an individual's internal state. We have just enumerated some of the possible causes of such a state: weak intellectual, sensory or characterological capacities. Other persons intervene with reference to the environment and mitigate these weaknesses.

Kelley and Thibaut have made the point well: "When the problem at issue requires opinions and judgements which cannot be validated by logic or empirical tests, people tend to seek support for their opinions through agreement with their associates. There appear to be at least two general types of relationship between the initiator and recipient of a suggestion that can function to determine the degree to which the recipient agrees with and accepts suggestion. In certain instances, the recipient may be viewed instrumentally as a "mediator of fact" by virtue of his perceived expertness, credibility and trustworthiness. In other instances, the recipient may be motivated to agree with the initiator without regard for his "correctness"; agreement may become an independent motive. The strength of this motive seems to depend partly on the strength of positive attachment to and affection for the initiator. Thus A can produce a change in B's opinion if he is liked by B or provides the means whereby B satisfies important motives. When the group member has a strong positive attachment to the group and its members, he will tend to the modal opinion expressed in the group" (1968, p. 743).

I will return to this statement later. For the moment I only want to draw attention to the fact that the intervention of a "mediator" between the individual and his environment is indispensable whenever the individual is incapable of coping with reality. But it should be remembered that in the case described by Sherif, the "third party" is the norm, while in the case described by Kelley and Thibaut, this "third party" is an individual, or the group, and so on. In the first case, influencing each other is tantamount to seeking a common outcome. In the second case, influencing someone means exploiting one's role—as expert, for example—in order to change the other's point of view or opinion. Nevertheless, whether this interaction is external or internal, it is not self-determined: it is determined by the relation to the object, and to the environment.

We can now add two further propositions to the two already put forward:

(c) The more uncertain a person is in his opinions and judgements, the greater his propensity to be influenced.

(d) The less certain a person is of his own sensory and intellectual capacities, the more willingly he accepts the influence of someone to whom he attributes greater sensory and intellectual capacities.

Attempts have been made to specify which of these effects can be ascribed to the uncertainty of the subject, and which to the ambiguity of the object, but the results are not conclusive.

There is no reason to challenge the soundness of these assertions. I would like to stress some of their corollaries that should, in my opinion, have received a greater share of attention:

(a) In a situation where both partners are certain of their judgements and opinions, there is no need for social influence, nor is there any way in which it can come into play, since there is no uncertainty to be reduced.

(b) Whenever a group, subgroup, or individual is certain about something, influence cannot be used to bring about changes in their opinions or judgements.

(c) When the stimulus is unambiguous, or when one can refer to an objective criterion, there can be no influence, since consensus validation and interaction take priority. "Under clear-cut and circumscribed conditions", Sherif concedes, "the opinions of a majority or a prestige source that contradicts our assessment of the conditions will be relatively ineffective in influencing our behaviour" (1969, p. 70).

The individual who has the environment on his side, if he is well adapted to it and responding correctly to it, is capable of resisting social pressures and of escaping the discomfort of interaction with others. When the environment is not on his side, and he is not adapted, and responds incorrectly to it, the individual yields to social pressures and cannot escape the discomfort of interaction. In brief, when one is in tune with nature one does not need society; when one is not in tune with nature, then one needs society. This is how the interplay is visualized in terms of relations with that part of the material world which is considered essential.

The notion of uncertainty thus plays in this theoretical model the same type of role as the anthropologist's key concept, promiscuity, or the economist's favourite, scarcity, in being a precondition for, and prime mover of, society. As is well known, anthropologists explain the emergence of social organization by the need to formulate rules (the prohibition of incest, for example) in order to avoid the fights and disorders which exist among animals in the natural state. In the same way, economists see in the behaviour and regulation of the market a sort of necessity imposed by the scarcity and uneven distribution of resources in nature. Similarly, to the social psychologist, certainty is a resource which is difficult to obtain, and it is in order to obtain it that a person comes to associate with, or submit to, others.

The presence or absence of this certainty brings out the contrast between the different forms of influence. If the individual, or subgroup, is uncertain, then the support of a "mediator of fact" is sought. This is justified influence. However, if he is *not* uncertain, and still conforms, other motives—subjective ones—are involved: the desire for group acceptance, the power of authority, and so on.

This type of analysis has been the motivation for the previously mentioned distinctions which have been made between informational and normative social influence, and between task-centred and group-centred conformity. "The distinction" writes Cohen (1964, p. 106), "an important one, is thus between need for status and need for information. Social influence may be accepted either to the degree that it evokes the desire of the individual to maintain his status vis-à-vis others or to the degree that it involves his dependence upon others for information about himself and the world around him. The first set of motives for acceding to the group we may call 'normative' or 'motivational' determinants: the second set are 'informational' or 'uncertainty' determinants. In the normative situation, the person's self-picture is reflected against the rewards and punishment he may gain from them. In the informational situation, the person accepts others as sources of influence because he uses them as stable sources of information for evaluating the world around him." In one case, then, the development and form of social influence correspond to the need of the individual; he submits because of his dependence. If the individual submits because of his dependence, it follows that if the individual had no need of the group, no group could have any hold over him.

This may be the appropriate place to express my bewilderment. What we have been told about the difference between physical reality and reality based on social consensus is entirely convincing, and has been repeatedly verified. But the very fact that conviction was so spontaneous, and verification so easy, should have made us *more* sceptical, and alerted our critical sense. Why should a person who is in no position to make an accurate judgement, for lack of adequate measuring instruments, assume that other persons sharing his predicament would be better

placed than he to make an accurate judgement? When there is no
certainty about physical or objective reality for any particular individual, there can be none for anyone. If there is no clock to tell the time,
or no hammer to test the hardness of a substance, then one individual
attempting to tell time by the position of the sun, or to gauge hardness
by touch or sight, will be no more and no less accurate than anyone else
using the same methods. The concept of ambiguity calls for similar
remarks. If individuals perceive a stimulus as ambiguous, lacking in
objectivity, as Sherif puts it, and if furthermore they know that this is
the case, then diversity of judgement is permissible and normal. One
can really see no reason why they should rush into agreement, nor how
such an agreement could reassure them of the validity of their opinions
and judgements. The arbitrary nature of the results of their exchanges
must be perfectly obvious to them. At best, they might feel relieved not
to be alone in making a mistake. But they have no reason at all to feel
sure that, together, they are right, or that the others are right. This is
all that need be said on this subject for the moment; we shall return to
it later.

To return to the question of uncertainty; it turns out that reduction
of uncertainty determines the boundary between real conformity and
mere compliance. There is no necessary relation between our conviction
about the degree of truth in the group's opinion, and our going along
with the group, if we are compelled to go along with the group or are
attracted by the desire to belong to it. We can perfectly well think one
thing, and say another, if we see an advantage in doing so, or if we wish
to obtain the approbation of our peers, or if we see some other good
reason for doing so. Conversely, when we do believe what we are told,
we accept the group's judgement only because our own is uncertain, or
difficult to verify, or for some such reason. In the first case, we are
dealing with compliance. In the second case, we are dealing with real
conformity. At least, that is how the theory goes.

One of the most commonly held interpretations of Asch's experiments
fits in with this line of thought. Take, for example, an individual who
is comparing a standard line with three other lines. Internal doubt is
not possible; external ambiguity is practically non-existent. Certainty
is thus complete. On the other hand, the judgements of the other individuals participating in this experiment are undeniably wrong. The
naive subject, our typical individual, has a clear choice. If he says what
he sees, and what he knows to be true, he is in agreement with himself

and with reality. On the other hand he risks the displeasure of the majority, who expect him to agree with them. Truth, often, is not the right thing to say or to hear; there is the possibility that the majority will feel ill-disposed towards one, or even hostile. In avoiding this risk, he gives an answer which is wrong, but which seems appropriate. The conformist thus resolves his dilemma by giving a public opinion which is contrary to his private one; and he remains convinced of the truth of his private opinion.

Neither this, nor other interpretations have been subjected to careful verification. This is particularly interesting, since the interpretation is a deduction from a proposition which precludes the possibility of change when there is no uncertainty. Since change was nevertheless observed, to everyone's surprise, when it should not have taken place, the only way out was to ascribe it to external circumstances and consider it as purely superficial compliance.

Let us recapitulate some relevant questions and answers:

— Why are people uncertain?
— Because the stimulus is ambiguous, or because people lack information, self-confidence, etc.
— What justifies the existence of social influence?
— The reduction of uncertainty in the internal state of the subject, or in the external state of the object.

There is one notable exception to all this. It is provided by Asch's work. He has not attributed any great importance to these states of certainty or uncertainty. He has not attempted to demonstrate either that uncertainty makes people susceptible to influence, or that, if people conform to the group, they have to pay the price of uncertainty in their own beliefs and judgements. Nevertheless, whenever his research has been related to the general trend (Deutsch and Gerard, 1955; Jackson and Saltzenstein, 1958), its exceptional character has been ignored.

We have already seen a few of the things which the above questions and answers have led to. I have not yet referred to the three underlying assumptions:

(a) Uncertainty is located only in the target, never in the source.

(b) Uncertainty is perceived as a *given* rather than as a *result* of social interaction; it originates in the organism or in the setting, but never in the group.

(c) Influence is motivated by *pre*-social or *non*-social* factors: it satisfies an individual's need by reducing uncertainty, and allows the individual to adapt to the environment, but nothing more.

On the whole, it would seem as if social conditions were leading individuals to conform. When they do conform, the intervention of the social system is limited to re-establishing the psychological equilibrium of individuals, and their transactions with the external world. In every other case, conformity is undesirable and in any case purely hypocritical, a matter of rendering unto Caesar that which is Caesar's. Unhappily, this cannot be done with impunity. One may begin by complying out of politeness, and end up by making emotional and intellectual compromises which are very real and far-reaching. As Diderot expressed it "men in the end believe the opinions that they are forced to express publicly". In the last analysis, it becomes difficult to differentiate between compliance and genuine conformity. But that is another story.

Proposition 5

The consensus aimed at by influence exchange is based on the norm of objectivity

This is probably not a very explicit assumption, but it is always involved in the analysis of social interactions, if only because of its consequences. First of all, it reflects the idea of social consensus as adaptation to the external world. No group, no society, no action can be conceived without the existence of an agreement, a contract between the participating individuals (Asch, 1952; Festinger, 1950). Rules of conduct, market prices, prohibitions, scientific methods, standards of judgement, all these are instances of such consensus in their own way. They intervene in human interactions both as preconditions and as goals.

Why are they pursued, and how does the pursuit of them influence exchange? The following quotation puts the answer to this question in the proper perspective: "A basic human requirement appears to be the need for validation of one's opinions. Although clear information from the physical environment contributes to satisfaction of this need, the behaviour of other persons also provides a source of validation. Par-

---

* "One of the major determinants of uncertainty, and this of the acceptance of informational social influence, is therefore the amount of ability a person feels he has for making the requisite judgement. Ability, then, may be one of the major bases for making direct social comparisons: in order to reduce uncertainty, a person feels a need to supplement his own ability" (Cohen 1964, p. 113).

ticularly in situations where he is uncertain or confused—where he does not know how to react—a person can turn to the behaviour of other persons to observe a stable world. This social reality provides him with a reference point for his own behaviour. The more ambiguous the non-social stimulus situation, the more likely he is to depend on social reality for orientation" (Secord and Backman 1964, p. 331).

Here the familiar dichotomy between society and environment is clearly expressed. Between the lines, one can read the sharp opposition between relations with objects and relations with other people. The individual is at the core of this opposition: on the one hand, he tries to make a correct judgement and to evaluate his capacities for doing so. On the other hand, the reality that he has to judge, and to which he has to adapt, is given to him. Reality perceived in this manner corresponds to physical reality. It is a *solipsistic reality* as well, since the subject has no need of anyone else in order to determine its dimensions and to identify it. All that one needs to do in order to determine the colour of a fabric, the hardness of a table, the time of the day, is to look at the fabric, strike the table, glance at a clock—and these are things which every person can do alone.

But in other circumstances, either because we are dealing with opinions which it is impossible to validate or with objects some charac-teristics of which are not stable, we are not capable of making an immediate judgement. It is then that an appeal to others becomes necessary to help us in our judgements. The view of "reality" which we achieve in this way can thus be characterized as conventional or com-municative. It is, of course, social, both because it is a group product and because it is accepted by the individual only on condition that it is accepted by others. Ascertaining the degree of democracy in a country, the beauty of a painting, or the time of day, in a traditional society, presupposes a collective consultation and agreement among the mem-bers of the group on the basis of the different observations they could make in order to support their opinions.

Men are thus presumed to live in two different kinds of reality; to have a split and heterogeneous existence corresponding to the split and heterogeneity between individual and society. This distinction reflects the structure of objects, and the disposition of the environment. It de-fines the external forces compelling the individual to make transactions and to reach consensus with others.

Are there any internal forces acting in the same direction? They would be derived from the attitude of the "judge" towards his own capacities. Festinger has interpreted as a fundamental need the urge to evaluate one's own capacities correctly; this represents an individual, not a social, need. If the individual is certain of his own capacities, he does not feel compelled to take the judgement or opinions of others into account. Conversely, when he lacks this certainty, he is obliged to compare himself with another person close to or similar to himself. The theory of social comparison that I have just briefly presented is intended to explain why we are inclined to stay in a group or move towards it, and to affiliate ourselves with others.

I am not disputing the reasonableness of the distinction between physical and social reality, nor that of the theory of social comparison. My only purpose is to show that they are meaningful only on the assumption that behaviour in society is guided by the norm of objectivity. The hierarchy and difference between these two realities, the former externally given, the latter socially produced, hinges on the fact that the former is supposedly more objective than the latter. Consensus, group agreement, are substitute mechanisms on which one must rely more heavily if objectivity becomes more elusive. It is not claimed that men with different experiences and different degrees of knowledge seek a common truth, try to discover an unknown aspect of reality or to solve a problem and reach a solution by previously agreed methods. It *is* said that where no objective truth immediately presents itself, men have no alternative but to seek a conventional truth which might serve as a substitute.

This simultaneously elucidates the concept of dependence. To put it briefly, dependence is coextensive with social relations, and social relations generate dependence. Indeed, as we have seen repeatedly, according to this model convergence or exchange between individuals is necessary only when there is no objective reality; when the circumstances are such that objective reality cannot be directly determined. Independence, on the other hand, is correlated with a proper grasp of reality, the possibility of immediately determining its essential features, and the certainty that one's personal capacities are adequate.

The opposition between relations with objects and relations with other people merely reflects the contrast between a relation in which the individual is self-sufficient, finding enough strength within himself to resist social pressure, and a relation in which he is forced to compare himself with others and to submit to influence by taking into account

the diversity of points of view. As a result, in most experiments on conformity, it is believed that autonomy is being reinforced when the
subject is asked to make an accurate statement and to say what he sees;
whereas social pressure is defined and manipulated as though it represented an obstacle to accuracy and a source of error. To accede to
the group, to expect to reach a consensus with it, amounts to becoming
dependent on it and giving up the independence guaranteed by the
physical world. It is significant, in this respect, that Milgram (1965)
felt obliged to devise an experiment showing that the group may, sometimes, be a factor of independence and of social refusal. Had the opposite
conception, namely, that all group interaction necessarily leads to dependence, not been so generally accepted, such an experiment could
hardly have been imagined necessary, let alone published.

 This fragmentation into a social and a non-social realm, with realities
and relations corresponding to each of them, this division into a realm
where consensus and the influence by means of which it is achieved are
indispensable, and a realm where they are superfluous, reflects, roughly
speaking, the absence or the presence of objectivity: objectivity therefore is the prior consideration in this conception. But consensus itself is
viewed as subject to the norm of objectivity, as is evidenced in studies
where the process of social influence is directly related to the degree of
structure in the stimulus. If individuals conform, it is not because they
cannot tolerate ambiguity, but largely because they think that diversity
is inconceivable, and that there must be a single response which corresponds to objective reality. If they did not think so, what motive could
they have for adopting an opinion different from their own? In an
experiment by Sperling (1946), subjects were told that the autokinetic
phenomenon was an optical illusion, so that they felt justified in emitting
subjective judgements. No convergence occurred, and thus no influence.
Something similar could be asserted in regard to Asch's experiments.
By stressing the required accuracy of responses and the objectivity of
the stimuli, one in a way compels the subject to submit to the group
rather than to resist it, since there cannot exist a private reality for a
physical or geometric object. "Under certain conditions" Asch writes,
"such as those prevailing in most of the situations described in this
chapter, the trend to reach agreement with the group is a *dynamic
requirement* of the situation. It is based first on a clear and reasonable
view of the conditions: each assumes that he sees what others see. On
these grounds he expects to come nearer to the group. This striving, far

from having its origin in blindly imitative tendencies, is the product of objective requirements" (1952, p. 484).

We can now better understand why an individual faced with a structured stimulus and other individuals who diverge from him, or who are no better placed than he to formulate an accurate judgement, disbelieves his own eyes in the first place, and tends to move towards the others, adopting their responses in part or in whole, instead of holding to his own position and trusting his own judgement. Since physical phenomena are involved, and it is a matter of measuring, multiple or complementary responses are precluded, and agreement can take place only around a single response. It is highly unlikely that agreement will take place around his own response, since the others are already wholly or partly in agreement; whence the tendency of some individuals to yield. The dynamic requirement of the situation to which Asch refers is precisely this consensus; however, this is a special sort of consensus; specifically, a consensus about what is true or false.

The norm of objectivity came to play an important role in the theoretical and experimental work on social influence. It is culturally meaningful, and has become an integral part of behaviour and of the principles defining inter-personal and inter-group relations. It has even been reified into an intrinsic dimension of social relations and behaviour, making it thereby appear as

(a) a quasi-biological need, that of evaluation, and

(b) as a quasi-physical property of the environment, through the opposition between a structured and an ambiguous environment (the former being more objective than the latter).

The outlook has thus been restricted, first of all, by disregarding what happens in the case of multiple judgements and view-points, all of which are equally accurate and plausible. Such a plurality is theoretically inconceivable, as long as one is convinced that objectivity implies a unique judgement. Secondly, the outlook has been restricted by retaining the view that social influence cannot be exerted with respect to "preference" judgements but only with respect to "attributional" judgements.

"Such personal preferences", writes Crutchfield, "being most isolated from the relevance of group standards, thus seem to be most immune to group pressures" (1955). Without any clear experimental verification, most explanations that have been given are based on the idea that attributional judgements have an objective foundation which is missing in preference judgements. While differences between individuals are intolerable when they relate to a physical attribute, they are perfectly acceptable in matters of preference, for "there's no accounting for taste". This is an indirect way of admitting that the latter could still be sources of conflict, but that conflict is avoided by social agreement. It might be added that we do, in fact, argue more about tastes and colours than about moving points and matching lines.

Finally, with few exceptions (Kelley and Shapiro, 1954), social psychologists have adopted the point of view that truth is more likely to be apprehended by the group or the individual with the necessary social and material resources to grasp it. Little attention has been given to conditions where the truth is not immediately apparent, or where it seems to be an error or an aberration (a fate that seems to have befallen most great scientific theories and discoveries).

The influence process has, thus, been conceived in association with the norm of objectivity. Since this is not the only norm regulating social exchanges, this seems to me to reflect a certain choice, a particular way of defining these exchanges. At a deeper level, this choice implies that relations with others are subordinated to relations with objects. It implies also that the latter are granted the decisive, active role, leaving a derivative or reactive role to the former as far as individual development and behaviour are concerned. Leaving it a ridiculously small role, in fact, since such an analysis means that the group or society plays a role only in cases of incompleteness or powerlessness. The proper, complete, and well-adapted human being stands on his own two feet and has no need of others.

But this theoretical choice is neither novel nor surprising. It reflects, as was noted above, the adoption by social psychology of the theory according to which men have produced rules and social relations in order to fill the gaps left by nature, and the epistemological theory according to which objective truth is the handiwork of groups. It was, and sometimes still is, believed that an individual acquires information through his senses, has direct access to the data, and that from these data he draws objective conclusions which, in fact, force themselves upon him. The situation has changed somewhat in the last twenty years. Genetic epistemology, on the one hand, has taught us that data are created by intellectual operations and the action of the perceiver; therefore the data are not unequivocal. In this sense Piaget speaks of "the myth of the given". The history of science, on the other hand, has arrived at the conclusion that whatever is considered to be true, real, and objective is a function of the paradigm (Kuhn, 1962) or of the discipline system of groups of scientists and research workers. This means that objectivity is as much an individual as a social product, and that no reality can be physical without being, to a large extent, social. The evidence of our senses thus becomes the evidence of our culture. Moreover, ethology has demonstrated that the social element is part and parcel of what is individual and biological. Society exists not only to fill a gap, to substitute for the state of nature, but to complement it. There is, therefore, no need to oppose individual to society, nor to think that there are areas of life where social influence is impossible or ineffective. Social influence does not entail an opposition between individual and society, and if this process is associated with the norm of objectivity, it is not thereby excluded from association with other norms which may determine the consensus between individuals and groups.

I do not want to become too metaphysical, so I will not insist further on this far-reaching problem. However, I shall return to it later in order to provide a scientific and empirical underpinning for this discussion.

Proposition 6

All influence processes are seen from the vantage point of conformity, and conformity alone is believed to underlie the essential features of these processes

This is what I would call the conformity bias in thinking about social influence and, more generally, in social psychology as a whole (Moscovici and Faucheux, 1972). I may seem to be seriously over-stating the case. It would be more polite, and perhaps even more effective, to under-state it. I would not deny that there has been a certain difference of opinion in this respect. But, on the whole, I am convinced that this proposition is true, and that it corresponds to the way in which people, whether they are scientists or not, see the influence processes.

There is little room for doubt if we carefully analyse the work which has been done in this area. It presumes that any sort of social influence leads to conformity, and that conformity is the only interaction phenomenon related to influence. When this identification is taken as a starting-point, it is not surprising that any movement must be seen as proceeding

away from the individual and towards the group, and that the changes
to be expected are changes in opinion on the part of the individual.
As Kiesler (1969) expresses it, after a survey of the specialized literature:
"When we study conformity" (and he uses this term to summarize
everything relating to social influence) "we study change towards the
group, i.e. movement in belief and behaviour that makes them more
like those of other group members" (p. 3), and he states that influence
manifests itself by "a change in behaviour or belief towards the group as
a result of real or imagined group pressure" (p. 2).

Starting out with this perspective, the research in this field has limited
itself exclusively to the exploration of:

(a) the nature of the individual and social factors determining an
individual's submission to the group

(b) the role of conformity pressures in the individual or collective
psychological equilibrium

(c) the internal conditions—anxiety, need for affiliation, etc.—
which make an individual dependent (rather than those which make
him independent)

(d) the external conditions—stimulus ambiguity, hierarchy, etc.—
which make an individual more (rather than less) susceptible to influence.

This research programme takes the functionalist model as its starting-
point, together with a few added axioms, namely:

(a) Consensus with the group and its representatives is under all
circumstances not only necessary but also preferable to isolation.

(b) Conformity is favourable to social and individual development.
Deviance is harmful, dangerous, and detrimental to this development.

(c) Successful socialization and learning lead to conformity, whereas
deviance is symptomatic of failure—a sign that rewards and punishments have not been correctly administered: 'These and similar findings" writes McGinnies, "taken together suggest that the relatively high
incidence of various kinds of non-conformity, which ordinarily should
produce aversive reactions from others, is attributable to the irregularity
with which such behavior is actually punished. For example, the reinforcements for criminal behavior (money, property, revenge) are
generally prompt and continuous, whereas the negative sanctions (fines,
imprisonment) are invoked only at some later time, if at all" (1970,
p. 104).

(d) exchanges between group and individual are mediated by conformity: "In general, conformity is viewed as the 'good' or commodity and social approval as the reinforcer or medium of exchange. The purpose of this is to demonstrate that social approval and conformity are exchanged in a manner analogous to the exchange of economic goods" (Nord, 1969, p. 183).

The conformity bias has not only determined the research programme. It has also affected the way in which the actions of individuals and innovation have been treated, in the rare cases in which they have been studied. Jones (1965) wondered, for instance, how a person with little power might modify the attitude of a person with more power. The only strategy that came to mind was that of ingratiation. The person occupying a rather unfavourable social position must, in order to counterbalance the asymmetry of the relation, resort to compliments and flattery, trying to present himself in the most favourable light to the more powerful person. As the dependent individual becomes more alluring, the powerful individual may become more inclined to bestow favours on him, rather than take them away. As can be seen, a kind of conformity is made use of in order to allow for the possibility of reciprocal influence, permitting the modification of existing relations, opinions and behaviours. We know that there are other ways: it is significant that nobody has taken them into account.

The study of innovation was undertaken in the same frame of mind. It must be remembered that, in certain sociological theories, particularly functionalist and utilitarian theories, innovation is viewed as a type of deviance, and innovators are considered as a sub-category of the general category of deviants. If innovation is defined in this way, and if innovators are placed under this heading, it is not surprising that investigations have concentrated on the following problem: in what conditions will it be possible for a minority to be deviant or nonconformist without being ejected from the group, or subjected to group sanctions? This amounts to asking who is entitled to deviate, and to assert his deviance, in a given society. The answer is self-evident: those who already have power.

Hollander (1958) has presented this conception in more detail than Kelley and Shapiro (1954), Ziller and Behringer (1960), or Harvey and Consalvi (1960). He proposed the hypothesis that each individual in a group has a certain "idiosyncrasy credit", representing an accumulation of favourable disposition on the part of others towards him. The greater his credit, the greater will be the confidence placed in him by his fellows, and the more favourable will be his position for deviating, for acting without taking majority opinion into account. Hollander has proved in several experiments that the individual with a large stock of credit of this sort, acquired either through his competence or by his adherence to group goals, can take the opportunity of acting in a non-conformist way, and still have influence.

The results of these experiments, and the underlying hypothesis, seemed to conflict with other experiments and the generally accepted opinion that leaders must usually be closer to group norms than other members of the group, and must respect these norms more closely. Hollander tried to reconcile the two sets of facts by proving experimentally that what is involved here is a temporal sequence of phenomena. The individual must first be conformist and attain a high status, a dominating position, or popularity. Then he can successfully demand changes, deviate from the norm, in proportion to the dependence he has imposed on others in relation to him, or the competence that others attribute to him.

These different investigations all postulate therefore that:

(a) It is possible to take an innovating initiative when the movement is from the top towards the bottom of the social or psychological scale.

(b) The minority may influence the majority on condition that it already has power or resources (the term "idiosyncrasy credit" serving generally to identify anything having to do with competence, affection, etc.) and can deviate with impunity.

(c) There is no conflict between the social agent introducing change and the group accepting it. On the contrary, this agent must distribute rewards and reinforcements if he hopes to succeed; "We would say that his behaviour must have become positively reinforcing to the other members of the group if it is to become a model for their performance" (McGinnies, 1970, p. 173).

The paradoxical aspect of these conjectures is that they serve to explain how innovation as an objective result is achieved by means of conformity. This becomes obvious when one examines more closely the different phases of the process just described:

Phase I: An individual acquires authority over the group by pretending to adhere to the norms and goals of the group.

Phase II: He modifies the norms and aims of the group, and others inevitably go along with him because of their dependence on him, and because he now represents the group.

In the first as well as in the second phase, conformity alone is at work. Remarkably enough, in both phases, nobody is ever deviant in the last analysis except, perhaps, the group. The leader, the individual endowed with power or competence, first makes the group aware of these qualities. Then all he does is to put to use the excess power implicitly granted him to modify judgements or attitudes. The customary theoretical and empirical framework of domination and social control is brought to bear on the two above-mentioned cases of innovation, that of a person with little power seeking to influence a more powerful person by means of ingratiation, and that of an individual using his idiosyncrasy credit to innovate.

But why would a person do it? What is the motivation for using up credit? What are the pressures inducing a person to promote change? Of course, there are open-minded individuals and leaders who are impelled forward by their "followers". But this is not a typical situation. In addition, strong intransigence and complete refusal to conform often typify the attitude of individuals and groups who have had great impact on our ideas and behaviour. We have telling examples in Copernicus in the context of astronomy, Galileo in mechanics, the millenarians in religious history, the levellers in social history, Robespierre and de Gaulle in politics, and so on. Characteristically, in social psychology, innovation or non-conformity are made to appear as an outgrowth of leadership and power, conducive to the preservation of the leader's dominance and of existing power relations: innovations are not seen as leading to the replacement of old leaders with new ones, or to a change in power relations. This blind spot is, in my opinion, a glaring symptom of the conformity bias.

The six propositions I have just presented are mutually redundant, as one might well expect, since they are derived from each other and are part of a single coherent model. Nevertheless, it was necessary to formulate each proposition separately, since each one illuminates a different facet of the same phenomenon, and, more broadly, of social behaviour as it is conceived today. Not all research work and theories have started from all propositions simultaneously, nor have they given equal weight to each proposition.

Taken as a whole, the propositions reflect a way of grasping social reality, and the selection from this reality of a segment or level considered worthy of scrutiny. Their popularity in textbooks has been partly responsible for their becoming crystallized and converted into elements of a commonsensical view. When they are made explicit, as they have been here, it is easier to grasp their scope and limits. They admittedly reflect something that corresponds to our experience, and that deserves to be known. Nothing gives us the right to call them wrong or irrelevant.

Nevertheless, we also have the distinct impression that by limiting ourselves to them we are leaving unacknowledged other aspects of our experience which also deserves to be known. A part of, or a level of reality seems to escape the reach of these propositions. More specifically, a large number of essential problems or elements relating to social influence are thrown indiscriminately into one category, or ignored altogether. Some of these confusions, inaccuracies, and enigmas will be dealt with more closely in the second part of this book. I will then turn to the more constructive elements of this study, which will help to broaden our view and open up new perspectives.

3

The Confrontation Between The Logic of Theories and The Logic of Facts

Why have certain aspects of reality been omitted from our field of investigation?

In any scientific endeavour, the aim of theories and methods is to probe the deepest significant layers of reality. It must be admitted that the current theories and methods of social psychology have tended to remain at the surface of reality in many places. The phenomenon of deviance has been barely skimmed, and viewed only in relation to conformity. Very few studies have looked at the conditions in which a minority may take innovative initiatives and change group norms. Nor has the function of independence within the group been the object of any research. It has been said before, and will be said again, that this selectivity is not a function of the theoretical foundations of the science; that it merely reflects the preferences of those who are active in the field. Choice of research topics is, after all, a matter of taste or inspiration. Indeed I would be the last to deny one of the few liberties that remain to a dwindling number of people. I would, however, protest against the implicit coercion, the subtle tyranny of the model I have outlined, which forbids the exploration of reality in its full richness and diversity. For, if there has been a choice, it has been a choice determined by the restrictions of the model. The model has placed limits on the questions which may be asked, and on the answers which may be sought. To prove the point, I will take two examples from fields with which I am particularly familiar, deviance and innovation.

The deviant has always been described as an individual who is in need of others; deprived of independent psychological resources, he is willing to subscribe to the opinions and judgements of the majority and of authority. The state of deviance, the state of being different, is thought of as an uncomfortable condition, one with purely negative connotations. The examples usually pointed to are delinquency, moral perversion, psychological and intellectual inferiority. Could anyone challenge, up to a point, the correctness of these assumptions? One is forced to admit that the deviant does appear in this light as long as he is viewed as a potential conformist. Seen in a different light, he may be equated with the individual who tries to be independent, who tends to reject group influence and authority, and who is inclined to try and get his own viewpoint accepted. In other circumstances, being different reflects a need to distinguish oneself from others and the desire to assert what one believes and considers important.

Being different involves problems and tensions. In a way, one needs to be stronger and tougher to go beyond conventional views and confront the majority, than one needs to be to go along with group opinions and shelter behind the majority. When Freud's works began to be known, he and "his followers were regarded not only as sexual perverts but also as either obsessional or paranoiac psychopaths, and the combination was felt to be a real danger to the community" (Jones, 1961, p. 299). His fellow neurologists, psychiatrists and psychologists were alarmed; hostile reviews and arguments were rampant in the professional journals and books. Psychoanalysis itself was thought to be un-Germanic (what an irony, when one remembers who the first psychoanalysts were!). In reaction to such attitudes, Freud showed himself unperturbed; "The only reply he ever deigned to make to the flood of criticism was the same as Darwin's: he merely published more evidence in support of his theories. He despised the stupidity of his opponents and deplored their bad manners" (Jones, 1961, p. 306).

Consider, in the field of politics, Senator Fulbright's attack on the communist purges of the dark McCarthy era. In the 1950's there began a campaign of hatred, a witchhunt after communists which often included anyone with leftist, or even liberal, tendencies. The Oppenheimer trial is still a recent memory. Fulbright was the only Senator who stood up against, and who dared refuse to vote in favour of an appropriation of $214,000 for McCarthy's subcommittee. The rest of the Senators bowed to the fear that had been instilled into the United States by McCarthy. Such a "deviant", isolated stand by Fulbright was not without danger. He was threatened and attacked, and even accused of being a communist. Such attacks did not deter him. He made speeches denouncing McCarthyism as dangerous to democratic principles. His philosophy was that a law-maker "must be prepared to accept banishment or destruction at the hands of the people because he has aroused their anger in the very act of serving them well" (Archer, 1968, p. 178). In time, and with the help of the televised hearings, McCarthy's political career petered out.

In all such examples, we have evidence that non-conformity and marginality entail the harsh experiences of insult, ostracism, or even persecution in the defence of a belief, behaviour, or area of knowledge. But the rewards are great. Otherwise one would not have seen so many religious, political, artistic, and scientific figures and subgroups taking the risks that they have, and braving severe pressure for such long periods—and finally succeeding in carrying through major changes. Historical monographs, the correspondence of exceptional personalities and of lesser figures, the biography of many a scholar or fighter for liberty and justice show that this is a condition that may be experienced as something which is psychologically and even socially positive. Someone who is different, and officially declared to be different, is not for that reason a person who is tempted to conform or obliged to conform.

Let us limit ourselves, for the moment, to the specialized literature. It has been claimed that deviants are more likely to yield than conformists. The experimental evidence on this topic is too slight, and has been too quickly accepted. Kelley and Lamb (1957) had occasion to observe that the most extreme individuals are also the least influenced. Jackson and Saltzenstein (1958) found in turn that those members who identify most closely with the group are more conformist than the marginal members. But the harvest is most abundant in the previously cited work by Freedman and Doob (1968). These authors set out to discover experimentally how deviance, perceived as such, influenced behaviour. They succeeded in highlighting the difference separating those individuals who think of themselves as deviants from those who do not. For this purpose, they asked their subjects to take personality tests and told them the results, together with some false results said to have been obtained from four or five other persons who had taken the same tests. This information played a feedback role: the subject was categorized either as a deviant, at the tail of the list, or as having an average score. Consequently, the subject was led to think of himself as similar to the group or as dissimilar with regard to certain personality traits. Then in a second experiment, the authors tried to measure the impact of this self-evaluation on the subject.

The results were that, first of all, the subjects identified as deviants changed more readily when the source of communication was one of their peers than when it was an authority figure, while the non-deviants reacted in the opposite way. Secondly, in a situation where compliance was expected, deviants submitted more readily to non-deviants than to other deviants. But non-deviants submitted more readily to deviants than to other non-deviants. Overall, it was the case that deviants conformed less than non-deviants.

To avoid jumping to conclusions, I will not go so far as to claim that deviants are less easily influenced than non-deviants, although this would not be astonishing, since a group includes individuals and sub-groups who have already conformed once, and have no reason for not continuing to do so. Respect for the facts, however, forces us to stress one idea that emerges from them, namely, that the relationship between deviance and dependence is not clear-cut, and that the deviant's propensity towards conformity is no greater, in any case, than his propensity towards autonomy. Deviant individuals resist influence and tend to be impervious to command from above. They may also have some influence on non-deviants, i.e. the group members making up the majority.

These conclusions are not surprising. What *is* surprising is that they have been recorded as a matter of course, without anyone's noticing that they went counter to the accepted theories. Obviously, it was a problem to correlate deviance and independence on the one hand, and conformity and independence on the other. If the link between the first two qualities had been emphasized, one would have had to examine more closely the concepts of "bad" and "good", the deviation from the group which is considered dysfunctional and intolerable; and the desire to be true to oneself, to be a unique individual, a desire which in our society is considered to have the highest ethical value. However, independence is never viewed as deviance, nor deviance as a form of independence, since the former remains within the limits of norms and decency, while the latter undermines the foundations of society and tends towards anomie. In relation to conformity, independence constitutes a boundary, a barrier raised against society, an alliance with physical reality against social reality, a tendency to look at a situation and draw objective conclusions instead of following the crowd. Conformity representing "weakness", and independence representing "strength"— the two can hardly be imagined as coexisting in a single individual.

There is a high-minded philosophy implicit in all of this, high-minded though controversial, and reasonable though not usually true to life. In real life, independence has a large element of non-conformity, of a desire to be different; truly independent individuals are inclined to express themselves, to try and influence the opinions of the group. Being more concerned with values than with real conditions, and preoccupied with dependence relations, the students of social influence have seen in deviance only that fragment which correlates with dependence.

Let us now look at the way in which innovation has been handled. It is a well-known fact that innovation has been the subject of little research, and has stimulated few attempts at theoretical analysis. My reason for giving innovation special attention is not so much, or not only, because of its importance as a social phenomenon which determines many social exchanges. Its special status is that it allows—indeed, forces us—to revise the entire empirical and theoretical context of our work and to see social exchanges in a new light. One may agree with Homans' sociological approach or reject it, but in any case one must give him credit for clearly stating a widespread conception, and for having stimulated the only systematic attempt which has been made in social psychology to study Hollander's theory of innovation. Homans tries to make clear why one encounters less conformity at both extremes of the social ladder. Individuals with high social status feel free to give responses different from the majority's, and to disregard the majority in their actions, because, even if they should prove to be mistaken (for example, by not responding like the majority in experiments where the essential manipulation was to make the majority give a response which appeared false, but was in fact correct) they will not be penalized. A small decrease in prestige is of no consequence to them. Conversely, if their independence has resulted in their making a correct choice, these individuals will then find their prestige reinforced and their high status confirmed. Thus, for individuals with high status, the balance tips in favour of non-conformity.

What about the low-status individual? Whether he goes along with the group or prefers an independent line of behaviour, he has little to lose, being already at the bottom. Even when making a mistake, saying something contrary to what he sees and thinks, merely in order to agree with the group, he will not attract much attention. Unfortunately, if his behaviour conforms to that of the group, and the group is right, he will gain even less, if that is possible, since he will have done nothing more than act like everyone else. On the other hand, if such an individual adopts an independent line of conduct and he proves to have recognized the correct response, there may be some chance that his talents and abilities will be acknowledged by the group. Non-conformity and rebellion against the majority have some obvious advantages; low-status persons or subgroups, like the proletariat (if we remember Marx), have nothing to lose but their chains.

This analysis by Homans (1961) explains why non-conformity, and impulsive initiatives and opposition to group norms, can be observed at both ends of the social hierarchy. Such an analysis, however, is rather short-sighted. It takes no account of the beliefs of individuals and groups, of their aspirations to change, for example, the power relations in a society, or the dogmas of a science. Nor does it take account of the fact that, in spite of the odds against them, individuals as well as groups will oppose majorities and try to change them. The motto of William of Orange is enlightening in this respect: "It is not necessary to hope before doing, nor to succeed before trying."

But let us accept, for the moment, Homans' analysis. If we do, it becomes all the more interesting that those who came after him have been solely concerned with innovating behaviour and non-conformity at the top end of the social scale. Hollander, for example, investigated only the behaviour of an individual anxious to be accepted and liked by the members of the group, in order to accumulate the "credits" required in order to become a leader, "by showing competence and by conforming to expectations" (Hollander, 1964, p. 195). After having attained this goal, the individual, now at the top, can bring about changes if he wishes, is allowed to deviate, and can still be influential. It seems that there is a consensus supporting the idea that, in a group, innovation originates from the leader.

Let me cite two passages on this subject which are very similar, but drawn from textbooks whose general orientation is very different. "Another part of the role of leader, however, requires him to break away from the norm at times. He has the greatest contact with parts of the social system external to the group. Under some circumstances, the group must change if it is to function efficiently. Then it is the role of the leader to introduce changes in the norm" (Secord and Backman, 1964, p. 345). "One of the responsibilities of leadership is innovation, the setting of new standards, and trying out new methods of coping with the world external to the group. The leader gets credit for this even though he is breaking away from the usual pattern of doing things. Often leaders are expected not to conform, and to do so would result in a loss of status" (Jones and Gerard, 1967, p. 416).

Taking these propositions literally, one would have to say that:

(1) pressures leading to innovation originate outside the group;

(2) the leader is the only member on whom this pressure to innovate is exerted, since he is the only one who is in contact with the outside world;

(3) innovation generally presupposes the risk of a loss in popularity, or reduction in idiosyncrasy credit, and so on.

The restrictiveness of the basic proposition on which these statements rest is obvious at a glance. The history of innovations and revolutions has amply demonstrated that individuals with low or marginal status, by virtue of their position at the periphery of the group, have closer contact with the outside world than high-status individuals, who are at the centre of the group. Even in the case of primates, it has been observed that initiatives with respect to food-gathering, for instance, originate in the subgroup of "bachelor" males, who are kept at the periphery of the group. Everyone is so familiar with the fact of the motivation of marginal individuals to introduce changes, and their high receptiveness to change, that I need not go further into this. Moreover, an original initiative, an innovating behaviour, constitute clear risks for any individual whose position in society is well established, whereas such an initiative on the part of an individual or subgroup hoping to move from the periphery to the centre of the social system quite as obviously has many, if not more, advantages than risks. Finally, we must remember that when leaders do innovate, it is often in response to internal group pressure exerted by subgroups or individuals occupying an inferior position.

Are these two analyses—Homans' "social calculus" and Hollander's "credit system"—really important in accounting for influence and innovation? At least for the time being, a study by Wahrman and Pugh (1972) shows that they are not. In their experiment, a group of three naive persons and one confederate were assigned a task which required a group choice regarding strategy. They were asked to agree on a row in a 7×7 matrix that would maximize their winnings if they also correctly anticipated the experimenter's choice of column. For example, if the subjects correctly guessed that the experimenter would choose the yellow column, then their choice of row "George" would maximize their winnings, i.e. gain them 10 points. If they chose row "George" on the guess that the experimenter would choose column "yellow", but the experimenter actually chose "black", for example, they would then lose 8 points. The subjects believed that the experimenter had a "system" which they were supposed to uncover and beat. Although separated into booths, they were allowed to talk to each other through microphones and headphones.

Matrix used in group task

	Green	Red	Blue	Yellow	Brown	Orange	Black
Able	−1	−12	+5	−1	−2	+15	−4
Baker	+10	−1	−2	−7	+4	−3	−1
Charlie	−5	+5	−3	+3	−11	−1	+12
Dog	+5	−7	+10	−2	−5	+1	−2
Easy	−4	−1	−1	+1	+13	−10	+2
Fox	−6	+15	−5	−1	−3	−1	+1
George	−1	−1	−2	+10	+4	−2	−8

Fig. 1

Reproduced from Hollander, E. P. Competence and conformity in the acceptance o influence. *Journal of Abnormal Psychology*, 1960, **61,** no. 3, pp. 365–639.

In four of the conditions, the confederate was correct on 11 of the 15 trials. On these trials, the confederate chose a row that had not been selected by any of the other subjects, and the experimenter then selected his column so as to give a high pay-off if the group had adopted the confederate's choice as their joint response. Thus, if three of the naive subjects suggested "Able" and the fourth suggested "Charlie", the confederate might choose, for example, "Dog". If he said "Dog", then the experimenter would choose the column "Blue". This would indicate that the confederate's choice of "Dog" (+10 points) was the best guess.

During the trials, the confederate's deviant behaviour included suggesting that majority rule was less efficient than following his choice, and that he ought to get a larger share of the winnings, since he would be making the greatest contributions and making unsupported challenges of the other people's choices. He also interrupted the others and made his choice before his turn. In one condition, this deviant behaviour began at trial 1 and continued throughout all 15 trials. On average, he did two of the above things on every trial. In a second condition, the deviance started on trial 6 and continued through to trial 15. In the third condition, deviance started at trial 11 and continued through to trial 15. In the fourth condition he conformed, i.e. showed no deviant behaviour on any of the 15 trials. A fifth condition was included in which the confederate was deviant in all 15 trials (as in condition 1), but where he was not correct in the majority of his choices—in fact, where he was correct in only four out of 15 trials.

The influence exerted by this confederate was defined as the number of trials on which the group voted to choose the row that the confederate had chosen. The findings show that, among the four conditions where the confederate was "competent", i.e. produced the best guess on 11 of the 15 trials, the condition in which he showed deviant behaviour right from the first trial and continued it throughout is the *most influential*. Even more interesting is the fact that, the earlier the deviance occurs in the 15 trials, the more influential the confederate is. The *least* influence occurs when he abides by the rules over all 15 trials (condition 4). In fact, even when the confederate is *incompetent*, i.e. correct on only four of the fifteen trials, and is deviant from the beginning, he is as influential as the competent conformer. Until the others learn that his choices do not enhance pay-off, he is much more influential than the conformer.

The authors of this study conclude: "Clearly when deciding on a group choice the group did not discount the non-conforming confederate's suggestions. Quite the contrary occurred. The confederate's non-conformity or obnoxious self-assertiveness apparently increased his influence. The equally competent conformer suffered for his virtue" (Wahrman and Pugh, 1972, p. 380). In other words, a history of conformity (accumulated credits) have nothing, or at most very little, to do with the impact one can have on other people. In fact, Hollander's and Homans' reasoning would have us infer that if a person deviates early, his influence will be drastically curtailed compared to a situation in which he deviates after he has become popular, recognized as a leader, etc. This does not happen. As we have seen, the reverse of that, although precluded by psycho-sociological theory, is not precluded in the real world. These are just preliminary remarks. Their only purpose is to recall the familiar fact that innovation is not linked with status, let alone high status. In this case, why have authors persisted in focusing only on innovation which comes from the top? The reason for this becomes clear when one looks at the current theoretical model. The model postulates that the influence process is asymmetrical. The source necessarily has higher status than the target. Authority, the majority, the group are always upholders of the norm; the minority, the individual must be content to submit to it. There is, by definition, an inequality in the respective degree of initiative permitted to each: "Someone who has built up a lot of credit has a great deal of freedom to do as he pleases whereas someone whose balance is thin must be careful in what he does lest he loses the little credit he has. The person is no longer regarded as a functioning member of the group when his balance reaches zero" (Jones and Gerard, 1967, p. 442).

What is there to prevent a person from subverting all group values and hierarchies, just because he has nothing more to lose and is no longer a member of the group? In any case, leaving aside the possibility of subversion that is implicit in the naive textbook assertions, we can see why, in their view, change or an initiative coming from the lower levels is precluded and even unthinkable. This is the point that I wanted to stress. The reason why a number of phenomena have been ignored by social psychology is not that these phenomena are insignificant or uninteresting; it is that they are incompatible with the theoretical position.

Does uncertainty deserve its central position in the theoretical model?

No matter what philosophers may say, consistency is not a cardinal virtue of scientific thinking. On the other hand, there is a limit to inconsistency even in non-scientific thinking. When one reads about the relations between uncertainty and influence, one constantly finds assertions that are either mutually contradictory or that are contradicted by experience. The concept of uncertainty unquestionably plays a crucial role in our current analysis of influence, in that it is believed that influence always reduces uncertainty. Similarly, the effectiveness of an influence source is measured by its ability to reduce uncertainty. An individual's informational dependence on others derives directly from uncertainty, and Jones and Gerard (1967) even blamed Lewin for not having taken it into account: "Lewin's characterization of the person's life space does not contain the critical feature that is the basis for information dependence, that is, uncertainty . . . In a few places in his writings he does acknowledge the existence of uncertainty in the person's life space, but he does not incorporate it as an essential characteristic of action. This cannot be an accurate characterization because, at any given moment, the person's particular vantage point from which he views action possibilities is characteristically one of incomplete knowledge. Often he has only a vague sense of what will follow particular action" (p. 189).

It is perfectly true that Lewin never referred to such a concept, and it is equally true that he never saw the need for it. In any case, this passage brings out the supposed basis of uncertainty: lack of information, lack of knowledge. It also makes clear what the usefulness of the concept is: to explain influence behaviour as information-exchanging behaviour. Thus influence *no longer seems to be related to the need of the emitter or source to modify the behaviour of the receiver or target. On the contrary, it stems from the need felt by the receiver to obtain information for coping with his environment. In other words, the existence of uncertainty not only makes an individual or sub-group more receptive, it also transforms the meaning of the relations and behaviours associated with influence.*

This raises many questions. Here are just a few of them. A distinction has been made between informational and normative influence, but would it not have been better to distinguish between covert influence, which seems to be informational, and overt influence, which appears as an explicit attempt to bring about or modify behaviour? Another question might be whether, in many cases, the influence that has been exerted is attributable to a reduction of uncertainty *per se*, or whether it is rather due to the fact that it has been covert influence because of the context of uncertainty in which it manifested itself. It is obvious at a glance that the relation between influence and uncertainty is much more complex than it has been described or anticipated as being.

Let us for the moment leave aside this question of complexity, and adopt the customary innocence. The propositions, as I have already pointed out, are accepted by everyone:

The more uncertain a person is, the easier he is to influence.

The more ambiguous the object, the greater the need for, and/or the greater the actual influence.

These propositions have two corollaries:

When a person is certain, there is neither influence nor the need for influence.

When the object is unambiguous, the consensus of other persons is irrelevant, and therefore there is no influence.

The three postulates underlying these propositions and their corrollaries should also be spelled out:

The state of uncertainty is internally given for the person, and is determined either by his means of obtaining information or by his psychological traits.

Environmental ambiguity or non-ambiguity is a characteristic which is distinct from the organism dealing with it.

Uncertainty and ambiguity exist before influence and interaction with others are set in motion: they are the preconditions for influence and interaction.

These propositions have supposedly been verified by experiment. It is difficult to believe that their corollaries have been examined with sufficient rigour.

Let us first consider stimulus ambiguity. Sherif and his disciples have fully explored this dimension in their studies. However, Asch's experiment's, and more recently our own (Moscovici *et al.*, 1969) have shown that there can be strong influence even when the stimuli are absolutely unambiguous. It must therefore be concluded that ambiguity, and consequently environmental fluidity and instability, are not a necessary condition for the establishment of a norm or the influencing of opinions. It is not at all clear why this proposition about the relation between degree of stimulus structuration and uncertainty is assumed to have been confirmed. No one denies that larger displacements are obtained when stimuli are more ambiguous than when they are less ambiguous. But we must not confuse the *possibility* of exerting influence, of moving from the state of rest to the state of motion, with the *ease or difficulty* of exerting influence, i.e. with the greater or smaller degree of acceleration; for the two are not identical.

The problem in fact only becomes interesting when this proposition is rejected, and for the following reason: there is no guarantee that what we have here is a continuous dimension. Either from the psychological or the social point of view, influencing someone with respect to an ambiguous object is not at all like influencing him with respect to a non-ambiguous object. In the one case, one is trying to limit the range of values which the object can assume, to reduce the number of dimensions according to which it can be evaluated. In the other case, on the contrary, one is trying to widen the range and increase the number of dimensions. Yielding does not have the same meaning in both contexts. An identically small difference in judgement is noticeable with respect to a non-ambiguous object, but may remain imperceptible when the object is ambiguous. Therefore, yielding in a situation where deviation is obvious reveals a much more pronounced psychological change than yielding where deviation is not so perceptible. A subject claiming that he sees blue slides as green, or objectively equal lines as unequal, has really undergone a change, and adopted a response that was not part of his repertoire. Conversely, a subject who claims that the point of light in the autokinetic illusion moves five centimetres instead of three centimetres is settling on a response that already exists in his repertoire. It is misleading to compare the degree of yielding in the two cases, because the results one is comparing may well derive from two distinct psychological processes. This possibility *must* be taken into consideration, for in certain studies we find that persons who conform with regard to ambiguous objects appear to have different psychological profiles from those persons who conform with regard to non-ambiguous objects (Allen, 1974).

Moreover, even assuming that the two processes are identical does influence hinge on the condition of the object, on the clarity of the criteria by which it is evaluated, that is, on the corresponding degree of certainty? We have no justification for making this assumption. In Sherif's experiments, the subjects establish a personal norm, a relatively stable estimate of light source displacement, before interacting. In Asch's experiments also, the subjects have a norm, a very definite idea about the equality or inequality of the lines they are shown. What difference is there between the two groups of subjects, making the former apparently easier to influence than the latter? Is it ambiguity in the stimulus? No, it is the fact that the norm relevant to the equality or inequality of lines has been repeatedly reinforced by society, whereas the norm relevant to the displacement of a point of light is new to the subjects and has not been previously reinforced. One of Mausner's experiments (1954) shows that if such reinforcement is supplied, estimates do not converge and there is no yielding. Everything therefore leads us to suspect that there is no direct causal link between the physical properties of the stimulus (or the environment) and influence—that influence is not a function of stimulus instability.

What about the more general status of uncertainty? Is it a necessary and sufficient condition of influence? Is uncertainty so intolerable that individuals will under all circumstances attempt to reduce it? Are there really any grounds for considering it a precondition of social interaction, and for believing that it is only reduced as a result of such interaction? These questions can be treated at several different levels. On the practical level, there are many situations where individuals or groups with wel-defined opinions, norms, and beliefs are influenced by other individuals or groups. Examples of religious, political, scientific, and aesthetic conversions abound. Even if these examples were exceptional, they would still be interesting, and contrary to the assertion that where there is certainty there can be no influence. On the experimental level, a large number of studies of change in firmly established behaviour and attitudes attest that doubt is not an indispensable part of the phenomenon we are interested in. Lewin's experiments on the modification of food preferences, the experiments based on dissonance theory, in which subjects asked to defend or expose themselves to opinions contrary to their own eventually modify their opinions, the studies of role-playing in which improvisations bring about similar changes—none of these are as remote from social influence experiments as may be imagined. In all these cases, subjects are asked to imagine a point of view different to their own, or to adopt alternative solutions to their usual ones. Despite initial certainties, the subjects yield.

There appears to be a lack of communication between theorists and experimentalists. The former maintain that influence is due to the *reduction* of uncertainty; the latter try to influence subjects in order to *increase* their uncertainty. Crutchfield (1955) has carefully observed what happens in the experimental room and has shown that the subjects, as they enter the room are not unsure of their intellectual or sensory abilities, nor are they worried about having the required knowledge for judging whether or not two lines are equal. It is only when they are faced with the unanimous group decisions that such doubts arise. "First," Crutchfield writes "for many persons the discrepancies tend to be solved through self-blame. They express doubt of their own accuracy of perception or judgement, confessing that they had probably misread or misperceived the slides" (1955). At first, then, each one thinks he is like the others, but gradually he is forced to think otherwise—to consider himself deviant in relation to the group. "Another noteworthy effect" Crutchfield continues "was the sense of increased psychological distance induced between the person himself and the group. He felt himself to be queer or different, or felt the group to be unlike what he had thought. With this went an arousal of considerable anxiety in most subjects; for some manifest anxiety was acute. The existence of these tensions within and between the subjects became dramatically manifest when, shortly after the end of the procedure, the experimenter confessed the deception he had practiced and explained the real situation. There were obvious and audible signs of relaxation and relief. . ." (1955).

It thus appears that the effect of the group is first of all to *produce* uncertainty and anxiety. It is in fact difficult to see how perceptions or responses could be modified at all if this did not happen. We have no reason to assume therefore, that influence is always a consequence of the *reduction*, rather than of the *production* of uncertainty. Still the theoretical question remains of how and why influence produces uncertainty, just as much as how and why influence allegedly reduces it.

One might conclude that all this hardly matters—but, from the scientific point of view, this is not so. When uncertainty or ambiguity (or deviance in general) are assumed to be *givens*, influence can be considered as having been caused; it is also justified, by extra-social factors, and the starting-point—the original need—seems to be *intra-individual*. On the other hand, when we look at the conditions in which ambiguity and uncertainty can be *produced*, deviance takes on a social aspect. In these conditions it results from social interaction, and the starting-point or need in this case appears to be *inter-individual*.

Festinger's first theory of pressures towards uniformity, though less general, is in this respect closer to reality than his second theory of social comparison. In fact, as he has clearly seen, the pressures which act in a group to change the opinions of a deviant originate from the divergence between the deviant and the majority. It is this divergence which obliges the members of a group to communicate in order to eliminate any possibility of having their decision brought into question. Such questioning, if persisted in, would provoke doubt and a revaluation of choices made in common, as De Monchaux and Shimmin (1955) have shown. Social comparison presupposes nothing more than this: the individual by himself lacks assurance of his value, his opinions, and his abilities, and it is for this reason that he seeks to compare himself with others who are similar to him. But, one could well ask, might not this lack of assurance itself result from self-comparison with other individuals, perhaps under the stress of competition, who appear more able and more assured of their personal opinions and values? This would seem to be a more realistic assumption.

To conclude, neither theoretical argument nor experimental evidence will permit us to base social influence, its origin or its effectiveness, on the concepts of ambiguity or uncertainty. The states of mind that these concepts describe are "results" rather than "givens", and one must investigate their origin and formation within social interaction, instead of limiting oneself to observing their existence and effects outside this interaction. In any case, there is no justification for considering them necessary and sufficient conditions for influence. I do not mean to imply that they have no function at all, but that the reduction of uncertainty or ambiguity should not be included among the general propositions relevant to the analysis of the influence process. At the very least, there is a need for a rigorous reformulation of what has been asserted in this respect up to now.

Is it legitimate to continue using the concepts of power and influence interchangeably?

I believe that too much has been expected of the concept of influence, mainly as a result of associating it too closely with different aspects of power. In this field, the more or less implicit assumption has always been that power is the sole source of influence, and that influence is the consequence or instrument of the exercise of power. Given this perspective, it was natural to think that the degree of conformity corresponds to an individual's social status, and that dependence on the authority of the group or the majority was the principal source of influence. Three questions must be raised: (a) has the relationship been empirically verified? (b) is the causal link between power and influence adequately spelled out? (c) is a more searching study of the influence process compatible with keeping it in the context of power processes? I shall attempt to answer each question in turn.

The reason why dependence has been given such an important role, to the extent of being considered a major independent variable, is that a relationship between hierarchy and conformity has been taken for granted. Hence, influence was defined as an extension of power. In the same perspective, it was assumed that a majority opinion is given greater weight than a minority opinion, since dependence on the majority is greater than dependence on the minority. However, a careful interpretation of the facts militates against this conclusion. There is no connection between dependence and conformity

For proof of this, let us go back to Asch's paradigm which, together with its variations, is of fundamental importance. As everyone knows, according to this paradigm the subject is confronted with the obviously erroneous responses of three to fifteen confederates, depending on the experimental conditions. Overall, it seems that the subject conforms to the group in one out of three responses (32%). Asch himself, and all who have discussed this experiment in articles and textbooks, have attributed this effect to dependence on the majority. This attribution must be challenged for reasons I shall recall briefly. The postulation of a majority effect implies certain consequences: (a) the greater the majority, the greater its influence; (b) an individual given the choice between an individual's (deviant's) judgement and the judgement of the majority, will choose the latter; (c) when an individual is removed from the supervision of the majority, and thereby freed from the dependence relation, he will tend to make correct judgements, and not conform; (d) no other feature of majority judgement and social interaction (such as unanimity, certainty, etc.) can account for a significant part of the conformist response.

None of these implications has been unequivocally verified. With respect to (a), we find that once the majority exceeds three, a further increase does not result in stronger influence. As for (b), it has been completely disproved. Several experiments have shown that the action of an isolated individual (Asch, 1955; Allen and Levine, 1971; Gerard and Greenbaum, 1962) or of a deviant (Kiesler, 1969) can have a very strong effect in reducing conformity and influencing the naive subject. The third implication has not yet been decisively verified. Several experiments have been devised to test it by placing the naive subject in an anonymous role; his response is not singled out socially, and it remains unknown to the group. In principle, he is thus not in a position to fear the disapproval of the group. It was expected that under these circumstances the percentage of conformist responses would decrease. In an experiment by Raven (1959), for example, they did decrease from 39% in the public condition to 26% in the anonymous condition. However, even 26% of conformity on the part of a subject with no apparent reason for submitting to the group is large enough to be psychologically significant.

These findings certainly cast doubt on the postulation of the majority effect as the determinant of influence, but there is still no alternative explanation in sight, except for one which emerges from the fourth implication (d). The "erroneous" judgement in all these experiments has had two characteristics; on the one hand, it has been a majority judgement, and on the other it has been unanimous. In other words, this judgement was persuasive because it came from the group and was organized in such a way as to make the group seem consistent. Let us assume—as has been done in some experiments—that there are two types of groups. In one, the members of the majority are unanimous, and in the other, they are not. In the first type of group, *regardless* of the number of members, the percentage of conformist responses is always the same: 32%, as we have seen. In the second type of group, where a confederate has been instructed to shatter the unanimity by giving a different response from the others, the percentage of conformist responses is only 10·4%, or as low as 5·5% in some cases.

Hence, it seems that a unanimous majority of three individuals is more influential than a non-unanimous majority of seven. This is enough to prove that unanimity, that is, the organization of responses which reflects inter-individual consistency and the existence of a common norm, is more important than the mere number of persons who adopt it. Other studies (Graham, 1962; Mouton, Blake and Olmstead, 1956) reach similar conclusions. For the sake of brevity, I will not go into other empirical findings proving that neither majority pressure, nor the opinion of a majority, is of more decisive importance than that of an isolated individual. All such findings challenge the belief that dependency is the sole source of influence.

The choice of dependency as a causal factor reveals the assumption of a link between power and real influence. But can we really be sure that the *direction* of this link has been accurately analysed? French and Raven (1959) have tried to clarify the theory of power as the origin of influence, and they proposed a fundamental distinction between two types of power: coercive and normative power. The former manifests itself by constraint, in terms of physical resources and the distribution of rewards and punishments. The latter is manifested analogously in terms of expertness and the legitimation of different roles on the basis of values and norms. The power of the expert or the well-informed person rests on the conviction held by most people that he has some specialized knowledge in situations where it is required: the doctor influences his patient, the mechanic the car owner, the experimenter the subject, and so on, because the patient, car owner and subject accept the authority of the institution, and the value of professional training and qualifications which guarantee the conduct of these persons. The power of parents, managers, officers, shop-stewards is also based on a system of values which, having been internalized by the child, the employee, the soldier and the worker, induces all of these to bestow a higher authority on the people who influence them. The degree of normative power varies with the extent of acceptance of the norms, just as the degree of coercive power varies with the amount of coercion and resistance which is at the disposal of the other members of society.

This is all perfectly reasonable and clear, until one asks the one question that is never raised: what is the origin of power? I shall not deal here with the question of coercive power, which is less interesting because it has a less obvious relationship with the processes that concern us here. Let us consider, however, some concrete examples of normative power in action. Imagine an individual or group placing confidence in a person whom they believe to be an expert, whose authority and knowledge they accept: a doctor, a psychoanalyst, an economist, an experimental psychologist, a "pop" musician. They attach much value to his opinions and behaviour and they follow his recommendations. But before the individual or group will submit to such a dependence, they have to be persuaded that the doctor is somehow preferable to the witch-doctor or faith-healer; that the psychoanalyst is more effective than the orthodox psychiatrist; that the economist knows better than the ordinary businessman; that the experimental psychologist is more scientific than anyone else who considers behaviour; that "pop" music is valid expression, and not just cacophony. Of course, such acceptance is not easily gained, and groups, classes and sub-cultures disagree about the value which should be accorded to each of these categories of experts.

In other words, dependence with respect to the power and effectiveness of experts is contingent on individuals having been previously influenced, having had their opinions changed with regard to what constitutes real knowledge, or real music. In order for the authority of parents, teachers, supervisors, etc. to be effective, it is equally necessary that certain values concerning the family, school, and work should be upheld and shared. As soon as these values are changed, weakened or abandoned, as has recently happened in the family and the university, for instance, power remains, but only as a naked coercive power. It cannot, as such, propagate or revive values, and it cannot legitimate itself. This is why all societies perpetually create and maintain parallel institutions designed to propagate values, norms, and ideologies—in short, to influence. The role of these institutions, among others, is precisely to legitimize power.

Therefore, if power presupposes influence, and is in part a result of influence, we cannot possibly consider it as the *cause* of influence. It cannot be both cause and effect. I do not mean to deny the analogy between power and influence phenomena, nor that they are associated in some way. But the link between them is not one-way, nor is the former a necessary condition for the latter. On the contrary, we know that influence procedures often fail because a dominant stance seems to be taken by the would-be influencer, who thereby appears as a threat to independence of choice and judgement. Societies, aware of this fact, carefully separate the instruments of their power from those of their influence. The police or the army are rarely used as channels for ideologies, norms and values; this role is reserved for educators, priests, propaganda specialists, and these latter are never charged with maintaining public order or with the political decisions which determine the rights of citizens. In their global strategies, neither individuals nor societies apply these two instruments indiscriminately. Influence may be used to bring about change or conformity, and if this fails, force may then be used instead and vice versa.

But all this is very familiar, and needs no further amplification. I began this discussion by stressing that there is a discrepancy between some implicit propositions in social psychology concerning the relationship between influence, power and dependence and the experimental evidence. It seems that there is no direct causal relation between hierarchy and conformity. The attribution of conformity effects to dependence seems to be a misinterpretation; the experimental findings lend themselves to entirely different interpretations from those that are currently accepted (Moscovici and Faucheux, 1972). On the theoretical level, equally, the description and definition of these relations leaves much room for doubt. This suggests that we should separate the treatment of power phenomena from the treatment of influence phenomena. Autonomous treatment of each area would be more likely to lead to satisfactory explanations of their underlying mechanisms. Only by rejecting the present exclusive and overwhelming preoccupation with dependence and the model of social relations which is built around it, shall we be able to extend our vision.

Final remarks

My purpose in the preceding pages has been not so much to criticize as to raise questions. I have thus been led to highlight incongruities and discrepancies between theory and experiment, and to lay stress on the more implicit contradictions and limitations of the functionalist model itself. The contradictions arise mainly from an inadequate analysis of the notions of ambiguity and uncertainty by theories which have made them the starting-points of social interaction, rather than taking the equally valid step of seeing them as the results of this interaction. The limitations of the functionalist model stem directly and exclusively from the conformity bias, which makes it impossible to take into account the influence exerted by individuals and minorities, and which projects such a gloomy picture of deviance. The unwarranted identification of influence phenomena with power phenomena probably has the same origin. In fact, power and influence act in the same direction, and through the same agency, *only* in the context of group conformity pressure on the individual.

Other contradictions and limitations are apparent. There is the contradiction between the habitually negative descriptions of persons and subgroups who are "different", or even merely marginal, and the praise bestowed on independence; surely independence is itself a quest for "difference" or the defence of difference, which carries with it the risk of isolation and deviance and which calls for unusual strength and qualities. There is also the limitation stemming from insistence on the norm of objectivity, the requirement of a correct response. Are not originality, innovation, and the need to state one's preferences equally relevant in the determination of relationships?

Part Two

Conflict, Innovation, and Social Recognition

Social influence from a genetic point of view

4

Minorities, Majorities, and Social Norms

It can be hoped that, with sufficient patience, the questions we have raised can be solved; but just as every question presupposes the glimpse of a possible answer, each answer inevitably provokes new questions. We are, therefore, making a fresh start in the field of social influence.

It should not be expected that the propositions I shall present here will be as accurate or as solidly grounded as those presented in the last three chapters; they are of too recent vintage for that. I have derived them from three questions:

— Why, and how, are majority and minority capable of exerting influence?
— Under what conditions will influence take the shape of either innovation or conformity?
— Which qualities in the individual help bring about change in the group or in society?

Proposition 1

Every group member, irrespective of his rank, is a potential source and receiver of influence

The most important point here is that a perspective different from the usual one must be taken. A full understanding of influence phenomena requires that we view the minority, individual or subgroup in terms of the impact they may have on group opinion. Hitherto, they have been viewed only as influence receivers or deviates; they must now be seen also as potential influence emitters and norm originators. The nature of social life is such that "the heresy of one generation becomes the common-place of the next".

If we took such a view, the conformity bias would be corrected. But I do not wish simply to correct the bias; I would like above all to emphasize two interrelated ideas. The first is that influence is exerted in two directions: from the majority towards the minority, *and* from the minority towards the majority. In other words, far from being a unilateral effect of the source on the target, influence is a reciprocal process, involving action and reaction of both source and target. By thinking of each group member, irrespective of whether he is in a position of authority, whether he is a deviate, whether he belongs to the majority or the minority, as both an emitter and a receiver of influence, we are better able to grasp what happens to him in a real social interaction. This means searching in all cases for *symmetrical* relationships.

The second idea underlies the first, and it is that each part of a group must be considered as emitting and receiving influence *simultaneously*. More concretely, every individual and subgroup, regardless of status, is both being acted upon *and* acting upon others at the same moment, whenever influence occurs. Thus, a majority which is attempting to impose its norms and point of view on a minority is at the same time under pressure from this minority to make itself understood and to make its norms and point of view acceptable. Conversely, when a minority accedes to a majority position, it must be able to understand the motivations and opinions which it is assuming, and this will involve a process of adjustment and modification of these motivations and ideas so that they will fit as far as possible the existing minority frame of reference. When we see a government or political party modifying its policies, adjusting the tenor of its arguments in the process of applying and presenting them, it is precisely because, at the same time, different sections of the population are attempting to propose or impose other policies and arguments. As everyone knows, the usual tactic in such cases is to incorporate some of the minority's proposals into the majority programme, in order to deprive the minority of its identity and means of action.

In short, we cannot separate the emission from the reception of influence, nor should we fragment these two aspects of a single process by attributing one exclusively to one partner (majority), and the other to the other partner (minority) of social interaction.

The question now arises of why and how a social actor, particularly one in a minority position, is capable of exerting influence. A few conjectures may help us to establish the basic elements of a theoretical analysis, which will be fully elaborated later.

The activities of society as a whole, or of a group, always result in the establishment of a norm and the consolidation of a majority response. Once such a norm and response have been elaborated, behaviours, opinions, the means of satisfying needs, and in fact all possible social acts are divided into four categories: what is permitted, and what is forbidden; what is included, and what is excluded. The incest taboo, for instance, divides women into those that are accessible, and those that are not. Traffic regulations determine when the driver must halt (red light), and when he may go ahead (green light), and so on. These norms or prescriptions, ranging from the most serious to the most trivial, separate a positive realm (true, good, beautiful, etc.) from a negative realm (false, bad, ugly, etc.), and every act takes on a social or deviant character depending on the realm to which it has previously been assigned.

There is nothing absolute about this categorization. Even an asocial or deviant act remains within the horizon of those who respect or apply the group regulation. It remains one of their potentialities, perhaps even assuming an exaggerated charm because it is forbidden or denied. Everyone knows what the actual situation is with regard to incest, violation of traffic lights, speed limits, and so on. An internal conflict is thus kept alive between the alternative behaviour or opinion, and group uniformity.

Groups and individuals differ greatly with respect to the degree of internalization of norms or social responses; it may be a question of deep commitment or merely superficial adherence—in extreme cases, nothing more than an automatic response. Studies made many years ago showed the discrepancy that may arise in a community between public and private behaviour and opinions (Schank, 1932). This may be considered as a state of pluralistic ignorance, in which individuals are not aware that their collective norms and responses have actually changed.

The existence of internal conflict, or discrepancy between degrees of adherence to norms and judgements, creates a predisposition towards, and potential for, change. *Hence the minority, which represents the repressed or rejected opinion or behaviour, boldly reveals in public what has been the case in private; it always has a certain hold on the majority, and can induce it to modify its behaviour or attitude,* so that it becomes more tolerant towards what was previously excluded or forbidden. Although no specific studies have been done on this, it is also well known that when an individual openly adopts a behaviour that most individuals would themselves like to carry out, *he serves as an example and has a liberating effect.* Of course, when a minority seeks to influence society with respect to very strongly internalized norms or responses, it meets with much greater resistance. Along these same lines, various studies have brought out the fact that original or extreme points of view, which are by definition expressed by individuals or minorities, are far more likely to exercise a strong attraction than to be rejected.

The need to reach a consensus, and the customary manner of reaching it, also open up an important field of influence to individuals, minorities, and non-conformists. The classic view stresses the contrast between physical and social reality. Let me recall that the former only requires the intervention of a sensory or technical apparatus for the validation of judgements and opinions, while the latter requires group consensus.

This contrast, which has a certain intuitive appeal, nevertheless arouses some reservations. As far as physical phenomena are concerned, there is a selection process operating which gives some dimensions of reality more importance than others. Thus some persons are inclined to organize the material world in terms of colours, flavours, etc., while others tend to focus on lengths, weights, speeds, and so on; and when they make a judgement and define an object, their attention to the object will be deployed in a manner contingent upon the framework they have chosen. Language and social learning each influence the varying degrees of refinement with which the texture of the environment may be discriminated. It is true, of course, that technical instruments permit an individual to make decisions about the environment by himself; but even these instruments conceal a consensus, since the mode of action of a tool or the appropriateness of a measuring device must be agreed upon by all if the result of such operations is to carry any information.

Thus, an isolated individual using these devices and drawing conclusions from their results is conscious of the attitude of his contemporaries with respect to them. The difference between physical and social reality, if there truly is one, does not consist in the presence or absence of a consensus. It consists in the fact that, under certain circumstances, consensus has an indirect role to play in the validation process, while under other circumstances it intervenes directly. When we measure length or compare lengths, consensus intervenes only indirectly, because we "know" that somewhere there exists the standard foot and the standard metre which define these measures unequivocally, and we also "know" that any individual who has normal eyesight can tell the difference between equal and unequal lines. Moreover, this equality or inequality matters to him. On the other hand, when it is a question of evaluating a personality trait, the severity of a punishment, the degree of democracy practiced in a given country, if we do not place faith in tests or statistical indices, then consensus with others has a direct part in our evaluation.

The force of consensus, whether it intervenes directly or indirectly, depends upon the degree of unanimity which it commands. No matter how small its numerical strength, or how great its dependence, the minority can always refuse this consensus, and this power of refusal gives it considerable strength. The majority will certainly expend a great deal of energy in attempting to protect itself from this eventuality. In Schachter's experiments (1951) on pressures towards uniformity, for instance, the whole group spends time trying to persuade the deviate to accept the group point of view, paying no heed to the *mode* and the *slider*, whose positions are, after all, closer to those of the group.

It can be said that, should the deviate fail to change, the group can always exclude him, and it is true that this possibility considerably reduces the weight of the minority. *It is odd that no thought has been given to the possibility of the deviate's leaving the group and splitting it, thereby diminishing the power of the consensus and unanimity*—but then, the stress has always been on conformity.

There are, doubtless, sufficient reasons for people to remain in a group, and not to leave it spontaneously even under very painful circumstances. Among the most notable reasons for this reluctance to shift are a lack of knowledge of what the alternatives might be, and a psychological inertia, which makes one prefer to expend an enormous amount of energy in order to preserve a relationship or to continue a task, however hopeless, rather than abandon it. Obedience to authority, as Milgram (1974) has demonstrated, is one of the most important reasons. But there is another side to this coin; people also tend to be attracted by, to migrate towards, certain groups because these groups actualize their needs and ideals, because they reinforce some important values and behaviours. The reassuring propensity of people to stay in a group and the menacing possibility that they will leave, exist side by side. The balance is even.

However, it has to be remembered that, in ordinary circumstances, recourse to expulsion is quite exceptional and often impossible. Can parents drive out their children, white majorities expel coloured minorities, or capitalists get rid of the workers? Obviously not, although there are methods of coercion at the disposal of these groups, such as food deprivation (a common punishment for children in the days of Victor Hugo's "dry bread in a dark closet"), denial of citizenship, and starvation wages which come close to being the social equivalent of excommunication. And there are certain extreme instances of which we are all aware, such as the massacres of Indians by American settlers, and Hitler's attempted "final solution" of the Jewish "problem" by outright extermination.

But generally speaking, temporary or definitive exclusion from the group, or the opportunity of leaving it, are extraordinary phenomena. American social psychologists have, however, considered these solutions as possibilities—mainly on the basis of the particular experience of American society, in which leaving the system seems easier or more acceptable than speaking up against it. According to Hirschman,

> exit has been accorded an extraordinarily privileged position in American tradition . . . This preference for the neatness of exit over the messiness and heartbreak of voice has then "persisted throughout our national history". The exit from Europe could be re-enacted within the United States by the progressive settlement of the frontier, which Frederick Jackson Turner characterized as the "gate of escape from the bondage of the past". Even after the closing of the frontier, the very vastness of the country combined with easy transportation made it far more possible for Americans than for most other people to think about solving their problems through "physical flight" than either through resignation or through amelioration and fighting *in situ* the particular conditions into which one has been "thrown". The curious conformism of Americans, noted by observers ever since de Tocqueville, may also be explained in this fashion. Why raise your voice in contradiction and get yourself into trouble as long as you can always remove yourself entirely from any given environment should it become too unpleasant (1970, p. 106–9).

In most societies, however, the expulsion or the flight of an individual or subgroup are limiting cases which could never be common procedure. Most often, the majority tries to move somewhat towards the minority, no matter how small the steps which may be taken in that direction;

or it may try to bring the minority as close to itself as possible—the integration of immigrants, the attempted rehabilitation of prisoners, are some examples of this. All this convinces us that a minority's disagreement has a blocking effect in every instance, and this provides minorities with the means by which to exert influence.

It would also be useful to take other sorts of evidence into account. By a series of indirect assertions, the impression has been created that resistant individuals or minorities are unattractive, held in low esteem, and generally rejected because they are deviants. In such a situation, it was natural to conclude that they could not possibly have any impact, or gain the favour of a majority. In this, too, Schachter's experiment has been thought to be conclusive, since it demonstrates that in a popularity vote the deviant comes in last.

It would be inaccurate to say either that this lack of popularity is exceptional, or that it is typical. The question is—does it *impede* the ability to influence? Although social psychologists have answered "yes", they have not substantiated their view. It does not require a great stretch of the imagination to see that a deviant, just by virtue of being what he is, can exert a considerable attraction—often greater than that of the so-called normal person. Why can he be attractive? There may be many reasons, but I want to stress only two.

Normal people and normal behaviours represent to a large extent the authority of the super-ego, evoking the mechanical and rigid aspects of life—the ordinary, predictable, even automatic sequences of familiar events, words, and gestures. In sharp contrast, deviant persons and behaviours suggest the possibility of denial of the super-ego, inviting the release of impulsive urges and endorsing spontaneity of behaviour—and even more, offering access to the unknown, novel, and surprising. Above all, the attraction of the deviant is confounded with the attraction of the forbidden, which he symbolizes, and we know the force of that attraction.

A second reason is what I will call social guilt. Many categories of deviants and minorities represent groups which have been placed in an inferior position, excluded from the society's idea of normality, by various forms of discrimination—economic, social, racial. They are blatantly, in a direct or a hypocritical manner, deprived of rights that the social system and political or religious values grant to everyone else. Such a conflict between principles and reality not only creates internal conflicts, but also a sense of guilt. For the Christian to have slaves, the democrat to prevent blacks from voting by insidious manoeuvres, the

egalitarian to live with striking inequalities all around him, all represent
contradictions.

It is true that the consciences of many will be relieved by theoretical
or religious justifications, which are passably satisfying and provided by
priests, ideologists, or social scientists, who perform this function very
well. But there will still be some people who feel very strongly that these
justifications are not adequate, and that the strain they feel can only
be reduced by identifying with or adopting the way of life and viewpoint of these excluded groups. It is for this reason that some young
people, and some older adults, renounce their social advantages and
adopt a frugal life-style; perhaps giving up wealth and settling for
manual labour, or even, like the Friars of the Middle Ages, becoming
mendicants and sharing the life of the very poor. Others may try to
break socially with their own class, and move into districts where they
can attempt to assimilate themselves with the minority. Of course, social
guilt is not the only explanation of this type of movement towards the
deviant. A sense of justice, political beliefs, philosophical positions, may
also be involved. My analysis is not meant to be exhaustive, but simply
to point out that contradictions between the real and the ideal in a
society will create conditions in which those who are pushed to the
periphery by the society will exert an attractive force.

In addition, some experiments which I shall describe in detail later
are beginning to show that a minority individual, while he may not
necessarily be liked, may nevertheless be admired for his courage, sincerity, originality, and so on, and this will open up a whole range
of initiatives to him when he tries to act on the majority. The history of
resistance movements in World War II provides a striking example of
this aspect of deviance. A different example is the well-known phenomenon of sympathy and admiration for certain types of daring criminals
and delinquents, which can sometimes provoke an unfortunate emulation of their activities. Furthermore, not all groups give the same
weight to success; the underprivileged, the underdog, the defeated, may
arouse powerful emotions and sympathies when they confront the
powerful and fortunate: *The conquering cause was pleasing to the Gods, but
the conquered one to Cato.*

There is nothing wrong in being a deviant; it is tragic to remain one.
A whole set of factors—internal conflict, the desire that consensus be
unanimous, the fact that the deviant can be attractive and positively
perceived, show that deviants and minorities have as good a chance of

exerting influence as the majority. On this point at least the two poles of the relationship are interdependent.

But who is the influence source, and who is the influence target, and under what circumstances? The description of what constitutes a minority or a majority, of what is and is not deviance, must be carried further. The elements which I can contribute are not altogether novel, but I would like to complement the list of known elements whose implications have unfortunately been overlooked. For the convenience of the reader, but without wishing to appear too pedantic, I would like to propose provisionally that a distinction be made first of all between *nomic* and *anomic* groups, individuals, etc., according to whether or not they possess a common code, a recognized norm, a dominant response, or an identified consensus. Let us examine the meaning of divergence or deviance in the light of this distinction.

On the one hand is implied a lack for an individual or a group of psychological or social means for grasping or recognizing the norm or dominant response. On the other hand is implied a denial of the norm or dominant response, because of the existence of an alternative, of counter-norms or counter-responses which correspond to the beliefs, needs, or actual reality of the individuals or groups adopting them. It is easy to see that not conforming to a new fashion in clothes because the fashion is not understood, or because one cannot afford to buy new clothes, is not the same—does not have the same meaning—as having a preference for other fashions, or preferring to dress idiosyncratically. Similarly, in the field of social issues, if one indulges in free love, homosexuality, group sex, or drugs merely in order to gratify personal desires or curiosity, this is not the same thing as adopting these behaviours because they are the badge of a generation, or because one supports the theoretical notion of sexual freedom. In the first case, divergence or deviance are a transgression, and may be viewed as anomic; in the second case they result from conscious opposition to a norm and the assertion of alternatives, and may be considered nomic.

Consequently, it is also necessary to distinguish between *anomic minorities*, individuals or sub-groups, who are defined with reference to the norm or response of the larger social system because the group to which they belong lacks norms and responses of its own; and *nomic minorities*, who take a distinct stand in contrast or opposition to the larger social system.

Majorities can also be categorized in this manner. We know that there are majorities characterized by strongly internalized common rules or codes, to which the term nomic is applicable; certain churches, political parties, social movements, for example. There are also majorities whose codes and rules are the results of precarious compromises between conflicting interests, the famous "silent majority" for instance, anonymous and lonely crowds, the serially structured groups of atomized individuals described by Jean-Paul Sartre, all of which are best characterized as anomic.

On the basis of this classification, I will make another provisional suggestion. In the functionalist model, the role of influence source and influence receiver are attributed according to the criterion of dependence; the former is that part of the group in whose hands authority rests, and the latter is that part of the group which submits to authority. In the theory which I am putting forward, the criterion for the attribution of influence roles is the possession or lack of possession of a norm or counter-norm, of a response or counter-response. For the sake of terminological simplicity, we will use the terms majority and minority norms and responses. The possession or lack of such norms and responses is what makes individuals active or passive partners in social relations. In truth, social psychologists have already used this criterion implicitly. In their experiments they have usually confronted a majority or a leader having well-defined and structured norms or opinions with a minority or an individual who simply deviated from that norm, lacking self-assurance or solutions of his own.

It has sometimes been recognized that not all deviants are alike, and that they do not all react in the same fashion. In other words, they may sometimes actively resist. This has been explained by the possibility that deviants have ties to external groups which have different criteria and values. Carrying this notion to the extreme, some authors have described deviants only in terms of these external ties, disregarding the possibility of internal consistency or autonomy: "In instances of deviance it is probable that another group is providing the reinforcements for the individuals. Deviation thus becomes in part a matter of conformity to the norms prevailing in a different group" (McGinnies, 1970).

What an innocent remark, and how scientific it sounds. So scientific, in fact, that one has difficulty in recognizing the familiar conspiracy thesis. Why has your child become a leftist? Because he has come under the influence of some long-haired lecturer or friends—not because he has thought for himself, or made a serious political choice. Why do nations revolt against an imperial power? Because some other imperial power is inciting them, not because, as Frederick Douglas has said "the limits of tyrants are prescribed by the endurance of those whom they oppress". More generally, behind any particular social movement or individual transgression one is led to see the hidden hand, not of God or economics, but that of a powerful and secret group controlling them.

Given the conformity bias, however, social psychologists had no other criterion for deviance, apart from internal weakness, than that of dependence on some external group. One may well wonder what group it was that Copernicus was dependent on, or Freud, or any of the other persons who have revolutionized science, art, and society?

What I mean to stress is that theoretical and experimental research has been primarily centred on *nomic* majorities and *anomic* minorities. The existence of nomic minorities whose behaviour differs from that of anomic minorities has been considered only as an afterthought. Moreover, within the framework of the previously noted asymmetrical relationships of the functionalist model, nomic minorities are viewed only as less tractable influence receivers, and not as potential influence sources.

This imbalance must be corrected. It will demand more than merely introducing reciprocity and symmetry where before there was unilaterality and asymmetry. It will mean studying the neglected cases. What are they? Using the distinctions that I have proposed, if a matrix is set up with + representing the cases that have been studied, and − representing those that have been ignored, the balance is easily seen.

TABLE 1

	Majority	
	Nomic	Anomic
Nomic minority	−	−
Anomic minority	+	−

The table reveals that the influence exerted by a nomic majority on an anomic minority, and on a nomic minority in so far as it resists, have been analysed in the literature; the other combinations have been overlooked. Nevertheless, it is almost certainly true that an active group or minority, confronted with an anomic majority, will act as an influence source. A similar argument seems to apply in the other cases.

As I said at the outset, these distinctions are based on established facts. To refresh the reader's memory, the purpose is to determine the different roles played with respect to influence, and to introduce activity or passivity on the part of the social actors, regardless of their status, as a determining factor. Activity or passivity, which depend on the existence or absence of specific, consistent identities, opinions, or behaviours, would then take the place of dependence as the crucial factor.

My aim here is to come to grips with what actually happens to the minority and to give a more complete description of its features. The first distinctive feature is that a minority either appears as being passive (anomic) or active (nomic). But if we consider minorities or deviants as having opinions, norms, and judgements, to follow the general tendency, we should then have to evaluate their capacity to influence and to effect changes in terms of their *divergence* from the majority. This would imply neglecting an important element: the social space is always a vectorial one. Opinions, norms, and especially attitudes necessarily represent the dispositions, either "for" or "against", of the individual or the group. It is desirable, therefore, to take into account the *direction* of the solutions advocated by the deviant or the minority.

As an illustration, in the context of a national problem, one may have the opportunity of encountering individuals or parties adhering to extremist political positions: reactionaries, racists, conservatives, and so on, at one end of the scale, radicals and anarchists, etc., at the other end. One of the minorities is *orthodox* (pro-normative) whereas the other is *heterodox* (counter-normative). The former outdoes the majority norm, while the latter opposes a minority norm to it. This constitutes a second distinctive feature for analysing the processes that concern us here. According to the generally accepted propositions, only the orthodox minority would have a chance of exerting influence on the group since it advocates an already socially accepted norm.

If we abandon these propositions, it immediately becomes apparent that the spokesmen for heterodox minorities do provide something new (information, arguments, styles, etc.) for the group; they do present a different perspective, and for this reason, they create a conflict which may induce the group to change. There is, as yet, little evidence to support these speculations, but some clues are already available.

To begin with, it seems that a heterodox minority has a better chance of influencing the group, the smaller the distance between its own position and that of the majority. This is what logic commands us to say, what common sense encourages us to believe; and a recent experiment of Nemeth and Endicott (1974) leads us to think that this is indeed the case. As we shall see, this experiment, although it does not directly confront a minority to a majority, clarifies the ideas that concern us here, for it shows us the link that exists between discrepancy and direction of opinions or judgements in the process of influence.

The problem is the following: most theories have tried to establish a relation between the amount of discrepancy between positions and the amount of attitude change. More exactly, they predict a curvilinear relation: change increases as does the distance between positions up to a certain point, after which it decreases drastically. But our problem is not concerned either with these theories or with their predictions, for they are perfectly compatible with our most spontaneous intuitions. The problem resides in the mixed results that have been obtained from various experiments carried out under the auspices of these theories over the last twenty years or so. All in all, they seem to be caused by the range of discrepancy that is involved in the experimentation, confusions between initial positions and discrepancy on the one hand, and sides of issues and discrepancy on the other.

In order to clarify this situation, the authors of the experiment I am about to describe assumed that in every social judgement there is a psycho-sociological mid-point which divides all judgements into two basic orientations: "own side" and "opposite side". Furthermore, this normative middle point functions as an anchor, much as the individual's own position, in the evaluation of a message concerning a controversial issue as well as the response that is given to it. From this hypothesis, the authors predicted that, in general, subjects will be more inclined to assimilate the positions that are on their "own side", and to contrast those on the "opposite side", even when the amount of discrepancy is constant. This general propensity, however, should be more effective when discrepancies are large. The motivation to preferring "own side" to "opposite side" is relevant, especially when the sender of the message takes a stand that is very distant from the anchor, that is the actual mid-point or the subject's own position. With small discrepancies, the subject will react by a change of attitude, regardless of whether the sender's message is on his "own side" or on the "opposite side". With large discrepancies, however, subjects should be more likely to react by an attitude change in the direction of a sender who takes an extreme position that is very discrepant on the subject's "own side", whereas he should not show any kind of attitude change if the extremely discrepant position is on the "opposite side", that is, across the mid-point. Thus, if you are slightly conservative in science or politics, you are likely to be equally influenced by a moderate radical as by a moderate conservative. But when it comes to extremes, you will only be influenced by an extreme conservative and not at all by an extreme radical. This presupposes that there is a basic tendency towards always holding an orthodox position, be it close or distant, and only sometimes holding a heterodox one. I do not agree with this point or with its implications, and I shall explain why below. But having made this reservation, let us see if and how the predictions are confirmed.

The materials were pre-tested in a series of nine situations involving a moral judgement. In each of the situations, damage has been done to some object (for instance, a ball has smashed the front window of a house), and the value or cost for replacing it is specified. This replacement value is considered to be at the psychological mid-point of the scale, and it can be compared to other values, such as, "more than replacement value" or "less than replacement value". It is understood that money was used because it is a convenient internal scale for individuals living in a society in which money is the measure of things.

The experiment was carried out as follows. When the subjects arrived, they were informed that they would hear a recorded interview between the experimenter and one of their fellow students. They were also informed that the recording was a discussion about one of the cases that they had read three weeks earlier, and they were asked to listen attentively since the experimenter wanted to know how the subjects understood what was said and what their reactions were to the student who was interviewed. The interview was recorded with a fourteen-year-old male confederate. The same recording was used in all the experimental conditions simply by dubbing in the "student's" position, in order to control for non-verbal and verbal cues throughout the experiment. A control condition was also run in which the subjects did not hear a recorded interview. After receiving their instructions, the subjects listened to the recording which corresponded to the condition in which they took part. At the end of the recording they were asked to complete a questionnaire in which they gave their own opinion about the issue, rated the range of judgements (from zero dollars to forty dollars) as being acceptable, unacceptable, or ridiculous positions, and expressed their reactions to the student who was interviewed. (Before presenting the results, one item of information should be added. In this particular study, subjects had an initial position of sixteen dollars or eighteen dollars on a scale that ranged from zero to forty dollars for the compensation given to a person whose window, which cost twenty dollars, had been broken. The mid-point here is twenty dollars which represents the exact replacement value.)

What do we observe? The change of attitude is significant for the subjects who listened to the interview which took the "own side" position, whether the discrepancy was small ($t = 2\cdot85$, $p < 0\cdot05$) or large ($t = 2\cdot14$, $p < 0\cdot05$), and for the subjects who listened to the "opposite side" interview in which the discrepancy was small ($t = 2\cdot85$, $p < 0\cdot05$). Some change, but not a significant one, was recorded for the "opposite side" interview with a large discrepancy ($t = 1\cdot44$, N.S.). Thus, and in line with the predictions, the subjects changed their judgements when they were exposed to someone who took a position which represented a small discrepancy, in this case, six dollars. No matter what side the small discrepancy was on, subjects responded by changing their judgements in the direction of the interviewee's position. In contrast, when discrepancies were large, subjects showed a change in judgement and acceptance in the direction of the interviewee who was on their "own side", but showed no change in judgement or acceptance when the interviewee was on the "opposite side".

In brief, we see that our initial speculation is confirmed. A heterodox minority is more influential when divergence from the majority does not exceed a certain threshold. When this minority becomes extreme, its likelihood of influencing the majority diminishes. But we should not therefore believe that a person is any happier just because the extreme minority whose judgement he follows is on his "own side". Nemeth and Endicott notice that "the relative effectiveness of large discrepancy when it is on the same side of the issue was not because it was seen as an acceptable position, right or reasonable. Main effects for discrepancy were consistently found for these items. Small discrepancies were seen as more right, reasonable and fair than were large discrepancies, regardless of the side of the issue. Yet, the large discrepancy on the same side did produce a feeling of uncertainty in the subjects. They were less sure that their position was fair or that people would agree with them" (p. 19). Paicheler (1974) observed similar reactions in her experimental results. The orthodox minority is preferred since there is no other way out, but one is not any the happier for it. But does one adopt this position in all circumstances? Will a man who is on the right politically invariably prefer a fascist to a socialist, a "law-and-order" man, who is actually a tyrant, to a popular representative body? That conservative democrats do support dictatorships abroad more readily than they will less conservative governments at home, we know of plenty of exceptions to these rules that are stated in innocent and neutral psychological terms. If these exceptions did not exist, no one would ever cross from one side to the other side of the dividing line of his society.

It can no longer be doubted that a heterodox minority can exert influence, at least when it is a matter of a small discrepancy. The experiment we just described confirms this, if only indirectly. But it was clear from the start: our speculation was too cautious. We can now go farther and say that there are circumstances in which the fact of being a heterodox minority is actually an advantage, corresponding to some of the preferences of the majority.

Another experiment, by Nemeth and Wachtler (1973), allows us to confirm this hunch. The authors presented to subjects nineteen pairs of paintings on slides. One member of each pair was randomly designated "Italian", the other "German". Subjects were simply invited to indicate their preferences. But, as usual, they were not alone. They were in groups of five with one confederate. The confederate consistently showed a preference for either "Italian" or "German" paintings. In one condition, the confederate was represented as being of Italian origin ("Angelo Milano"); in a second condition he was introduced as being of German origin ("Fritz Mueller"), and in a third condition no mention was made of his national origin ("Bob Jones"). A control condition was run with the naive subjects only, without the confederate. This control group was not neutral in its preferences, but preferred the paintings labelled Italian—revealing that the majority norm is pro-Italian.

What influence did the minority represented by the confederate exert? When he was represented as German, the subjects of the experimental groups tended to become *more* pro-German (or *less* pro-Italian) than the subjects of the control group. But they became equally *less* pro-Italian when the confederate was represented as being Italian. The authors write "Thus, rather than a situation where the majority of subjects took a stand of equal preference and were faced with a single individual who had either a German or an Italian preference, we had a situation where the majority position was already pro-Italian. In that sense, a confederate who took the Italian position was actually over-espousing the majority position to an extreme degree" (p. 77). The German position, on the other hand, being counter-normative, or a real minority norm, represents an alternative, and helps or obliges the group to reassess its values and judgements. The authors of this elegant experiment explain it thus:

> If we take, as a starting point, the fact that the German position is a minority position in the classic sense while the Italian position is an extremization of the majority viewpoint, we come to an interesting conclusion. A single con-federate, who takes a consistent minority position which is different from that of the majority, is effective in inducing the majority to change its judg-ments in the direction of the minority. However, if he over-espouses a ma-jority position or takes a position more extremely than does the majority itself, the effect is to polarize the subjects away from his position rather than to influence them in his direction. He is still effecting a change, but in the opposite direction. It is possible that the deviate's taking a counter-position brings something new into the situation, causing subjects to consider aspects of reality which they had not previously considered. There is an element of courage in his behaviour. The deviate who over-espouses the majority posi-tion, however, offers nothing new and his rigidity may cause polarization from his position. Another possible explanation for the present data revolves around the possibility that all subjects in the experimental conditions may have been moving toward more "fairness" or showing more equal preferences between German and Italian choices. It is possible that, when a confederate consistently espoused a given position, the concept of nationality and bias became a salient factor and caused subjects to reassess their own positions. The result of such reassessment may have been a response on the basis of a norm of fairness. Thus, while subjects were overwhelmingly pro-Italian when in control groups, they may have been made aware of their own nationality bias by a confederate who consistently chose on the basis of nationality. They may, then, have attempted to deny or reduce their own bias by equalizing their preferences between two nationalities (pp. 77–78).

Another study by Biener (1971) provides equally startling results. In this study, the target of influence was the subjects' perceptions of colour. The task was for the subjects to make judgements on a series of twenty-three colour chips in the blue to green spectrum by assigning each chip to a place on a scale that ranged from the label "very blue" on the one end to "very green" on the other. Out of the twenty-three chips, fifteen displayed the "critical" colour which, objectively, was more on the blue side of the spectrum. The aim of the influence was to have the subjects believe that the "critical" colour was green when the blue versus green comparison had to be made. The following justification was presented in order to facilitate the manipulation of the main variables: subjects were told that the experimenter was interested in determining whether they preferred to make judgements alone or in groups. They were also informed that in several of the trials, before they expressed their own judgements about the colour chips, they would be presented with the dichotomous (blue or green) judgements of one or two other persons like them who had participated in the experiment in the past. The frequency of exposure to a discrepant (green) response was manipulated by informing the subjects on either six or twelve of the critical trials that a past participant had called green what were actually bluish chips. The author of the experiment made the hypothesis that resistance to the discrepant information would increase, on the one hand, the less the subject was exposed to it, and, secondly, the more his judgements were reinforced by giving him supportive information prior to his seeing the colour chip in question. The degree of resistance was manipulated by varying the number of trials in which the subjects were also presented with perception-bolstering information, that is, the response of a second past participant who had called the bluish chip blue, on zero, six, or twelve of the fifteen critical trials. The order of presentation of the supportive and discrepant information was counter-balanced so that half of the subjects received the supportive information from the first past participant, and the discrepant information from the second past participant (S-D condition), and the other half of the subjects received the information in the reverse order (D-S condition).

There were, in fact, two phases of this experiment. In the first phase, the subjects (1) were presented with the colour chips, (2) received a message about the first past participant's judgement of that chip (or a message that the first past participant's judgement would not be given), (3) received a message about the second past participant's judgement of that chip (or a "no response" message), and (4) were presented with a scale on which they were to make their own judgement about that chip. In the second phase of the experiment, the subjects were invited to make dichotomous (green or blue) judgements with twelve colour chips. After this second task, they filled out a questionnaire in which they expressed their attitude towards the two past participants.

The effect of the discrepant information was measured (1) by the tendency to judge the critical colour as more and more green, and,

(2) by the displacement of the threshold for scoring ambiguous colours green.

As one can imagine, and in line with the current thinking about the so-called informational social influence, it was predicted that the more support the subjects received, the less they would be influenced by the discrepant information. The results turned out to be rather surprising. They showed that a different mechanism was operating, one which contradicted what was generally thought to occur. While it was predicted that the existence of social support would bolster the individual against the impact of discrepant information, the data suggest that, in some circumstances, the presence of social support diminishes the individual's resistance to it. We should point out in passing that increasing a person's certainty and reinforcing his judgement does not necessarily make him impervious to influence, far from it. But let us look more closely at Biener's interesting results and comments. The only reliable effect, observes Biener, was due to the order of presentation of the information. Among the subjects who were presented with twelve supportive past participant's responses, those in the S-D condition were more influenced by the discrepant information than those in the D-S condition. It is immediately obvious, however, that when subjects receive a reinforcing message stating that the colour is "blue" *before* they receive the contradictory "green" message, they will be tempted to perceive more "green" in the critical colour chip that they are presented with just *after* (p is significant at less than 0·05 level). Those in the S-D con-

TABLE 2

Certainty that ambiguous colours were green

Number of trials containing discrepant information:	Order of presentation	
	S-D	D-S
6	165·7	61·2
12	147·9	33·9

* A score of −468 would represent absolute certainty that ambiguous colour chips were blue; a score of +468 would represent absolute certainty that they were green.

dition also indicated a greater certainty, on the discrimination task in the second phase of the experiment, in calling the ambiguous colours green (see Table 2).

Responses to the post-experimental questionnaire are even more persuasive. When the past participant who supposedly sees "green" says so after the past participant who supposedly sees "blue", thereby adopting a manifestly contrasting deviant position, he receives more positive sociometric choices and arouses more favourable attitudes than otherwise. Excerpts from the interviews reveal that he is also quite highly regarded: "Someone interesting who looks into things", "Really funny, sort of brilliant". Conversely, subjects in the S-D condition wrote the following about the supportive past participant: "Because he basically always said 'blue', I felt he was a little narrow-minded", "He seemed kind of dull, not too thought-provoking—probably because he thought so much like me".

Biener writes:

> The present results, provide no support for the hypothesis that the availability of external mechanisms of resistance reduces the tendency to accept a discrepant point of view. They suggest, on the contrary, that the knowledge that there are others who agree with the subject may under the same conditions increase his receptivity to the discrepant communication. It was assumed at the outset that the mere exposure of an individual to information which was discrepant to his own belief would arouse motivation to resist it. This assumption seems to be quite common in studies of attitude change. The influence situation is often seen as a conflict in which the influencer and the influencee are conceptualized as adversaries. Viewed in this way, the outcome of the attitudinal conflict can be manipulated by varying the power of each of the parties. Thus, we often find persuasion attributed to the power of the communicator to reward or punish; or to expertise or authority of the communicator as compared to the receiver; or to the subtle tricks of message construction designed to short-circuit the subject's defensive machinery. These kinds of conclusions and the models from which they were derived are, to be sure, quite valuable. However, the results of the present study suggest that in our preoccupation with the competitive orientation toward the influence situation we may have ignored some important aspects of the process of attitude change (p. 44).

They certainly have been ignored. What has been ignored above all else is the fact that human beings always preserve a certain curiosity and open-mindedness, and that, more often than not, they esteem those who have the intellectual or physical courage to leave the beaten track. This is why individuals or groups, when they are exposed to the influence of an orthodox (pro-normative) minority, may find the norm (and the minority) to be less attractive; this has the effect of facilitating the influence of an alternative heterodox (counter-normative) minority which, by way of contrast, appears to be interesting and original.

*

But social phenomena are hardly so simple. It would be absurd to assume that only heterodox minorities exert influence while orthodox minorities do not. We should first examine what kind of influence each type of minority exerts, and even then we must be wary of generalizing too rapidly, for we must also know more about their modes of action. But in the light of historical and political experiences, we should not be far off the mark in advancing the hypothesis that an orthodox minority is frequently able to oblige the group to share its attitudes and beliefs, while a heterodox minority in the same conditions, creates a split in the attitudes and beliefs of the group. It is also possible for the heterodox minority to be completely rejected, to have the contrary effect to what it intends, and we shall return to this question later.

A recent study by Paicheler (1974) allows us to confirm this hypothesis. The study deals with the polarization of attitudes in groups, that is, the fact that during and after social interaction groups tend to adopt more extreme positions than those of its members before the interaction. Let us first describe the experimental material and procedure that were used in Paicheler's experiments. First, the subjects are individually presented with a questionnaire consisting of eight items concerned with attitudes towards women. Each item describes an aspect of women's lives and problems, and offers several alternative responses, some of which are basically pro-feminist and others basically anti-feminist. For each of the eight items the subjects are asked to indicate which alternative they prefer (pre-consensus). After they have completed the questionnaire, the experimenter places them in groups of four, gives them a second copy of the same questionnaire and asks them to discuss each item and to come to a unanimous decision about each one. The decisions reached by the groups are then recorded on a second copy of the questionnaire (consensus). After this phase, the subjects are again asked to express their individual opinions for each item (post-consensus). Thus, the experiment is divided into three phases: pre-consensus, consensus, and post-consensus. If the group were unable to reach a consensus, the discussion on that item was interrupted after eight minutes; subjects were then asked to write down their individual position at that time.

The experimental conditions were the following: (a) the presence of an external person. A confederate of the experimenter was placed in each group. He was instructed to take an extreme position and to abide by it no matter how great the pressure from the other group members. He was to adopt this extreme position consistently throughout the group discussion, answering every item in the same way. (b) The orthodox and the heterodox norm. The confederate expressed either a pro-feminist attitude, which goes in the direction of the norm for the student groups who participated in the experiment, or an anti-feminist attitude, which goes against the norm for student groups. By constantly and consistently adopting an extreme, and therefore deviant position, the confederate either places himself in the direction of the contemporary evolution of the norm, or in the counter-current.

The results were as follows: when a feminist and extremist confederate is placed in the group, the polarization of attitudes is very strong, and in the majority of cases corresponds to an agreement with the confederate on the most extreme feminist positions. In 94% of the cases the subjects allied themselves with the confederate's point of view. It is even more remarkable to note that the subjects maintained these extreme attitudes in the post-consensus phase of the experiment when they responded alone. In short, the norm was considerably changed by the presence of an orthodox minority individual who stood firmly by his position. When the confederate was inconsistent, the change or polarization is much smaller than in groups in which he was consistent; and this in both the consensus phase ($F = 13 \cdot 8$, $p < 0 \cdot 02$) and the post-consensus phase ($F = 7 \cdot 29$, $p < 0 \cdot 02$).

But the picture is altered in those groups which had an anti-feminist confederate. We must first emphasize, as the author of these experiments has pointed out, that in 94% of the cases a consensus was not reached by the group members, and the discussion on that item was interrupted after eight minutes. This inability to establish an agreement is felt to be a great frustration for the subjects, which is only exacerbated by the rigidity of the confederate, and it leads to a deadlock in the discussion. However, we cannot support the conclusion that the presence of the confederate leads only to an opposition to, rejection of, or agreement with his intransigent and extreme position. The processes which are involved are much more complicated. In some ways, they are similar to those described by Sherif and Hovland (1961) as the assimilation and contrast mechanisms. According to these authors, the recipients of a message shift their attitude in the direction closer to the source of the message when the position of the source is near to their own—the assimilation effect; and in the direction opposite to the attitude of the source of the message when its position is remote from the recipients' attitude—the contrast effect. But in their studies, Sherif and Hovland considered these effects as separate ones, leading sometimes to conformity and sometimes to polarization.

In bipolarization a phenomenon of differential influence can be observed. The views of the minority confederate have the effect of shifting towards anti-feminism those subjects who already had some anti-feminist tendencies, and towards pro-feminism the subjects who already were to some extent pro-feminist—thus, assimilation and contrast operate simultaneously. It is true, however, that although the processes postulated here imply a symmetry of the two effects, our results show a dissymmetry, since the assimilation effect is more marked in them than the contrast effect. Indeed, we can notice very different shifts for the subjects who tended towards a feminist position before the group discussion and those who tended towards a less feminist one. The former returned to their initial positions, or, in a few cases, to more markedly feminist positions after the exchange of ideas in the group. There are here signs of resistance to the confederate's influence, but not a clear contrast effect. Other subjects adopted the confederate's position, both during and after the exchange. Their slight resistance lets us suppose that the confederate's anti-feminist arguments resonated with their own and entailed a clear assimilation effect (see Table 3).

TABLE 3

Average differential evolution in groups with an anti-feminist confederate

Subjects:	Phase of experiment		
	Pre-consensus	Consensus	Post-consensus
the least feminist	0·02	−0·89	−0·44
the most feminist	1·46	1·03	1·55

Thus, the consistent expression of a heterodox attitude had a very pronounced effect of bipolarization; as was expected, the members' position tended to move away from one another. Although we do not have as yet a clear explanation of these findings, this is an important effect, and it has rarely been obtained experimentally. It corresponds to the kind of influence that a heterodox person can exert by increasing the divergence of opinions, by arousing conflicts between the group members and blocking the consensus between them. This shows that it is just as possible to increase the influence of a minority which agrees with the norms as it is to make two opposing influences appear simultaneously when the minority disagrees with the norms.

Because of the richness of these experiments, there would be much more to say about them and many considerations to add. But we can see that the two minorities, one deviating in an orthodox way and the other deviating in a heterodox way, induce different types of change, and for the moment this is the main point of these results. One question remains to be solved. The first statement made above was that only nomic minorities which have a definite point of view are in a position to influence the group. Then it was asserted, and I hope demonstrated, that the orthodox or heterodox character of this point of view, of the norm it represents, determines the degree and especially the nature of the minority's influence. Nevertheless we may wonder how this influence is related to the way the minority expresses its own views. In other words, we need to know whether the rigidity or the flexibility of the arguments which are presented have the same effects in the use of orthodoxy as in the use of heterodoxy.

Mugny (1974) studied this problem and tested the hypothesis that the orthodox point of view will tend to be more influential when it is presented in a rigid manner than when it is presented in a hesitant way, and that the opposite is true of a heterodox point of view. The rationale for the hypothesis is fairly simple: in the former case, a message containing coherent arguments reinforces the attitudes of the group; in the latter, it threatens these attitudes and provokes rejection. The real situation is, however, more complicated. The material used in this experiment concerned attitudes towards foreigners as measured by a questionnaire consisting of sixteen items. Each item is composed of a phrase expressing a judgement on the problems raised by the presence of foreigners in Switzerland. Half of the items represent anti-foreigner attitudes, and half pro-foreign attitudes. The items deal with problems of housing, political rights, culture, and economics as they relate to the presence of foreigners. For each item the subjects were to indicate whether they considered the judgement "valid" or "not valid" on a seven point scale. The subjects, young Swiss junior high school students, were administered the experiment in their classrooms. They were first asked to answer the questionnaire. After having completed the questionnaire, they were each given a tract to read; they were told that there were several different tracts, and were therefore asked to read them alone and silently. There were, in fact, four different tracts which all followed a similar outline: the first paragraph stated the problem which the presence of foreigners in Switzerland raised, and indicated the position of the authors of the tract. The three following paragraphs briefly presented issues relevant to housing, labour union rights, and political rights of foreigners. Out of the four tracts, two represented the orthodox, pro-normative anti-xenophobic position, and two represented a heterodox xenophobic position. Moreover, in each of the two categories of tracts, one presented the attitude for (or against) the presence of foreigners in a consistent way while the other was more "hesitant", less consistent than the next. Each subject read one only of the tracts, the class having been divided into four sub-groups. The tracts were collected after the students had read them, and they were again asked to fill out the questionnaire on attitudes towards foreigners. The task was justified by saying that merely reading a text often allowed people to clarify their thoughts and ideas.

The experimental situation involved here is certainly too constraining. Yet the results provide us with some interesting tendencies. Table 4 presents the change of attitude on all the items in the four experimental conditions.

TABLE 4

Average index of attitude change on the
sixteen items of the questionnaire*

Source:	Type of message	
	Nomic	Anomic
Orthodox	+2·92	−1·32
Heterodox	+1·76	−1·76

* N = 25 for each square

We can observe that the subjects who read the orthodox tracts which contained a coherent point of view are positively influenced, while the subjects presented with an orthodox tract which is relatively flexible tend to be influenced in the opposite direction, becoming more xenophobic instead of more anti-xenophobic. The tendency, however, is not statistically significant. What about the subjects who were presented with a heterodox tract expressing a xenophobic point of view? Their reaction was almost the opposite. Those who read the heterodox tract written to present an absolutely xenophobic group show a tendency, which happily is not significant, to become xenophobic. In contrast, the subjects who read the "hesitant" heterodox tract changed in the opposite direction of the message to which they had been exposed, since they became more anti-xenophobic than before ($t = 1.77, p < 0.05$).

An analysis of variance of the two independent factors reveals a significant difference ($F = 9.136, p < 0.005$) between the "rigid" and "flexible" messages, which indicates that the style and organization of arguments play an important role. Nevertheless it appears that the "rigid" ones induced a greater change when the message was orthodox than when it was heterodox ($F = 5.645, p < 0.05$). Orthodoxy therefore has a greater impact than heterodoxy, but only if the positions are presented in a coherent way.

One could object, and rightly so, that these results do not, strictly speaking, concern the influence of a minority, since the tracts are presented to the students by a group of adults and in the classroom setting. For this reason I underlined the tentative nature of the present results. Let us recall however the experiment of Paicheler (1974), in which there is a minority, and we observe that the minority's impact is significant only when it abides firmly by a single specific position from the beginning to the end of the group discussion, to when it is expressed as a nomic minority. With all these reservations in mind, however, we are led to conclude that only a nomic group, be it for or against the norm, is in a position to exert an influence over its social environment.

In summary, the reciprocal influence of a minority is conceivable because of the permanent existence of internal conflicts, because of the quest for a unanimous consensus, and because individual are often perceived favourably even when they have no special status or power. But the mere fact of being a minority, a deviant, does not in itself transform the individual or the group into a target or a source of influence, into a passive or an active part of the group or society. What transforms the minority into a source or a target of influence is determined by the absence or presence of a definite stand, of a coherent point of view, of a norm of its own. In other words, it is the nomic or anomic character of the social grouping that counts, and not the fact that it is, or is not, in a position of power or that it does, or fails to, constitute a majority. Finally, it is not the sheer distance between positions—the discrepancy between majority and minority judgements or attitudes—that determines their respective impact, although such discrepancies must be taken into account. The meaning of this distance deserves a more rigorous examination. We could thus have observed that their influence depends on the different directions which exist between the two poles of interaction: *orthodox* when it moves in the same direction as the norm, and *heterodox* when it goes against the direction of the norm. If we look closely at the data, we can see that a deviant heterodox minority has a good chance of influencing a group, of attracting its members, of making them think through their beliefs and judgements, and even of winning a certain amount of esteem. But we have to examine the facts as well, for beyond its polemical value such a conclusion is somewhat removed from reality. By analysing what this reality can teach us we are forced to think in different terms, that is, to examine the nature of the influence exerted by one type or another of minority. In general, orthodoxy implies a greater uniformity of opinions and beliefs in the group, a global influence of the minority's point of view. On the other hand, heterodoxy by blocking the communication and interactions among the group members and by making a consensus impossible, produces a sharp differentiation between opinions and beliefs in the group, and a displacement in the direction opposite to the group norm. Sometimes such an effect is unintentional; at other times, it corresponds to a manifest goal of increasing the distance between the heterodox minority and the orthodox majority. In any case, the conditions for exerting influence remain unchanged: one must exist and be active.

5

The Knot of Change: Conflict

Proposition 2

Social change is as much an objective of influence as social control

All societies are heterogeneous by definition, and people do not all share the same world within a society. Individuals, classes, and professional interests are in conflict, and their objectives and modes of action are incompatible. Laws, conventions, administrative regulations attempt to transform these centrifugal forces into centripetal ones. Order crystallizes out of the shifting mass of virtual disorder. And what applies to society as a whole applies also within each group. Social control and social change, sometimes complement each other and sometimes oppose each other. But these two forces are not equally strong in all sectors of social life, or in all parts of society or groups. Nor do they have equal impact on all developmental phases of a collective system. These are commonplace observations, but they do call attention to some neglected implications.

Off-hand, one might assume that groups such as the family, the church, school, industry, the army, certain political movements, would act to maintain social control as the dominant force. In these groups, the requirement of continuity, the need to transmit practices and values, the need to maintain hierarchic relationships, entail a constant supervision of individual behaviour and a no less constant vigilance to prevent or eliminate deviance whenever it occurs. Consensus, submission to norms, the suppression of strong personal preferences, and the need for guidance and approbation seem to be necessary preconditions for any coordinated and conflict-free interaction.

This does not hold true for science, art, fashion, or technology. In these areas, originality, the clash of ideas, the search for new ideas and techniques count among the highest and most rewarded values, and indeed survival depends on them. In these spheres of activity, the aim of all exchange and communication is to disseminate new elements, to modify methods, concepts, tastes, and behaviours, and to establish differences between groups and individuals. There is little desire to maintain the *status quo*: on the contrary, it is viewed with repugnance. The driving force of these behaviours is not affiliation with others, or the need to share their opinions and codes. The motive is the renewal and replacement of what is in existence, the recognition of the individuality of each contribution and each position.

I am, of course, somewhat overstating the case. However, one can see here that the tendency towards social control and the tendency towards social change are not working in the same direction. At times, the antagonism between these tendencies is clearly revealed. In scientific and technical groups, for instance, examinations, evaluation, and the nature of the literature contribute to the shaping of individuals, to the perpetuation of ways of thinking and of working, and the perpetuation of certain topics and models. What is considered "scientific" at any given time is usually sharply defined and constitutes the measure of a person's fitness to become a member of a given group. Participation in conferences and symposia, election to professional organizations, and the winning of prizes complete the scientist's integration into the group. By respecting the various techniques and rules with which he has become familiar, he gains recognition for his competence and is awarded membership in a group which in turn gives him access, according to his ability and accomplishments, to positions in the academy, industry, or government.

At the same time, by the choice of examples worthy of emulation, the stress placed on the discovery of new phenomena and techniques, the award of prestige in return for successes in innovation, one is encouraged to shun accepted ideas and seek for new stimulation and perspectives. The honour accorded to the man of genius, the discoverer of a new phenomenon, the creator of a new theory or technique, and particularly of a new science, enter into the collective consciousness and create the conviction that, in the last analysis, it is the upsetting of established principles, techniques, and concepts which is the highest goal and the most secure basis for lasting recognition. In this same group, however, the elaboration of existing knowledge, the refining of techniques, and the validation of ideas by routine and detailed experimentation are also usually valued, and indeed this is what most scientists are actually doing. Their work can easily be assessed and integrated within a particular field, according to whether it has improved something that needed improving, or whether it has solved a troublesome problem.

But, by the same token, in periods when scientists do agree in their basic orientation, and are thus making small advances and steady progress on a limited scale, a strange thing happens. The normal lacunae and deficiencies of knowledge become magnified, and there is a pervasive sentiment of boredom and discontent. The small-scale, plodding routine loses significance, and everyone seems to be waiting for something new to happen—for someone to bring forth a truly new and exciting idea. So the normal periods of steady, piecemeal progress, such as we are living through today, are experienced and judged at the time as periods of crisis; and the exceptional, agitated periods in which everything is re-worked and turned upside down are experienced and judged as times of growth and achievement.

The delicate balancing-act between the desire for constant change and the need to evolve new means for keeping change in check is illustrated by the unceasing subdivision of scientific disciplines, the unending stream of new periodicals, the steady creation of new research establishments, the relatively rapid progress from the periphery to the centre of the scientific community, the tolerance towards marginal individuals and subgroups, and the severity with which work offered for publication is judged. Irrespective of the accuracy or otherwise of this description of the scientific community, it is a fact that social change is more important than social control in certain areas of activity, and that communications, influence processes, and the organization of relations between individuals and subgroups are all deeply affected by this situation.

Although either change or control may be dominant in a society, it goes without saying that not all groups within the society will agree as to the desirability of the predominant force. Social control is usually valued by authorities and majorities. Their ideal, and indeed their business is equilibrium, the painless resolution of conflicts, unquestioning adherence to existing opinions and laws, and the propagation of a single view of reality. Of course, everyone benefits from this to a certain extent, but the differences in the extent of the benefit are important.

Social change, on the other hand, will clearly be desired by deviant or marginal individuals and subgroups. For them, the struggle against the "establishment" and discriminations of all kinds predominates over the need for stability and respect for rules.

The terms that I have been using might seem to imply that my observations apply only to the economic and political sphere. A moment's thought, however, will reveal that they are equally applicable to the scientific and artistic sphere, and even to relations between parents and children, married couples, teachers and students. This analysis applies to confrontations within the university, struggles against colonialism and racism, and conflict between generations and sexes. It is true that such instances of conflict are not as widespread as situations of stability and cohesion, but they are nonetheless crucial for our lives and culture. One cannot hope to grasp the fundamental nature of individual or group behaviour without taking phenomena of this sort into account. This truth needed to be clearly stated, for, on the one hand, many social psychologists have tended to neglect structural differences in the spheres of social action, and on the other hand they have assumed that individuals and groups obey the same motives or interests regardless of their position in the society.

Up to this point, I have discussed social control and social change in general terms, in order to be able to grasp them in perspective. But we now need to ask the question—what is the meaning of this opposition between control and change in terms of social influence? This meaning is contained in our definitions of source and target of change. This comes out clearly in studies relating to power, communication in small groups, decision-making, and modification of attitudes and behaviour. Groups, majorities, and leaders appear determined to strengthen their control and attain their objectives by putting pressure on individuals and minorities in order to make them change. Lewin's (1948) concept of group dynamics, as well as work by Coch and French (1948), are based on the belief that the group is the most effective instrument for altering behaviours or opinions, and for bringing about the integration of the individual. Lazarsfeld's theory of the two-step flow of communication uses an analogous framework, and the prolific literature on attitude change betrays the same bias.

The attitude to be changed is that of the individual. Most theories formulated on this—including the dissonance, reinforcement and attribution theories, are theories which deal with individual rather than collective attitudes. This was in fact inevitable, since the individual was always considered as a potential deviant, a possible obstacle to group locomotion, and as maladjusted if resistant to group demands. We will only finally be able to speak of genuine social change when we invert the terms and make the group as a whole, *its* norms and *its* attitudes the target of change, and make individuals and minorities the source of these changes.

It now becomes clear that social change is the central process of influence, in its individual and collective manifestations. The opposition between social change and social control, that I have laid so much stress on is intimately linked with the direction, origin and effects of influence. The crucial nature of this opposition lies in the fact that it channels and directs our whole approach to social relations and the questions we raise about them. There is another reason why it is important: it forces us to revise our theories about attitude change, if these are to be applicable to groups as well as to individuals. By concentrating on the pressures which produce social change, we will come to recognize the need to describe and account for *innovation*.

Proposition 3

Influence processes are directly related to the production and resolution of conflicts

> War is a kind of exchange that binds together the very ones it tears asunder
>
> *Joubert*

Social influence is not necessarily associated with either uncertainty or disagreement. Everything around us is arranged in such a way as to confirm us in our attitudes, strengthen our agreement with each other, and forestall anything that might unsettle this state of affairs. All means of communication, from the daily newspaper to prayers, from harmless conversations about the weather to political speeches, are used in such a way as to avoid the slightest awakening of curiosity. But when influence is exerted in the direction of change, disagreement is inevitable. As soon as disagreement makes itself felt, it is experienced as a threatening, anxiety-inducing state. It gives notice that the fragile contract of relations, beliefs, and consensus is about to be challenged.

The very expectation of disagreement and divergent opinion has analogous physiological effects. There is a common expression used of a crossed person—that he or she is "bristling". C. E. Smith (1936) set out to measure this response in terms of variations in the galvanic skin response. In his experiment, subjects are told that their opinions are in agreement or disagreement with a fictitious majority. In cases of disagreement, the reactions recorded on the psycho-galvanometer are stronger. The reaction is also more pronounced when subjects defend their opinions heatedly, than when their convictions are not so strong.

Burdick and Burnes (1958) carried out a similar study. Adolescent boys were given two topics to prepare for discussion with a teacher—"life after death", and "conscription". During the discussion, the teacher would consistently agree with the subject on one topic, but disagree consistently on the other. A more pronounced psycho-physiological reaction was observed when the subject was being contradicted.

These experiments and several others like them (Steiner, 1966) give some support to the idea that people normally expect others to agree with them, that they will feel tense if this expectation is not met, and that it will take them some time to perceive the existence of disagreement. Asch (1952) has observed that individuals who are subject to majority pressure hesitate a long time before accepting the notion of a conflict with the majority. Among these subjects, "none are prepared for the fundamental disagreement; instead, they look for a more obvious source of misunderstanding. The subjects are not yet fully in the conflict; they are in fact resisting it as a real possibility by searching for a simpler explanation. They hope that the early disagreements were episodic and that they will give way to solid unanimity. As the disagreements persist, they can no longer cling to this hope. They now believe that they are perceiving in one way, the group in another."

But this rule that individuals expect the agreement of others is "proved" by its exception. Smith has shown that individuals who have profound conviction show no signs of tension when they encounter disagreement. He suggests the following interpretation; persons who are sure that they are right do not feel challenged by contrary opinions.

I will return later to the question of such exceptions, in order to dispute the hasty conclusion that people prefer harmony to argument, love to hate. Present or future differences of opinion or belief, as such, are not at issue. What matters is that they are signs of imminent conflict. Steiner, to whom we are indebted for this insight, observes: "Even when they are anticipated, interpersonal controversies may presage impending disaster, predict future hardship, or confirm the existence of personal faults. Undoubtedly it is the *symbolic meaning* of a disagreement, rather than its inherent qualities, that is inconsistent with valued goals" (Steiner, 1966, p. 223).

But, in the final analysis, what is threatening about divergence is (1) the threat of a different norm or response, and (2) the uncertainty about one's own ability to resist or modify the other norm or response. Beyond the other viewpoint, there is also the personality of the other person or persons to be taken into account. When there is a clash of ideas or judgements, doubt is made all the stronger because of the belief that there cannot be more than one acceptable, or accepted, idea or judgement. The individual loses confidence in what he sees or thinks, or, if he remains confident, he cannot understand how and why another individual can have a different point of view, and he is led to concern himself about the validity and generality of this other point of view.

The resulting feeling of inadequacy not only has intellectual roots, but interpersonal and social roots as well. As we have seen before, an individual or a group are at the same time sources and receivers of influence. That is, depending on their stand, they can expect to influence others, or to be influenced, to a certain extent. If disagreement persists, their expectancy is not met, and they may experience failure instead of success.

Failure, when it occurs, is less drastic, or can be accepted more easily when it is a case of a minority confronting a majority. Success, on the other hand, is experienced as an absolute triumph. The opposite is true for majorities. The failure of attempts to influence is profoundly disturbing, while success is nothing exceptional. In short, the persistence of divergent attitudes and judgements constitutes a blow to people's anticipated power to effect change, and as a result of this, confidence in either one's own abilities or one's own opinions and beliefs is lost.

Disagreement, as well as the threat of conflict, thus has a disturbing effect, and creates uncertainty. In Sherif's experimental paradigm, it is possible almost to put one's finger exactly on this development. Subjects watch a point of light for a certain number of trials, during which they are asked to evaluate its displacement. They are uncertain at first, but after a few trials they reach an opinion of which they are almost convinced. Now they are brought together as a group, and discover that they all have different opinions. There are distinct signs of a anxiety .

each subject deals with his uncertainty by making his opinion converge towards the common judgemental norm.

Asch's experiments are based on a device which creates and necessitates an extreme opposition: error replaces truth. The interaction in the laboratory leads to loss of self-confidence and the destruction of a stable frame of reference. "Yet this clearness of perception" writes Samelson (1957) "combined with the similarly unequivocal but contradictory evaluation by the other observers do create an unstable total situation for the naive subject . . . Since at the outset the task seemed quite simple, the initial expectation of observer agreement was presumably very high. The surprising discrepancy between the subject's perceptions and those of a number of other subjects, unanimous among themselves, created a conflict in the cognitive field which could not be resolved in a satisfactory manner by simply denying or disregarding the socially transmitted information" (p. 182).

The subjects actually feel quite remote from each other: in a way, they begin thinking of themselves as deviants and behaving accordingly. In order to escape this diagnosis, they submit to self-criticism. They question their outlook and judgemental ability, avowing that they might have made a mistake and given a wrong evaluation. Reality seems to evade them. Crutchfield also observes: "Another noteworthy effect was the sense of increased psychological distance induced between the person himself and the group. He felt himself to be queer or different, or felt the group to be quite unlike what he had thought. With this went an arousal of considerable anxiety in most subjects; for some, manifest anxiety was acute" (Crutchfield, 1955).

I have quoted from these reports about a specific situation in order to remind us that, even where certainty exists at the beginning, it can be undermined by divergence. As can be observed by anyone following these experiments, the self-confidence of the naive subject is gradually eroded. Gerard and Greenbaum have explained this in terms of the following process: at each trial, the subject's uncertainty increases. On the other hand, when a supporting confederate joins the naive subject, uncertainty decreases; but if a confederate is introduced who does not give support until the *end* of a set of trials, his support will be experienced as much more positive.

Gerard and Greenbaum (1962) used Asch's material. The customary trials are followed by twelve other trials during which a partner (confederate) joins the naive subject, whose judgement he at first contradicts, but eventually agrees with. After this eventual agreement (switch-trial condition), the confederate agrees with the subject in all remaining trials, moving away from the majority in order to do so.

The important manipulation here is the timing of the switch-trial, and the effects of it can be clearly seen in the results. The later the switch, the more the subject's confidence increases and the more positive is his perception of the "partner". The authors' conjectures are confirmed: during interaction with the majority, the subject's uncertainty increases, but if one helps him to reduce this uncertainty, positive reactions towards the person contributing to this reduction are aroused. An additional conjecture might be added: the subject's attitude towards the confederate can probably also be attributed to the fact that he believes he has convinced him. The greater the effort expended in this direction, the more the subject's self-confidence increases, and the more kindly he is inclined to feel towards the person who symbolizes and supports the value of this effort.

There is nothing problematic about divergences in judgements and certainty. The problem for the individual is not so much to reduce his uncertainty, as to reduce the underlying disagreement or to persuade the other that he is right. The latter is accomplished when he wins someone else's support, and the former can be accomplished by yielding. One of Brodbeck's experiments (1956) reveals that if subjects who have lost confidence in their opinions are given the opportunity to exchange views with other members of their group, they do not change their minds, but they do change their minds if this opportunity is not given.

It is therefore conflict which is at the root of uncertainty. Before trying to persuade a person to believe us, we first attempt to make that person unsure of his own opinions. Lewin called this the "cognitive thaw". The proponents of the dissonance theory are doing the same thing when they ask subjects in their experiments to contradict themselves, to defend a point of view which is not their own, or to do something that they would normally be reluctant to do. If conflict produces uncertainty, and if it is a prerequisite of influence, then the greater the conflict the more profound the influence.

This proposition has not yet been tested directly, but I am inclined to believe that it is correct. There are several indirect clues in support of it. In experiments on conformity, a unanimous majority is usually opposed to an isolated individual. The conflict is most intense when physical stimuli are at issue. In certain conditions, the confederate

breaks up the unanimity in giving the correct response, thereby lessen-
ing the conflict. In such conditions, it is observed that influence diminishes. Mead's observation that "conflict is a social act that calls out
the response of change" therefore seems plausible. But the change can
take place in several ways. Let us imagine that a person is confronted
with the divergent opinions of another: there is an interpersonal conflict
because his judgements are challenged and he is obliged to choose. At
the same time, the conflict is an intrapersonal one, for giving in would
imply submitting to the other person, thereby suffering a loss in terms
of identity and self-esteem. What are the possible solutions to such a
conflict? The first conflict can only be resolved by changing or by seeking a reasonable compromise with the other; but the second conflict is
resolved as soon as the person decides to maintain his own position even
more strongly. In other words, when he decides to suppress any response
that is different from his own. This type of solution reminds us of certain
situations of daily life in which new ideas are not recognized as long as
the innovator is present, or have a significant impact only after his
death.

Moscovici and Nève (1971) attempted to explore this problem experimentally. The authors tried to show that an individual accepts another
person's opinion more easily if the other person is not actually present.
The experimental material consisted of the well-known autokinetic
phenomenon. The subjects, in a totally darkened room, are told to
indicate the amplitude of displacement of a point of light located a few
meters away which appeared for several seconds. In the first phase of
the experiment, after familiarization with the task, a subject and a
confederate write down their judgements individually on twenty-five
trials. During the second phase, first the subject, then the confederate
give their responses orally on fifty trials. The confederate consistently
maintains that he sees the displacement of the point of light as being
some ten or fifteen centimeters more than the naive subject. In this
experimental group, an announcement over the inter-com system invites the confederate to leave the room after the fortieth trial, but he
stays on for another ten trials. In the third phase, the subject gives his
responses alone for twenty-five trials. In the control group, the confederate stays in the room until the end of the experiment. The results
confirmed our predictions concerning the effect of the presence and
absence of the source of influence. Control group estimates in phase
three are significantly more divergent from the confederate's estimates

than they are in phase two ($p < 0.008$ by Wilcoxon's test, one-tailed). Subjects therefore tend to polarize when the influence source remains present. Subjects in the experimental groups revealed an opposite tendency; their estimates in phase three (after the withdrawal of the confederate) are significantly less divergent from those of the confederate than they are in phase two ($p < 0.05$ by the same test). Comparing between groups, we find that the estimates evolve in opposite directions for the two groups between phase two and phase three ($t = 4.77$, $p < 0.001$). In the experimental group, ten out of twelve subjects gave estimates *closer* to those of the confederate when he is *absent*, whereas in the control group, eleven out of twelve subjects *diverge* from the confederate who is always *present*. Therefore, as we predicted, being "out of sight" can be a necessary condition for *not* being "out of mind".

The post-experimental questionnaire also yielded results that agreed with our hypothesis. In response to the questions "to what extent do you think that you were helped by the other person?", and "to what extent do you think that you were hindered by the other person?" control group subjects replied that the direction of their judgements had been dependent on the other person more frequently than the experimental group subjects. (For each of these questions, Fisher's test of exact probability was significant at 0.026 and 0.08 respectively). Finally, in response to the more direct question, "to what extent do you think that your judgement was influenced by the other person?", control group subjects reported more frequently than experimental group subjects that they had been influenced (Fisher's exact probability test significant at 0.05).

In summary, the evaluations are closer to those provided by the source of influence when the confederate is absent, and less close when he remains present. However, as we pointed out, even if the other's judgement is denied, it does not cease to exist "internally", and, in due course, it has its impact. The absence of the partner modifies the situation by allowing the subject to cease considering himself as a target of influence, which considerably reduces the interpersonal conflict. He is then in a position to resolve his intrapersonal conflict by examining the cognitive alternatives concerning the object and the stimulus more "objectively".

Are the submissions that are generally observed due to a tendency to avoid conflict? Of course, this tendency does play a role. It all depends, however, on the nomic or anomic character of the majority or minority. Whoever is sure of his judgement seems to face conflict willingly, or even to seek it out. Schachter's experiment (1951) on uniformity pressure showed us a majority willing to cross swords with a minority in order to bring it round to the point of view of the group. In Smith's (1936), and in Steiner's (1966) experiments, individuals with extreme convictions or a firm response display little anxiety in the face of a threat of divergence. Such individuals are clearly not anxious to avoid conflict.

An elegant demonstration of this has been given by Gordon (1966). He made one group of individuals believe that their judgements were incorrect. They were then asked whether they wished to participate in a group whose judgements differed from theirs. He observed that the subjects with greater confidence in their judgements were more willing to do this than subjects who were uncertain. It seems almost as if individuals whose judgement was correct felt the need to influence others by stating their opinion in the face of a significant divergence of view. Conversely, those whose judgement was incorrect could not place confidence in their own opinion. They had no wish to influence others, and preferred to remain in a group which shared their opinion and reinforced their individual position. It is surely a well-established phenomenon that new converts have a burning desire to convert others.

Let us repeat, therefore, that conflict is a necessary condition of influence. It is the starting-point and the means of changing others, of establishing new relations or consolidating old ones. *Uncertainty and ambiguity are concepts and states derived from conflict.* Doubt grows out of the encounter with another who is different, and in most experiments doubt appears not as a given, but as the product of influence. Certain objects that are part of the physical world are, of course, more structured than others. Even so, it is still possible to make a highly structured object psychologically ambiguous by bringing out unknown or neglected dimensions, by bringing about a divergence of judgements. Here, for instance, is an individual naming colours without hesitation. He sees a slide as blue, and names it blue. Another individual tells him that it is green. The first will feel compelled to look again in order to see whether there is in fact anything green about the slide, and indeed he will find a trace of it. Blue has become blue-green.

Everything must therefore be seen in the context of interaction. This is a consequence of the emphasis placed on conflict. As long as influence was held to be a matter of reducing uncertainty or ambiguity, the other person, the source of influence, had the role of *mediator of facts* with regard to the environment. In other words, using persons or relying on them amounted to an alternative way of using or relying on physical objects; other persons served as a sort of remote sensor or grappler, permitting the subject to extend his resources for dealing with the material world. But it must be recognized that the other person, the source of influence, will obviously tend to encourage a need of this kind, in order to serve his own interests. He will tend to provoke the state that forces the subject to rely on him, since he is the *antagonist* with whom the subject must come to terms. If this is the case, we certainly cannot continue to conceive of him merely as a "mediator of facts". Relative strengths, feelings, intentions, sincerity, courage, and so on, all must be taken into account, and they are very easily overlooked when we are dealing with non-personal, non-social entities.

With these factors acknowledged, the divergence between alternative solutions represents a sort of conflict with respect to consensus. Such conflict is inevitable if consensus matters to us, especially if we have nowhere else to go in order to find it. *In short, in social influence, relations with others take precedence over relations with objects, and inter-individual dynamics take precedence over intra-individual dynamics. This constitutes exactly the reverse of what has been accepted up to now.*

At this level, interaction is characterized by divergence and antagonism. In dealings with other persons or subgroups, each person or subgroup brings to bear a value system and characteristic reactions which are unique. It has a certain margin for accepting or rejecting the value system and reactions of its antagonists. Confrontations of frequently incompatible systems entail the risk of rapid termination of exchanges, in so far as the parties give preference to their own mode of thinking and seek to affirm their own point of view as against that of the antagonists. The tensions resulting from such confrontations may quickly lead to a breakdown of communication, the isolation of the participants, and inability to achieve the purpose of the social exchange in which they were taking part. Furthermore, self-confidence has been shaken and anxiety has been produced.

In order to avoid this kind of situation, the parties are compelled to attempt a readjustment of the system which will lead to a reduction or resolution of opposition, and this is done at the cost of a few concessions. To the extent that the influence process takes place in such a context of conflict, and tends to lead to readjustment procedures, it would seem to be closely related to the process of negotiation. The connection between influence and negotiation has not been recognized until now. Inasmuch as consensus was viewed as a secondary phenomenon, and the link with society, with others, was identified with a link to physical reality, this omission is not at all surprising. But it has been a mistake to view everything in terms of information-gathering, for at least two reasons. Firstly because every exchange of information takes place within a certain process of work and structuring of the opinions, values, and ultimately the meanings involved. The whole idea of informational social influence is very partial and superficial, and what is surprising is the success which the idea has had.

Allen (1974) reports an experiment which makes this very clear. College students were asked to formulate their interpretations of six statements that were projected on a screen one after the other. Based on preliminary findings, known alternative meanings were provided for each statement. In a first condition of this experiment, along with the attitude statements, the subjects were presented with the allegedly extreme positions of a group that gave unanimously unpopular interpretations. In a second condition, the same extreme position of the group was presented, but one member of the group gave the popular answer. In a third condition, the group gave unanimously popular answers. In the control condition, the statements were projected without any accompanying answers from the group. Of course, the subjects never expressed their own attitudes; they merely indicated what they believed the statement *meant*. It is nevertheless important to remember that in several of the conditions the subjects responded while being informed of the responses of other persons. The results show a significant shift of meaning on most of the statements when projected in the context of a group's unanimous unpopular response. In the non-unanimous condition, the meaning of a statement was similar to what it was when the subjects answered without knowing the attitudes of the group. Therefore, receiving information about opinions or judgements does not simply permit an individual to get a better idea of his own opinions or judgements, or to compare his judgements with those of others more validly. Actually, such information instigates a process of internal restructuring of intellectual and attitudinal elements that leads to a new context of interpretation for the subject, and a new meaning for the object. In this experiment we can see that the process of change in the meaning of statements is instigated only when the group is unanimous; otherwise nothing happens. It follows, therefore, that information *per se* is a rather secondary factor in any kind of phenomena related to influence.

The second reason is that, even in the purest of judgements, it is never a question of sheer information-processing, never an individualistic and solipsistic evaluation of stimuli coming directly or indirectly from the external world. There is always a dialogue or debate, as well. As Churchman writes:

> Essentially, a judgement is a group opinion. The "group" may consist of the same individual at different points in his reflective life, but for all practical purposes we can talk as though the group in question has several different members. We shall argue that judgement is a group belief which occurs when there are differences of opinion among the group members, because, in the spirit of the earlier discussion, we want to say that such judgement occurs when the judgement is the establishment of "agreement" in the context of disagreements. Judgement is a type of negotiation (1961, p. 293).

What do we have in mind when we try to persuade others, other than the intention to establish a hierarchy of new responses, or to eliminate responses incompatible with our own—that is, the intention of eliminating dissonance or conflict? Whether it is a matter of beliefs, judgements, or attitudes, influence must be conceived as a process occurring between persons, or groups, in which consensus establishes a contract (norm) which permits comfortable transactions, i.e. a system which makes certain reactions and choices more probable than others. It might be said that in most social psychology experiments a *tacit* negotiation is being carried on, during which each participant is trying to have his own view prevail or to discover the import of potential concessions on his part. If this is in fact what is happening, then each type of influence corresponds to a particular type of negotiation, or method for dealing with social conflict. And, just as conflict can be dealt with by different methods, so *there are several different influence modalities corresponding to these methods of handling conflict*, and we shall undertake to define these later.

6

Behavioural Styles

Proposition 4

When an individual or subgroup influences a group, the main factor of success is behavioural style

As I have already pointed out, social influence involves tacit negotiations, confrontation of view-points and the eventual search for a solution which will be acceptable to everyone. But what determines the outcome?

As long as we look at this question from the point of view of power relations, that is, from the point of view which determines current concepts and experiments, dependence appears to be the decisive factor. In so far as a differential status or a socially validated competence emerges, there appears to be a certain conformity with individuals who control the distribution of rewards and punishments, who have more extensive knowledge, or who have greater experience in a given field. The existence of a majority or a leader establishes a right to guide and change the behaviour of individuals or subgroups. In such a situation, the lower the status of individuals, or the less their recognized competence, the more they will feel assigned to a minority position and dependent on the evaluation of others. If they are so assigned and dependent, they will be all the more likely to yield, and to cease defending their point of view.

This is not a valid approach when dealing with social influence, which should be studied independently of power processes. Leadership, competence, majority, may play a certain role as external parameters of dependence, but this role is not crucial to the influence process. What *is* crucial is the *behavioural style* of each social partner. Why should this variable be substituted for that of dependence? First of all because, as I have already stressed, behavioural style is *specifically* related to influence phenomena, whereas dependence is more closely linked with the power dimension of social relations. Secondly, dependence upon an individual or subgroup in the process of innovating may be a consequence of the influence process, rather than its cause. For example, the need to follow expert advice with regard to the use of videotape or computer follows from the decision to use videotape or computer. Finally, any minority that brings about genuine innovation must start and continue for a certain length of time, with no advantages in the way of power, status, resources, or competence.

Dependence is not, therefore, an *independent* or *general* variable which can explain the kind of influence to which I am referring. I believe that the only variable with explanatory power is that of behavioural style, which is entirely independent of majority, minority, or authority in its determination of influence.

Behavioural style is a novel, and yet familiar, concept. It refers to the organization of behaviours and opinions, and the timing and intensity of their expression—in short, it refers to the "rhetoric" of behaviour and opinion. Behaviours *per se*, like the individual sounds of a language, have no meaning of their own. Only in combination, as determined by the individual or group, and as interpreted by those to whom they are addressed, can they have meaning and arouse reaction. Repetition of the same gesture or word may, on one occasion, reflect stubbornness and rigidity; on another occasion it may express certainty. Conversely, stubbornness and certainty can be manifested in many different ways: by repetition, rejection, intensity of gestures or words.

Each of these styles functions as the projection of subjective states into the social environment; they are the objective counterpart of subjective experience and the structure of subjective identity, their surface in relief which facilitates articulation with the social environment. By the same token, behaviour appears not as directly given, but as encoded fragments of an underlying content. This underlying content therefore has to be *inferred*, the visible fragments decoded and given meaning. In social exchanges, the role of participants can only be guessed at, provisionally attributed, and never apprehended directly at their so-called face value. Because of this, role behaviour is necessarily tentative, and constantly tested during the course of exchange. It is only in exceptional situations that everything is clearly, immediately, and irrevocably set forth. Knowledge of the other person or group is usually increased as a result of this involved interaction.

What are the implications of this state of affairs? They are, simply, that any sequence of behaviour has two aspects. One is instrumental, defining and providing information about its object. The other is symbolic, and gives information about and defines the state of the actor, the source of the behaviours. Thus, when a naive subject in the laboratory hears a person repeat twenty times over "line A is the same length as line B", or that the slide which the subject sees as blue, is green, he infers two different orders of things. One is that line A may be equal in length to line B, or that the blue slide may be green. The other is that the person making these statements is either certain or uncertain, and may be seeking to influence him.

In general, then, behavioural styles have both a symbolic and an instrumental aspect, relating by their form to the actor, and by their content to the object of action. Correspondingly, they give rise to inferences concerning these two aspects of their meaning. Behavioural styles both convey meanings and bring about reactions which are a function of these meanings. This insistence on the *meaning* of behaviour will seem futile to many readers. But, in fact, it is very important, because all the emphasis until now has been on the meaninglessness of behaviour.

We will now consider some more concrete points about behavioural style. The person or group who adopts one of these styles must, if the style is to be socially recognized and identified, meet the following three conditions:

(a) be aware of the relationship between their internal state and the external signals they are using. Certainty is manifested by an affirmative, confident tone; for example, the intention not to make any concessions is expressed by consistency of the appropriate behaviour;

(b) use signals systematically and consistently, so as to prevent misunderstanding on the part of the receiver;

(c) preserve the same relationships between behaviours and meanings throughout an interaction—in other words, ensure that words do not change their meaning during the course of an interaction.

In order for the eye to see an object, spatial relations must be transformed correctly into temporal relations between impulses sent along the optic nerve. Similarly, for a communication to be persuasive, or for a person to be perceived as credible and trustworthy, elements inspiring credibility and trust must be present in the manner of representation.

In an extremely interesting experiment, Hewgill and Miller (1965) presented a message-sender to subjects as a person who was credible and trustworthy. At the same time, they varied the degree of non-fluency and redundancy in his speech. Their hypothesis was that, the greater the non-fluency and redundancy in the speech of the message-sender, the less the credibility of the message, and this expectation was confirmed by the results. There is, therefore, an important relationship between the way in which the message-sender is characterized and the way in which the message-sender is expected to behave. If a relationship defined initially on the social level by factors such as competence, rank superiority, etc., is not confirmed by the expected style at the level of speech behaviour, the relationship will not in fact come into existence as initially defined.

In social interaction, these conventional ways of organizing behaviour are meant to give the other group or person information about the position and motivation of the person or group initiating the interaction. They may, for example, indicate a degree of openness, certainty, or commitment. They may also signal a desire to influence. Thus, behavioural styles are purposeful arrangements of verbal and/or non-verbal signals which express the meaning of the present state and intended development of those who display them.

To return to the non-fluency example, it is obvious that if the frequency of non-fluencies is normal, this will indicate to those listening the speaker's mastery and conviction in regard to his subject. But if the non-fluencies exceed the normal frequency, or if they occur at inappropriate moments, their meaning will change: they will be interpreted as a symptom of uncertainty or insincerity, and so on. Whatever is "normal", "excessive", "inappropriate", etc. is obviously defined by a common social code which furnishes all participants with the means of distinguishing between styles, motivations, and intentions of various kinds.

Why are behavioural styles effective in influencing people? I have not yet found a satisfactory answer to this question. It may be assumed that they simply arouse positive or negative attitudes, but this does not lead us very far. They may possibly determine psychological fields, or focus attention by giving differential weights to items of information or highlighting particular events and objects in the environment.

Non-violent resistance, for instance, by means of calm strength of purpose and demonstration of the futility of physical repression, may simultaneously arouse interest in the cause it is serving and compel a change of method in dealing with this cause, since conventional methods will prove ineffective against it. In the same way, when a child expresses his desire for a particular toy by crying and screaming for it, refusing to accept a substitute or to be consoled, his parents are forced to take some account of his viewpoint and scale of preferences. But little is really known about the underlying mechanisms of behavioural style; the notion is, after all, a new one, and its importance for our understanding of phenomena in social psychology is only beginning to be recognized.

There are five behavioural styles that can be objectively described: (a) investment (b) autonomy (c) consistency (d) rigidity (e) fairness. The only one of the five which has been the object of serious attention is consistency, and this is probably the most fundamental one.

INVESTMENT

Research on cognitive dissonance (e.g. Festinger, 1957; Brehm and Cohen, 1962; Zimbardo, 1960) and social learning (e.g. Bandura and Walters, 1963) has highlighted the role played by the effort, or psychological investment, which is put into justifying and changing behaviour. If an individual or group take great pains to achieve some particular end, two implications will be conveyed to others: (1) that they have great confidence in the option they have chosen and (2) that they have great capacity for self-reinforcement.

There are many examples which show that behaviour reflecting a strong investment will have a decisive influence. One need only think of the mythology surrounding great figures of science and art to realize how the knowledge of their tenacity, sacrifices, and ability to identify themselves with a particular enterprise has contributed to the success and influence of their work.

Taking an imaginary example, let us consider a situation in which funds are being raised. It is known that most individual donors converge towards an "average" donation, thereby establishing a norm which is more or less appropriate for everyone. It is likely that each donor presumes that the others are making a sacrifice which is comparable to his, or proportional to their means in the same way as his. If it should happen that, on the list of previous donors which is usually presented by fund-raisers, there is displayed the information that a poor individual has made an exceptional sacrifice, there is every reason to expect that this information will influence most of the other donors to take this sacrifice as their reference point for determining how much they should give.

Hain *et al* (1956) have studied the conditions determining the signing of petitions. They observed that the number of signatures already visible is not the decisive factor. What matters most is the conviction and urgency with which the appeal to sign is made. They write: "The findings cast doubt on the validity of the unrestricted assertion that the larger the number of signatures for a petition, the more widespread the sentiment in favour of the proposed change" (p. 389).

On the whole, one might say that styles of behaviour which indicate that the individual or group involved are strongly committed by free choice, and that the goal pursued is highly valued to the point that personal sacrifices are readily made, will be influential in social exchanges.

AUTONOMY

Autonomy is an asset which, when displayed, arouses positive reactions. It is seen as an exemplary attitude encouraging emulation. How can it be defined? Autonomy has several facets. First of all, there is independence of judgement and attitude, which reflects the determination to act according to one's own principles. Objectivity is also involved—the ability to take into account all relevant factors and to draw conclusion from them in a rigorous manner without being deflected by subjective interests. Extremism may also be an element of autonomy, to the extent that extremism implies a consistent and uncompromising attitude.

De Monchaux and Shimmin (1955) have demonstrated the effect of independence in their analysis of a study made in Britain by Schachter. In this study, several groups were asked to select a model for an aeroplane of which they were later to simulate the production. The confederate of the experimenter had been instructed to choose consistently the model most rejected by the group; the group, on the other hand, had been instructed to reach a unanimous decision. Out of 32 groups, 12 reached an agreement which ignored the confederate's choice, 6 adopted his choice, and 14 failed to reach agreement. The authors write in conclusion:

Our assumption has been that, as discussion progressed, the need to reach a group decision would master individual needs. But it is possible that the behaviour of the deviate in persisting quietly and unaggressively with his own choice may have reinforced the strength of individual goal preference ("If he won't give up his choice, why should I?"). We have therefore to consider the possibility that the presence of the deviate may have worked as a pressure towards individuality of choice rather than towards group unanimity (p. 59).

It is apparent from this study that behaviour perceived as independent may *either* influence group decision in its favour (six groups did opt for the model chosen by the confederate), *or* encourage an independent attitude in the individuals of the group. Either case reflects the influence exerted by the confederate. When an individual appears to have autonomous opinions and judgement, and is neither domineering nor yet inclined to compromise, he will be perceived, characterized, and probably responded to as an advocate of a particular model or set of values. He will, consequently, give the impression that he is in control of his behaviour. In a way, he is the initiator of a set of actions. What little we do know of indirect communication and social causality indicates that such an individual (or subgroup) will not only gain a hearing, but will have some power in relation to other individuals who lack this degree of autonomy. Autonomous behaviour, like behaviour which expresses investment, is apparently not perceived as intending to influence.

In all likelihood, innovations in the artistic, cultural and scientific spheres, and in the world of fashion, are launched by autonomous individuals. Such persons reject the gregarious, sheep-like behaviour accepted by the group. Their initiatives appear bold, their solutions novel and original, liberating them from the routines that restrict the behaviour of others. There is an undeniable attraction in novelty, independently of its intrinsic value, and it sooner or later gives rise to imitation. Individuals are less content to inhabit their customary world after they have had a glimpse of unsuspected possibilities. Faced with the new, the old becomes intolerably dull. Imagine a Picasso placed next to a classical portrait: the Picasso may be shocking, but it gives new insight into the subject of the painting, as well as into painting itself. In contrast, the straightforward copy of reality, the slavish imitation of a model, appears deficient. In this way, art extends its influence.

Individuals in a group are always suspicious of manipulative intentions. Such intentions are not, and cannot, be attributed to an individual whose integrity and lack of ulterior motive are taken for granted. Because of this, such an individual gains ascendancy over others, and his opinions and judgement carry more weight. If he is present when a consensus has to be reached, during a meeting, for instance, or in team-work, or when an opinion must be given on a controversial question, and he behaves in a manner which conveys the impression that he is in command of many relevant and well-considered facts, he will prob-ably exert a high degree of influence on the collective result. His thoughtfulness and independence, as manifested in his behaviour, will inspire respect and win support.

This explains, incidentally, why the affirmations of scientists, religious authorities, and panels of experts are readily, and perhaps too readily, accepted by us. Often rightly, but sometimes mistakenly, we assume that their opinions have been carefully weighed, and that there are no personal interests or concealed motives in the solutions they propose.

A study that tends to support my analysis was conducted by Myers and Goldberg (1970). Three hundred and thirty-seven students were asked to read a brief "magazine article" on air pollution. Unknown to the subjects, this article had been composed by the experimenters. The opinion expressed in the article was that air pollution is not dangerous. Air pollution was selected as a topic because it was assumed that subjects would share the widespread belief that air pollution does constitute a danger. The possibility therefore existed that the subjects could be made to change their opinions in the direction suggested by the persuasive message.

For our purposes, the results of only three of the experimental con-ditions will be reported here. In one condition, "high ethics *group*", the subjects were told that the position of the article represented the con-clusion reached by a panel of experts after three hours' discussion. In a second condition, "high ethics *individuals*", the subjects were informed that the article was based on a poll conducted among a small group of leading scientists. In a third condition, "high ethics *individual*", the sub-jects learned that the article represented the conclusion reached by one of the most prominent scientists in the United States.

We can assume that there was no difference in the prestige of the experts in the three conditions. However, the greatest influence was observed in the "high ethics *group*" condition, in which the subjects believed that the article represented the result of a common deliberation, and in which they presumably thought that an exceptionally careful review of the question had been made.

But deliberation is apparently not enough. More is required in order for autonomy to be perceived. There must be the conviction that the person or group expressing the ideas in question occupies a particular social position, is the originator of the ideas, and has freely chosen this stance. An experiment by Nemeth and Wachtler (1973) is particularly relevant here.

In their experiment, they brought together groups of five persons as simulated juries. Each group was given a case study to read. In one particular case, an individual had claimed damages for an injury sustained during the course of his work. While repairing a washing machine, this person had fallen down some steps and torn a cartilage in his knee. The maximum compensation allowable by law was $25,000. Most of the subjects, when asked individually in private, believed that heavy compensation should be paid: the mean sum suggested was $14,560.

In the experimental conditions, however, subjects were exposed to a confederate who consistently suggested the amount of $3,000. The five people in each jury group (four subjects and one confederate) discussed the case for 45 minutes, during which time the confederate presented seven arguments which he had previously memorized. Among these were: questioning the magnitude of the injury, suggesting that the jury should consider what was a truly fair compensation, rather than allowing the maximum just because the insurance company could afford it, and indicating that $3,000 was really quite a large sum of money. A control condition was also run, in which five subjects deliberated on the case with no confederate present.

There was also a variation introduced which is of special interest. (Some research on trial juries has supported the belief that, in our culture, the position of the seat occupied by a person reflects their status, and their power to influence. In particular, the position at the head of a table is usually associated with power and prestige. It may well be that the person who takes this seat thereby calls attention to himself, affirming his mastery and competence and his intention to act as leader. If the occupation of the head seat *causes* others to attribute leadership characteristics, an individual may be better placed to exert influence by the adoption of this behavioural style.) In their experiment, Nemeth and Wachtler used a table with the seating arrangement as shown in

Fig. 2. The head seat is S, the side seats Q and R. The confederate, according to the experimental condition, sat either at the head, or in one of the side positions. The crucial variation was that, in some conditions, the confederate *chose* a seat, while in others he was *assigned* a seat. In all conditions, and this is an important point, the confederate presented exactly the same arguments (which amounted to defending a deviant viewpoint) during the 45 minutes' discussion of the case.

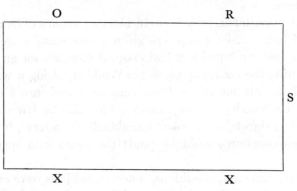

Fig. 2. Seating arrangement in simulated jury study.

The difference between choosing a seat and having a seat assigned to one is that the former is a sign of autonomy, while the latter indicates compliance to a system of rules and authority. We may therefore expect that, other things being equal, the confederate will be most influential when he has chosen his seat. This expectation is borne out by the experimental results. Analyses of the confederate's effectiveness show that it was only when he *chose* the head seat that he exerted influence. When he was *assigned* the head seat, or occupied a side seat (by choice or assignment), he exerted no influence ($t = 1.53; p < 0.07$).

The authors observe that "the taking of the head seat, being a behavioural style, could be interpreted by others as a sign of confidence, the attribution of which then renders the individual effective. Occupation of that seat, if not by choice, would reveal no information about the actor regarding such traits" (p. 20). However, there is more to it than this. Reacting in a firm manner to the hostility or reluctance of the others, the individual in turn gives credibility to the traits the others attribute to him. Nemeth and Wachtler report that "In this study, the majority was quite resistant to the views of the confederate. On numerous occasions, the majority harassed or ridiculed the confederate for his very deviant position. One even threatened to break the confederate's leg after the experiment was over to demonstrate the pain and suffering that is involved in such an injury. Thus, we can see that the majority did not accede easily, yet they were influenced by this same confederate with the same arguments when his style included an indication of particular confidence—taking the head seat" (p. 21).

Another way of illustrating the effect of autonomy and objectivity is as follows. Society always assumes that individuals have concealed interests and motives. Their judgements and opinions are attributed to external biases (class membership, family background, etc.) or internal ones (jealousy, ambition, etc.). As a result, it is also assumed that behaviour is not really free, either in its content or purpose. However, it is safe to predict that the response of a person who seems to be independent of external agents or internal drives will easily be accepted by the majority of individuals.

There have been many studies in the field of communication which have been based on the dependence paradigm. They have been successful in proving their postulate, that the prestige or credibility of the sender of a message is the major factor in the effectiveness of the communication. More precisely, all other things being equal, the greater the credibility, the greater the change in the opinions of the receiver. It was always assumed, moreover, that the message bore no relation to the interests of either the sender or the receiver—that people did not consider the possibility of any such relation. Walster *et al.* (1966) set out to show that there *is* perception of relationships between messages and interests, and that this has an effect on communication and on the formation of attitudes and judgements. They started from the assumption that a person will be perceived as more sincere and trustworthy if he advocates a point of view which is contrary to this obvious self-interest. In their investigation, subjects were divided into four experimental groups. The first group received a communication from a high-prestige individual (prosecuting attorney) arguing for a position favourable to his own interests; the second group received a communication from a low-prestige individual (criminal) arguing for a position favourable to his own interests; the third group received a communication from the high-prestige individual arguing for a position unfavourable to his interests; and the fourth group received a communication from the low-prestige individual arguing for a position unfavourable to his interests.

When the two individuals advocated points of view which were opposed to their own interests, they were more influential, regardless of their status. In fact, the low-prestige individual was *more* influential than the high-prestige individual when taking a position opposed to self-interest. Therefore the communication which appears to be unbiased is interpreted as being more honest and more expert, and is more influential. Powell and Miller (1967) also clearly found that a source would appear more trustworthy when he was considered as not benefiting from the target's behaviour. Subjects were exposed to tape-recorded messages advocating the donation of one's blood to the Red Cross without payment. The persuasive messages were attributed to a known physician and to a chairman of a blood donor recruiting unit of the Red Cross, i.e. an anonymous person. The physician, a disinterested party, was viewed as more trustworthy and was more influential than the chairman of the recruiting unit who, of course, appeared to be more interested and selfish. Mills and Jellison (1967) exposed students to a speech of an alleged candidate for the local elections. Subjects were induced to believe that the speech proposing a bill to triple licensing fees of tractor-trailers was made either to a group of railway men or to truck drivers. The results are neat: subjects changed their own opinion to agree with the communication when the source was perceived as delivering his speech to a less popular group, i.e. where it appears as more objective.

Politicians are aware of this, since they never miss a chance to proclaim that they are capable of rising above their narrow interests in order to espouse the general interest. It is often seen that conservative politicians have less difficulty in passing "leftist" socialist legislation: they meet with less resistance and can make the legislation appear unavoidable. In the United States, it is a common experience that the Republican Party implements many policies that the Democratic Party has advocated. The same pattern was observed in France concerning the granting of independence to the colonies—it was always advocated by the Left, but more often implemented by the Right.

Extremism is not a popular subject of study, and it has been dealt with only when defined as deviant behaviour. Theoreticians have tended to consider it as less accepted, and particularly as less effective, than moderate behaviour. The balance theory even supposes the existence of a "bias against extremism". "If the focal person" writes Taylor (1969) "is communicating with another about some issue or topic, then either the focal person or the other can state his position in a 'moderate' way, or he can state it in a more 'extreme' way. It is postulated that people, in general, will have a preference for moderately worded communication over strongly worded communication. It is a bias against 'extremism'. The implication is that a moderate communication from the other or the focal person is more likely to induce attitude or sentiment change in the focal person than a strongly worded communication" (p. 122). Despite this postulate, the few studies available provide a less negative picture of the chances that an extremist has of exerting influence, given his deviant or "unbalanced" character. A little known experiment by Mulder (1960) helps to restore the balance. The small businessmen of an urban community were called together and informed of the future implantation of a supermarket in the area. They were faced with the necessity of defending their rights and property against the menace which the supermarket represented for their businesses. One of the businessmen, actually a confederate of the experimenter, took a hard-line position, refusing all compromises and insisting on the necessity of organizing the community and actively resisting the construction of the supermarket. He advocated the creation of a local trade union for their mutual defence. A second businessman, also a confederate, took a moderate position, defending the same ideas but with less insistence. The participants were to decide whether or not to form a trade union, and eventually to elect delegates who would represent and defend them. The experimental results show that the participants adopted the hard-line position. The radical confederate was the most frequently chosen as their representative, and the moderate confederate was most frequently rejected. Given the experimental conditions, we can be sure that the participants' involvement was greater than it would have been had the task consisted in estimating the number of dots in a cartoon. The businessmen of Mulder's experiment were polarized over clear-cut, coherent, and radical alternatives. The unyielding position of the extremist confederate, far from blocking their interaction, allowed the participants to establish a solid group position.

Some time ago, Brehm and Lipsher (1959) carried out an experiment in which they studied the relation between the degree of divergence separating the sender of a message from the receiver, and the trust placed in the sender by the receiver. Contrary to the prediction of most

theories that the confidence of the receiver would be inversely proportional to the degree of divergence, this experiment demonstrated
that the receiver's confidence in the opinion or judgement of the sender
is at its greatest when the divergence is at its maximum.

More recently, Eisinger and Mills (1968) tried to show that if an
individual sending a message is "on the same side" as his listeners, he
will be judged more sincere than a sender on the opposite "side", for
the apparently obvious reason that he will be more popular. The
authors also postulated that an extremist message-sender would be less
popular, and judged less sincere, than a moderate. Generally, however,
the findings show that extremist individuals arouse more positive reactions than moderate individuals. The authors had not anticipated such
an outcome, and they comment: "It is possible that the greater liking
for the communicator on the opposite side was also counteracted by the
perception that the communicator on the opposite side was subjecting
himself to more social disapproval" (p. 231). In other words, the extremist's standing is enhanced by the courage he demonstrates in facing
risks—and when he is compared with a moderate of the same party,
he is given preference because he is "rated as more sincere, more competent, more likeable and more trustworthy" (p. 231).

Not only is virtue not rewarded, but, worse still, the type and style
of response which, ever since Allport, had been expected to arouse
antipathy, on the contrary awakens admiration and is taken as evidence
of serious-mindedness and credibility. None of these experiments constitute a definite proof, yet, inconclusive as they are, they do suggest that
a new orientation is due. Moreover they are strong witness in favour
of autonomy in its various manifestations as a distinctive behavioural
style.

CONSISTENCY

Behavioural consistency is perceived as a sign of certainty, affirming a
decision to adhere unswervingly to a given point of view, and reflecting
commitment to a coherent, uncompromising choice. The potency of
this influence source can be attributed neither to a difference in capacity, nor to an explicit form of dependence. It is true that "behavioural
consistency" embraces many forms of behaviour, from the persistent
repetition of a phrase, through the avoidance of contradictory behaviour, all the way up to the elaboration of a system of logical proof.
For my present purposes, this is not an important point; intuition and

experimentation will determine the range. I shall limit myself here to analysing the implications of consistency for a view of social influence.

Let us first re-state the hypothesis that each individual or group attempts to impose some organization on the material and social environment, validate their knowledge of it, and confirm the rules they have adopted for dealing with it. They come to terms with reality, make predictions about it, and gain some control over it by separating ephemeral and variable behaviours and events from their permanent and invariable foundations; they introduce a temporal and causal sequence into a situation where everything might seem accidental and arbitrary. When two people meet, the only way in which they can communicate and adopt mutually satisfactory behaviours is by filtering a few predominant features out of the mass of inchoate impressions: intentions, feelings, capacities, and so on. Material objects give rise to the same operation, involving comparison, classification, selection of the transmitted stimuli; this results in a characterization of the object's dimensions, colour, speed, and so on, and in a determination of its possible application to some goal. Whether one is dealing with persons or objects, an inferential process about their dispositional properties is set in motion.

Heider (1958) has listed the following conditions for the differentiation of social and physical entities, and describes how a person endows these entities with stable distinctive features: (a) the presence of an effect is noted when its presumed cause is absent; (b) reaction to an effect produced by a person or object remains invariant, regardless of different forms which may be assumed by the person or object; (c) the response that is made agrees with the response of other individuals placed in the same situation in relation to the same effect. More succinctly, distinctiveness, consistency over time, consistency in modality, and consensus are the four criteria which allow one to distinguish between "ephemeral" (phenotypical) and "permanent" (genotypical) properties, as well as to validate information received with respect to them (Kelley, 1967).

If this line of thought is pursued further, it becomes clear that consistency plays a decisive role in the process of acquiring and organizing information from the environment. Consistency takes the role of either internal, intra-*individual* consistency (consistency in time and modality, in Hieder's terminology), or that of inter-individual, *social* consistency. These two really amount to the same thing, since consistency in time and modality is simply a sort of consensus which each person establishes internally in order to harmonize different sets of information and actions; while consensus itself is a form of consistency imposed on, or sought by, different individuals. Both forms of consistency result in reducing response variability. This reduction is the customary, visible manifestation of an action model through which the desired features are revealed, and through which the invariant dimensions of the social and material world, i.e. the norms which determine behaviour, are validated. At least, the individual *feels* that this is the effect of the reduction of response variability, and this therefore becomes its meaning.

Bearing this meaning in mind, it becomes easy to see why behavioural consistency is so influential. On the one hand, it expresses either very strong conviction in circumstances where opinions are usually more unstable, or a valuable alternative to predominant opinions. On the other hand, an individual displaying consistent behaviour not only seems very self-assured, but also guarantees that agreement with him will lead to solid and lasting consensus. Consistency also appeals to a general desire to espouse relatively clear and simple opinions or judgements, and to define unambiguously those realities with which one is commonly faced. An undue amount of attention may seem to be demanded, and the behaviour may seem extreme or odd, but it may also have an attraction, and may constitute a rallying point for latent group tendencies. These considerations make sense of the determination of Cato the Elder to end every one of his speeches, regardless of the topic, with the famous "Carthage must be destroyed", until the Senate agreed with his views and sent an expedition against Rome's rival city.

There is by now support for the contentions I have made regarding consistency as a behavioural style. Evidence is provided by two experiments carried out by Moscovici and Faucheux (1972).

First Experiment

Experimental procedure The experiment is presented to the subjects as an investigation of a problem in applied psychology. They are told that, in connection with recent developments in information transmission, notably in aerial and space navigation, operators have to read information projected on cathode screens. Because of this, it is important to determine people's preferences for different codes so that the legibility and discriminability of the transmitted information can be improved. A concrete example is offered: airport control tower operators must simultaneously track and guide large numbers of planes which are preparing to land or take off. From the point of view of airport safety, the work of these operators should be simplified as much as possible. The information they have to make use of (altitude, position, speed, priority, etc.) should be presented to them in the clearest possible way, with the most appropriate symbols and signals, so that they can make accurate and rapid decisions.

The subjects are then told that they will take part in an experiment which is a simplified version of the conditions in the control tower, but requiring the same kinds of selective attention and decision-making. For this purpose, they will be shown a series of drawings differing in four respects: *size* (large or small); *colour* (red or green); *shape* (round or angular); and *line* (dotted or continuous). The subjects are shown a sample of each type of drawing. They are then informed that they will be shown a long series of drawings, and that for each drawing there will always be four correct answers possible. However, they are asked to give only *one* answer—the one which, for whatever reason, seems to them to be the most appropriate for a given drawing in the circumstances. Answers were to be given either orally or in writing. The order of answers was systematically varied: the first subject to give an answer on the initial trial would be the last to give an answer on the next trial, and so on.

The series of stimuli consists of 64 drawings which are shown in sequence such that only a single dimension remains constant from one drawing to the next, for example, one drawing would be large, green, rounded, dotted; the next would then be large, red, angular, continuous, and the next would be small, red, rounded, dotted, and so on. The subjects, who are in groups of four or five, are positioned round three sides of a rectangular table. The fourth side is reserved to the experimenter, who presents the drawings in sequence for inspection. A confederate of the experimenter consistently gives a *colour* answer throughout. Control groups consist of naive subjects only, with no confederate.

Results Table 4 shows that the number of "colour" responses increased significantly in the experimental groups, as compared to the control groups. It is noticeable that this increase in "colour" responses accompanies a significant decrease in the number of "shape" responses, but this latter variation cannot be attributed to any specific factor. The "shape" dimension is not the one chosen most frequently by the control groups, and does not seem to be related in any special way to "colour". There is a second measure of the influence of the minority subject.

TABLE 5

First Experiment: Average number of choices in each dimension; comparison of experimental and control groups

Dimension	Colour	Line	Size	Shape
Experimental groups (k = 8)	20·86	16·18	16·09	10·88
Control groups (k = 6)	15·28	18·93	14·20	15·59
Student's t	2·46	1·67	0·75	2·74
Significance level	p<·2	p>·10	p>·10	·2>p>·05

Normally, when expressing a preferential choice, subjects do not respond in an isolated manner, but rather in a series of two or more successive responses. It can be seen that in the experimental groups, the "colour" judgements are more frequently given in series of two or more responses ($X^2 = 17·84, p < 0·001$). In the case of the other dimensions, however, there is either no significant difference ("size"), or else the number of isolated responses increases ("shape": $X^2 = 5·45, 0·05 > p > 0·02$; "line": $X^2 = 22·397, p < 0·001$). Thus, the consistent behaviour of a minority determines not only the frequency of responses of the majority, but also their organization.

Second Experiment

Experimental procedure An implicit norm is a norm which regulates behaviour without our being clearly conscious of its general nature, or of the fact that it determines most of our decisions. Such norms are ubiquitous in the realms of fashion, food, language, taste, etc. For convenience, we chose linguistic material for this experiment. Verbal habits may be defined as normative regularities in a collectivity which shares these habits.

Eighty-nine word associations were chosen from a list compiled by Nunnally and Hussek (1958), who measured the frequency of certain word associations in an American student population. For each stimulus word (e.g. "orange") there are two corresponding associations, one of which is qualitative ("round"), and one of which is superordinate ("fruit"). The subject is given a set of five pages on which the 89 associations are printed. As the experimenter reads out a stimulus word, the subject selects and repeats whichever of the two associations printed on the same line as the stimulus word seems most closely related to the stimulus; the subject also keeps a record of his own responses. The order in which responses are elicited is systematically varied as in the first experiment. The seating arrangement is also like that in the first experiment. The experimental groups consist of three naive subjects and one confederate. The control groups contain only naive subjects. The confederates in the experimental groups always choose the superordinate association.

The word associations were organized into two different lists according to increasing or decreasing probability of the choice of the superordinate association among the general population. In the first list (list A) the probability of a superordinate association to the stimulus word is greater at the beginning; thus, for these stimuli, the association "chosen" by the confederate happens to correspond to the norm. As the probability of his responses decreases, his behaviour appears as more "conservative", impeding adaptation to the shift in verbal habits. In the second list (list B), in which the probability of superordinate associations is smaller at the beginning, the confederate's responses appear as "deviant".

These two lists were used in order to show that: (a) the true source of influence is the *consistency* of the minority's behaviour, not its degree of deviance; (b) the initial conformity of a minority, contrary to what seem to be the findings of Kelley and Shapiro (1954) and Hollander (1960), may enhance its influence, but is not the cause of its influence.

Results Regardless of the order in which the lists are used, the increase in superordinate responses in the experimental as compared to the control groups is significant. The influence of the confederate on the majority's responses is undeniable, whether he acts as a "conservative" or as a "deviant" (see Table 6). It may be questioned whether the *minority*

TABLE 6

Average number of "Superordinate" responses; comparison of experimental and control groups

	List A	List B
Experimental group averages ($k = 6$)	74·01	63·67
Control group averages ($k = 6$)	57·61	53·89
Student's t	2·24	1·91
Significance level	$p < 0·05$	$0·10 > p > 0·05$

individual's choice affected the *majority individuals*' choice over the whole list, or only for that part of the list where he was nearer the norm. If all responses were influenced, there would be a modification of the majority norm away from the original American norm. Such a modification can indeed be observed; the proportion of superordinate associations chosen by the experimental groups is significantly higher than that chosen by the control groups in the second half of list A

$$(t = 3\cdot41, v = 34; 0\cdot01 > p > 0\cdot001)$$

and in the first half of list B

$$(t = 2\cdot38, v = 34; 0\cdot01 > p > 0\cdot001).$$

Is there any difference in the extent of the confederate's influence according to whether he is "deviant" or "conservative"? Our evidence showed that the order of list presentation did not affect the direction of associations. The proportion of superordinate responses in the control groups is identical for both lists. Whatever difference appears in the experimental groups must be due to the stance of the confederate. For list A, from which the confederate made conservative choices, the frequency of superordinate responses is higher

$$(t = 1\cdot91, v = 10; 0\cdot10 > p > 0\cdot05)$$

than for list B, from which the confederate made deviant choices. Thus the initial conformity of a minority increases its influence, but initial conformity is not a necessary condition of influence.

The two experiments reported have been the first to study the effects of behavioural consistency. Other experiments which have replicated them have confirmed the general trend of the original findings, while raising some new problems.

RIGIDITY

These experiments on behavioural style have raised some new problems. One of the problems is awkward; how is consistency expressed: by repetition, or by patterning of behaviour? More directly, the problem is that rigid behaviour can be a cause, but also sometimes an obstacle, to influence. First of all, repugnance is aroused by behaviour lacking in subtlety, flexibility, and sensitivity to the reactions of others. Secondly, rigid behaviour is a symptom of conflict, of refusal to compromise or to make concessions, and of the will to impose one's own point of view at any cost. Such rigidity may sometimes be attributed to an individual's or group's incapacity to appreciate certain aspects of reality, or to emerge from self-imposed limitations of viewpoint. However, it should not be forgotten that rigid behaviour may merely be the outcome of a situation in which concession and compromise are in fact not possible.

The question of the extent to which consistent behaviour is to be interpreted as rigid behaviour, and the psychological significance of this behaviour, must also be dealt with. For the moment, however, I only want to show that such rigidity is not only a function of the behaviour of minorities, but also a function of the way in which others in turn are led to categorize rigid behaviour. That is to say, rigidity is not only in the behaviour of the person or subgroup, but is also in the eye of the beholder.

Ricateau (1971) brought together a group of three people to discuss the case of a young criminal, Johnny Rocco, and asked them to decide what type of punishment or treatment was appropriate for him. In general, the majority were rather indulgent towards him; but the minority, a confederate of the experimenter, consistently made more severe recommendations. Majority and minority had to confront each other's views before reaching individual decisions. Decisions were based on a seven-point scale of indulgence/severity. Two individual decisions were taken during the course of the experiment. The first was made before there had been any discussion at all. The second was made after thirty minutes of discussion (which had been divided into three blocks of ten minutes each). Three experimental conditions were set up in order to determine degrees of rigidity in the "mode of interpersonal perception". This was defined as the way in which the members of a group judge and categorize each other. How can we discover or manipulate these modes of perception? By obliging subjects to judge themselves or others according to a more or less large number of categories. In real life, for instance, dogmatic or racist individuals judge themselves, and particularly others, according to very few categories—usually two—while more open-minded individuals will make use of more categories.

Ricateau invited his subjects to judge themselves and the other members of the group according to a scale derived from Osgood's semantic differential. Subjects were to categorize each other in terms of polarities such as active/passive, realistic/romantic, and so on. These polarities were the extreme points of six-point scales on which subjects marked with a letter of the alphabet the position judged most closely descriptive of each member of the group in turn. In the first experimental condition (I), subjects were given only two polarity scales on which to indicate their judgements. In the second condition (II) they used five scales, and in the third condition (III) they used eight scales. These scales were filled in at regular intervals—every ten minutes—during the course of the discussion on the young delinquent Johnny Rocco.

As I have indicated, this judging activity using two, five, or eight scales was meant to provide the subjects with a specific code for the perception of others, which differed in the number of dimensions available according to the experimental condition. It was therefore a matter of inducing a certain preparedness to categorize in such a way that the image of the minority (which was elaborated during the course of discussion) was constructed out of a variable number of dimensions. The content of the scales of judgement had been selected in such a way that it had no direct correspondence with the content of the discussion itself. By changing the narrowness of the perceptual code from one experimental condition to another, the experimenter hoped to induce a greater or lesser degree of differentiation in the real image of the behaviour of others, and in this way to modify the relative salience of certain dimensions, and therefore the influencing capacity of the deviant individual. The assumption was that he would be more influential when perceived through a larger number of dimensions.

Ricateau confirmed that subjects in condition I were significantly less displaced towards the minority norm than the subjects in condition II

$$(X^2 = 4\cdot99, 0\cdot02 < p < 0\cdot05)$$

and in condition III

$$(X^2 = 3\cdot92, p < 0\cdot05).$$

Also, subjects in condition II were less displaced towards the minority norm than subjects in condition III

$$(X^2 = 2\cdot72, p < 0\cdot10).$$

The indices of displacement, when arranged in rank order, showed that the degree of influence exerted by the minority was in inverse proportion to the number of categories used in the induction of "modes of interpersonal perception" (see Table 7). From this, we can conclude that a majority will be less likely to accept the views of a minority if

TABLE 7
Degree of influence and the breadth of category decisions

Order established as a function of increasing uniformity	III < II < I
Order established as a function of increasing submission to the influence exerted	I < II < III

their interaction is perceived "dogmatically", a situation in which the consistent behaviour of the minority will be seen as more rigid. In contrast, the same behaviour will have an undeniable influence on a less dogmatic majority.

A study by Nemeth *et al.* (1974) has demonstrated that less "dogmatic", more "flexible" behaviour can be more effective in the "patterning" of its responses than in the repetition of its responses. The stimuli used in the experiment were blue slides. Groups of six subjects were made up of two confederates and four naive subjects. In one part of the experiment, the confederates claimed that they saw "green" on 50% of the trials, and "green and blue" on the rest of the trials. In one condition, these responses of "green" and "green and blue" were given randomly; in a second condition, the confederates said that they saw "green" on the 12 slides that were dimmest in intensity, and that they saw "green and blue" on the 12 slides that were brightest in intensity (Correlated I condition). In a third condition, the reverse was the case: the confederates said that they saw "green and blue" on the dimmest slides, and that they saw "blue" on the brightest slides (Correlated II condition). Thus, in these latter two conditions, the confederates patterned their responses according to the intensity of the stimuli. A control condition was also run, in which there were no confederates.

The first dependent variable showing influence was the mean number of trials in which "green" was a response. The second dependent variable was the proportion of total responses of "green". Table 8 shows the mean for all conditions of both variables. Comparing the "random" and "correlated" conditions (in which 50% of the confederates' responses were "green", and 50% were "green and blue"), it is clear that the minority exerts influence when it gives a patterned set of responses, but exerts no influence at all when its responses are random. The differences are all statistically significant ($t = 1.94$, $p < 0.05$). Furthermore, if the conditions in which the confederates behaved consistently, by repetition, are compared, it appears that the "patterned" condi-

TABLE 8
Mean number of trials on which subjects responded "Green"

Repetitive "green" responses	Repetitive "green and blue" responses	Patterned or Correlated responses (I and II)	Random responses	Control
0·69	4·00	5·84	0·06	0·00

tions were equivalent to the "repetitive" "green and blue" conditions, but significantly more effective than the "repetitive" "green" condition ($t = 1·883$, $p < 0·05$). As is obvious from the data, the "patterned" (correlated) conditions showed significant minority influence as compared to the control condition (in which there were no confederates). The "repetitive" "green and blue" condition was partially effective as compared to the control condition ($t = 1·3$, $p < 0·10$). The "repetitive" "green" condition, in contrast, was not effective at all. The authors conclude "it is clear that the patterned response of a minority was at least as effective in modifying the majority's opinion as was simply repeating a position" (p. 15).

What can we learn from this experiment? First of all that a behavioural style, in this case consistency, is defined by a certain degree of rigidity, and that when this rigidity is visible, it exerts influence. In theory a less rigid style of behaviour ought to have a greater effect than a more rigid style. But secondly, we learn that the minority's rigidity is a function of the social meaning attributed to it by the majority, one of the inferences resulting from the deviant minority's behaviour. If flexibility signifies compromise and submission to the pressure of the group, then the chances of changing the group's opinions are certainly reduced. This has recently been demonstrated by Kiesler and Pallak (1975). In this experiment, which is actually more complex and subtle than I shall present here, the authors invite the subjects to participate in a study of group decision making, informing them that a group decision would be made about a human relations case. Subjects read the case and privately communicate their personal recommendations. The case was about a fifteen-year-old delinquent named Johnny Politano. The personal history of the boy was written in such a way as to make the reader feel relatively unsympathetic towards him. He was presented as being disruptive and aggressive, a selfish character who preyed on others in spite of the warm and lenient treatment he received from them. After giving his personal recommendation, each subject was shown a distribution of opinions with a majority of six and a minority of two. In seeing the distribution, each subject could perceive himself as belonging to the majority. Allegedly, because of a technical error involving a lack of complete information, the subjects were asked to vote again, and each subject saw some of part of the opinion distribution change. There were six experimental conditions:

(a) Subjects in the control situation saw the same distribution as before the "technical error".

(b) Subjects in the "minority compromise" condition saw that both minority members changed their recommendations two units in the direction of the majority position.

(c) Subjects in the "reactionary condition" observed that one member of the majority became even more negative, polarizing against the minority position.

(d) Subjects in the "mixed condition" noted a polarization movement against the minority and, at the same time, a movement of compromise by the deviant minority.

(e) Subjects in the "majority compromise" saw that one of the majority members who previously held the modal majority position had changed his recommendation by two units in the direction of the deviant minority.

(f) Subjects in the "majority defector condition" observed, by examining the new distribution of opinions, that one of the majority members had defected by adopting entirely the minority position.

Thus, in two conditions the minority seems to move towards the majority, in two other conditions we observe a movement of the majority towards the minority, and in the two remaining conditions there are indications of polarization against the minority. In addition, in order to induce even more change, each subject "received" a note from one of the minority members advocating a more open and positive attitude towards the delinquent boy and indicating a feeling that he would certainly improve during his probation period. After reading the note, the subject filled out three sorts of attitude scales: (a) what he thinks the group should do; this judgement was presumably to be distributed to the other members of the group and used as a starting point for group discussion; (b) what he positively thinks should not be done; (c) his guess as to the final recommendation of the group. Other measurements were also taken, but they do not concern us directly here.

The results show that the members of the majority changed their opinions when the minority was able to entice a majority member to compromise ("majority compromise") or to defect ("majority defector"). In both cases the impact of the deviant minority is significantly different when compared to the control condition ($t = 2.24$ and 5.63 respectively, $p < 0.001$). Moreover, defection of one of the majority members shattered the majority opinion more than the compromise condition ($t = 3.39$, $p < 0.0002$). And as we expected, the minority compromise did not produce any change in the attitude of the majority. Likewise, the "reaction" of the majority ("reactionary condition") had no sizeable impact. In other words, a consistent (uncompromising) minority can influence a group, while an inconsistent (compromising) minority has no such power. Actually, the three attitude measures show us the differential impact. The strongest influence, that is, the greatest move towards the minority position, was observed when subjects predicted the final group decision. The weakest influence was noted in the subjects' private opinions. The subject's own change towards the opinion expressed by the deviant minority was located between the two.

While this experiment demonstrates, in an original way, the impact of the minority's behavioural style, it also points out that, although it is a necessary condition, it is not always a sufficient one. In the control condition the minority was consistent but did not produce a greater change than the inconsistent, compromising minority. Only when the minority was able to produce some movement of opinion on the part of a majority member did the differential and full effect related to behavioural style become apparent. This is not at all surprising. Conversions have always been used by scientific, religious, or political minorities to point to the correctness of their point of view, as an example which others should follow, and as a means of legitimizing their position. Innovation always requires what has been called a "demonstration effect", the beginning of the minority's encroachment and the dislocation of the majority through the movement of one of its members to a new position. What is more surprising is the fact that the moderation and the compromise of the minority is hardly ever rewarded and their "reasonable" attitude does not make them any more influential. But why does the majority change when the movement of the minority proves the correctness of their own positions? This is surprising for a certain common sense view and any theory which wants to include its principles. It is less so for certain social and political *praxis* and the perspective which I am trying to present here.

But for the moment, the essential lesson of this experiment is that while there is a limit to rigidity, there is also a limit to flexibility, namely, of appearing as a concession or a submission to the majority. It is certain, however, that this statement is ambiguous. In fact what we should say is that if an individual or a group wish to create a distance between themselves and another individual or group or wish to make them adopt an extreme position opposite to their own, then they should adopt a rigid style of behaviour. Conversely, if an individual or a group wish to bring about a convergence with another individual or group, then the theoretical statement holds: a less rigid style of behaviour will be more influential, provided that a certain distance remains between the two parts of the group—the majority and the minority—and that flexibility does not seem to be the result of a submission to an external pressure. This, of course, is difficult to achieve, although it is desirable in many respects.

It is certain that a rigid style of behaviour can have several negative effects on direct influence:

(1) Firstly, it can provoke an attitude of rejection, since it may be perceived as a kind of violence or unacceptable constraint, particularly if the other person only has a limited number of possible reactions open to him. This is nicely illustrated in an experiment by Paicheler and Bouchet (1973).

The experiment took place in the academic year following the May 1968 student rebellion in France. The subjects were all students, invited to discuss items which covered various aspects of the issues raised by the student movement. As in all such kinds of experiment, they first expressed, individually, their opinions. Secondly, brought together in groups of four, they were to discuss and reach a consensus on each item. Finally, they again expressed individually their opinions on the same items. There were three kinds of measures: pre-consensus, consensus, and post-consensus. Some of the groups contained one or two extremist members, while other groups did not.

Comparing these two types of group, the results show that the consensus of the moderate groups is more extreme than the individual judgements of its members; and that, after consensus has been reached, the individuals adopt the group norm without any tendency to revert to their previous individual judgement. Conversely, in the groups containing one or more extremists (radicals), while a strong extremism occurs in the consensus, there is marked regression to previous individual judgements in the post-consensus phase.

It seems clear that what happened in the latter case was that the strength of the consensus norm made it impossible for firm opposition to arise in the course of group discussion. The minority succeeded in compelling other group members to give unwilling assent to the norm. One result of this was, as the data show, that extremists were even more extreme after the group interaction. In parallel, moderates became more conservative (23%) than they had been before discussion. It can thus be assumed that some subjects reacted to the somewhat unjustified pressure they felt had been exerted on them.

TABLE 9

Comparison of averages obtained in the most and the least extreme groups

Phases	Pre-consensus	Consensus	Post-consensus
Groups			
Most extreme	1·37	2·22	1·73
Least extreme	0·75	1·17	1·07

(2) The second negative effect that a rigid behavioural style can have on its influence is therefore a *displaced* one, which occurs where least expected. This is because, even if a person wants to agree with another individual or sub-group on some topic, the rigidity of that individual's or subgroup's behaviour may be sufficiently repulsive to prevent him from doing so. An experiment by Mugny (1974a) shows that this is indeed the case. During a preliminary survey, Mugny found that the junior high school students not only held industry strongly responsible for polluting the environment, but they were also undecided as to how to attribute this responsibility. Based on this survey, Mugny constructed a questionnaire measuring the attitude of the subjects towards imputing responsibility for pollution. A Likert-type questionnaire was composed of twenty phrases, eight of which either accused or defended industry; eight others accused or defended individuals and the idea that "every litter-bit counts", and four phrases accused or defended both individuals and industry. The experiment was administered in the students' classrooms. The subjects first answered the questionnaire, indicating

their position on each item. Then they were asked to read a tract dealing with some possible remedies for the problem of pollution. There were two types of tracts: one tract (F) took a position with respect to pollution and proposed "reasonable" solutions (restrictions on industrial production, fines, etc.), while the other tract (R) presented the authors as being intransigent and advocated very firm measures (shutting down the factories that pollute the environment, forbidding picnics in natural settings, etc.). The subjects were asked to answer the questionnaire a second time after having read one of the two tracts. In analysing the results, Mugny distinguished between changes on the items that were linked to the source of influence, that is, whose content was treated in the tracts (D), and changes on items the content of which was not treated in the tracts (ND). An analysis of variance shows that there is more change on the indirect items (ND) than on the direct ones (D). But in fact, as Table 10 shows, when the subjects were given a text that is coherent without being rigid, the influence is evenly distributed among both types of items, while the influence is practically nil for the direct items and, on the contrary, very strong for the indirect items when the subjects were given a text which presented its authors as being rigid ($F = 5.761, p < 0.025$).

TABLE 10

Change on the direct and indirect items and
behavioural style

Behavioural style:	Items	
	Direct	Indirect
Consistent but not rigid	+3.52	+3.40
Consistent and rigid	−0.84	+6.04

This demonstrates that even when a rigid behavioural style produces a change, its influence remains an indirect one. But is this rigidity invariably experienced as a blockage? We might suppose that this is the case only when there is a perceived or an actual disagreement between the sender and the receiver of influence. Hence the impression of there being an agreement on basic attitudes would tend to diminish the feeling of being blocked and the rejection of attempts at influence. In a new experiment, Mugny (1974b) used the same questionnaire and tracts as in the preceding experiment, only changing the procedure of the experiment. The subjects are first asked to complete the questionnaire. After this is done, the experimenter announces that he will return a week later, and that in the meantime he will show the subjects' responses to competent people belonging to a (fictitious) group of environmentalists who would be asked to respond to each subject individually. The experimenter himself was presented as a member of a study group on opinion surveys and therefore completely independent of the organization interested in problems of pollution. In the second phase of the experiment, the subjects were given two sheets of paper. The first sheet informed the subject whether his responses agreed or disagreed with the opinions of the fictitious research team of environmentalists. The second sheet was a text on pollution which was either the (F) tract or the (R) tract from the experiment described above. Just after having read these documents the subjects were again asked to answer the questionnaire. In analysing the results, as in the preceding experiment, Mugny distinguished between direct items (D) and indirect items (ND). The changes that were observed are the following: for the most part, the subjects who received the messages of the "rigid" tract were less influenced (F = 6·745, $p < 0.025$) than the subjects who received the messages of the other tract. The perceived agreement or disagreement of opinion had a very clear effect here. If the subjects believed that there was an agreement between them and the source of influence, the first type of message (R) induced a change only on the indirect items (ND) without effecting any change whatsoever on the direct items (D), whereas the second type of message (F) had the same influence on both direct (D) and indirect (ND) items. In other words, when the subject feels a constraint, the resistance to the source of influence is accompanied by a very strong displacement of the centre of gravity of the concessions he is willing to make. On the other hand, when the subject is in disagreement with the source, the flexible message (F) modifies especially, and even more strongly, the indirect opinions (ND), not related to the content of the message, while the rigid message (R) also affects these opinions (ND), but to a much smaller extent. The presence or absence of agreement, then, has more pronounced consequences when the source appears to be rigid than when it appears to be flexible (see Table 11).

The reasons for these phenomena are still unclear, and one should not venture to speculate about them before we get to know much more about the underlying mechanisms of interaction in such conditions. It is enough to underline the fact that the impact and the type of impact

TABLE 11

Change of attitude according to the perception of the relationship with the source of influence

Perceived relation between sender and receiver:	Behavioural style			
	Flexible (F)		Rigid (R)	
	Direct items	Indirect items	Direct items	Indirect items
Agreement	4·07	4·57	0·89	9·14
Disagreement	3·85	10·39	1·60	4·142

which behavioural styles have are very much dependent upon the social context in which they occur.

Admittedly this conclusion does not carry us very far forward. However, if we take this dependence on the social context seriously into account, we can better understand the subtle operations of the "grammar of behaviours" and the role which they play in processes of influence. By spinning a web of rules and meanings, it transforms every information, every attitude, and every sign into an *action* directed towards (or against) someone or something. With this in mind, we can affirm that consistency is not the feature or miracle solution of interaction; its primary function is to call attention to the existence of a coherent point of view, to something powerful, and, of course, to a norm. In a word, it forcefully indicates the nomic quality of an individual or a group. Beyond this, we know that consistency can appear in a thousand different ways, some productive and some counter-productive for the individual or the group in question. This observation is not very surprising, but it is just as well to have grounded it experimentally. It was time for some restraint to be introduced into the rather extreme notion that behavioural style is always effective no matter what the circumstances.

FAIRNESS

What is the consequence of rigid, monolithic, repetitive behaviour when two people, two groups, a majority and a minority, find themselves face to face? As we have already seen, there will be failure of communication, refusal to take into consideration the interests, opinions, and point of view of the other person or group. This is a serious matter;

because, as we have suggested, each social actor, even if he expects to change to some extent himself, expects also to be able to bring about some change in others. People may be quite willing to accept that they are sometimes wrong, but not that they are always wrong. One may wish others to be right, but it is painful to have to believe that right is *always* on their side. So it is that, from one angle, the autonomous, consistent behaviour of a minority will appear firm and resolute to the majority; but from another angle, this same behaviour may appear as stubborn and out of touch with reality.

But which behavioural style escapes this taint of rigidity? There is one, and I have defined it as a state of "fairness", for two reasons. One reason is that this style presents a certain solidity, a certain salience which permits the position of the individual or collective actor to be easily seen in the field of social action. In this respect, the style is close to consistency, and is perceived as such. The second reason is this: it expresses a concern to take into account the positions of others. It makes felt, in interactions with others, a desire for reciprocity and interdependence, a will to enter into genuine dialogue. The person or group present themselves as open-minded; they can be influenced to some extent, and they can also influence others. Lack of agreement with them does not give rise to animosity or a sense of failure, and it does not preclude further contact with them. There is no attempt to coerce, although preferences, beliefs and opinions will be made clear. They are neither indifferent, nor necessarily looking for, or willing to compromise; but they are ready to consider any possibility. In other words, everyone has a chance to be understood, and the game is left open up to a certain point. In such conditions, people are more prepared to submit to influence, to change, because they feel that they are not the only ones doing so.

The most striking example of this style in modern history is that of Pope John XXIII. He succeeded Pius XII, who, in the language we are using, was not open to dialogue with other Christian groups, nor with the representatives of other social and political movements. Many judged his attitude towards the modern world a rigid one, and saw his attitudes as determined by a strict adherence to traditional dogmas. John XXIII was no less faithful to the teachings of the Catholic church, and no less careful of its interests, or of the authority of the Pope, than his predecessor. But in addition to all this—and herein lies his historical importance—he declared himself ready to re-open issues which had been closed to discussion for catholics for centuries, ready to listen, to enter into dialogue with other Christian religions, to bring bishops into direct participation in Church government, to re-examine the Church's relationship with socialist countries, and to take account of the evolution in mores and mentality in the western world and elsewhere. In other words, without necessarily abandoning secular powers and traditions, he showed himself ready to change if it was necessary, ready to be convinced of the need to modify institutions and secular opinions—while at the same time expecting and calling for corresponding changes on the part of others. His aim, ultimately, was to bring the Church out of its rather isolated position and to widen its influence in ways which were better adapted to the condition of the times.

Fairness means exactly this: *simultaneous* expression of a particular viewpoint, and concern for the mutuality of the relationship in which views are expressed. Experimental evidence concerning this behavioural style is scarce, but it does exist. Mugny, Humbert and Zubel (1973), and Mugny (1973) have studied this style in a relatively detailed way in a series of experiments on interaction between a minority and a majority. The problem they began with is already somewhat familiar to us. By consistently adopting an attitude of rejection towards majority norms, a minority places itself in conflict with the majority. From the outset, therefore, the majority has no tendency to move towards the minority norms, even when these are in the direction of its own interests. To reject any approach, any possibility of change, signifies the intention to maintain the conflict at its highest pitch, to block any attempt at communication or negotiation with the rest of the community. This tends to diminish the minority's chances of success, since it will be perceived as dogmatic and hostile.

The authors hypothesized that such an extreme form of behaviour, together with rigid views and excessive demands, is a less efficient style of behaviour than the fair style, which allows the majority a certain latitude to influence the minority. The fair style, while conserving consistency of behaviour, allows concessions in a spirit of latitude which in turn, if responded to by the majority, will make consistent behaviour in deviants more acceptable. While being flexible, in order to influence, a minority must nevertheless remain nomic, avoiding the disunity which could lead to anomie. At least, this is true if the genetic view is correct.

The facts we have to work on were provided by the following experimental procedure. There were three phases:

Pre-test phase Subjects were first of all introduced to each other in groups of three (two naive subjects and one confederate). They then proceeded individually, to give the following pre-test data:

since the topic of discussion was to be military service in Switzerland, the subject was asked to express an opinion on this topic by selecting a position on an eight-point scale;

in order to measure underlying opinions, subjects were asked to fill in a 40-item yes/no questionnaire of adjectives which were to be judged descriptive or not descriptive of the Swiss Army.

On the sheet displaying the eight-point scale, and this is important, subjects were able to read that they would later be asked to express their opinion orally. There was no such information on the questionnaire sheet. Two measures were therefore available—one of manifest attitudes, and one of latent opinions.

Interaction phase This began by having subjects express their opinions. In order to emphasize the "public" character of this opinion disclosure, a display board was placed conspicuously in the room, on which each subject's response to each questionnaire item was marked with an A, B, or C (C always represented the confederate). Discussion was then begun. Subjects were given a booklet containing six questions of the type: "Bearing in mind the current military and political forces on the international scene, do you think that the Swiss national defence budget should be adjusted? Your opinion is that the Army's budget should be *discontinued, much reduced, doubled . . .*" For each question, subjects chose one of eight possible responses expressed orally, and then began the discussion, during the course of which they had to defend their positions. The confederates defended their positions with arguments which had been prepared in advance, and which were based on the decisions of military tribunals in cases of conscientious objectors. Questions which might be embarrassing to subjects had been anticipated from the arguments presented by conscientious objectors at these same tribunals.

Confederates defended their positions in two ways. In one experimental condition (R), they were rigid and adhered to the same extreme position throughout. In the other condition (F), they took extreme positions on the first three questions, but took rather less extreme positions on the remaining three questions. The deviant position was to be favourable towards the Swiss Army, since the Swiss student body is not generally favourable towards it.

Post-test phase After the discussion, subjects were asked to fill in the questionnaire once more. Naive subjects were then interviewed individually about their perception of the other subjects, their certainty of opinion, and so on.

The results of this experiment were as follows. At the level of manifest attitude, there was no difference between the two experimental conditions. Whether the confederate was "rigid" or "fair" made no difference. However, the picture is different when we look at latent opinions. As expected, the "fair" confederate changes more opinions in his favour, and gives rise to fewer negative reactions, than the "rigid" confederate (see Table 12).

TABLE 12

Change in underlying opinion after interaction with a "Rigid" or a "Fair" minority *

	Change favourable to the minority %	No change %	Change unfavourable to the minority %
Condition R	11	28	61
Condition F	39	28	33

* Significant at 0·04 by the Mann-Whitney test

The most interesting results have to do with the *relationship* between the two types of response according to the experimental condition, and this reveals clearly the problem of their psychological significance. The following relationships were found: in condition (R), there was a strong negative correlation between the change in manifest attitudes and the change in latent attitudes. Subjects whose latent attitudes were most divergent from the minority had overt attitudes which were closest to those of the minority. In condition (F), the correlation was positive. In this case, manifest changes were the same in direction and extent, as latent changes of opinion.

At first, the effect of a minority which refuses to recognize the position of the majority exerts a kind of pressure on individuals to follow it, if only because there appears to be no alternative; but the more an individual follows, the more hostile he becomes, and the more his conscience is opposed to it. In contrast, a "fair" minority can induce individuals to follow without producing this delayed reaction of hostility and reluctance. There seems to be at least some advantage in fairness.

However, things are not quite as simple as we would wish. Considering the extent to which any behavioural style might produce a similar effect, Mugny (1973) simplified his experimental procedure. In a first phase, subjects filled in a series of questionnaires relating to their attitude towards the Swiss Army, and their attitude towards other subjects. In a second phase, subjects listened to a speech on the Swiss Army which represented the position of an extreme left anti-militarist group. In this population, the subjects were rather favourable towards the Army. The speech, read by a confederate, consisted of a three-pronged attack:

(a) economic argument: the Army is the economic support of the class in power;

(b) ideological argument: the Army is an ideological "bludgeon", regimenting and reinforcing the work hierarchy in the capitalist division of labour;

(c) political argument: the speech ends with a denunciation of the Army as an instrument of repression of progressive struggles, controlled by the bourgeoisie. This is illustrated with examples from history.

Between points (a) and (b), and (b) and (c) was interposed a short discussion of the question of conscientious objectors, who are generally recognized as taking an ideological stand against the Army. This discussion indicated an extreme left-wing attitude, which accepts conscientious objection as an individual, personal solution, but not as a method of bringing about a fundamental change in the nature of military institutions. A variation in this short discussion was the major difference between experimental conditions (R) and (F):

(1) Between points (a) and (b), the discussion was the same in both conditions: "We think that the only effective way of weakening the Army is to carry out revolutionary activities within it and against it. We think that conscientious objection is too individualist to succeed as a means of undermining the Army."

(2) Between points (b) and (c), individuals in the (R) condition heard the same idea, but slightly more forcefully: "In the struggle against ideological regimentation, we believe that methods such as conscientious objection are insincere, individualistic, petty-bourgeois and quasi-reactionary. We must fight within and against the Army." In the (F) condition, the confederate made his position slightly more conciliatory between (b) and (c): "I would like to return to the question of conscientious objection, which I did not deal with very well before. Our position is that collective conscientious objection, if well organized,

is a useful and valuable method of struggle against the Army. However, we also believe it is important to carry on the struggle from within the Army itself."

In these two conditions, the fundamental ideological position is the same. What distinguishes the conditions is that, in (R), the minority takes no account of the possible opinions of the audience, and adheres to an inflexible point of view; in (F), the minority takes the step of acknowledging the possible views of the audience, and seems to imply: "I know your views on this, and I am ready to acknowledge and consider them." The two minorities, of course, behave with equal consistency.

In this experiment, the behavioural style labelled "fair" was more effective in inducing change than was the rigid behavioural style ($t = 1.821, p < 0.05$). However, each one did have a certain impact of its own. If 70% of subjects in the (F) condition changed their opinions in the direction of the confederate, so did 57% of subjects in the (R) condition.

Mugny has obtained similar results in two other unpublished experiments using extreme left-wing tracts, which the subjects read individually, as the method of communication. But he also observed that a rigid, dogmatic minority has more of a chance of affecting subjects whose positions are already close to those of the minority than it has of affecting subjects whose positions are more distant. On the other hand, a minority which presents itself in a "fair" manner has a greater chance of exerting influence widely and evenly on all subjects. The initial difference of positions between sender and receiver therefore considerably complicates the picture.

This is an old problem in studies of social influence. We know, for instance, that influence is directly proportional to the differences of position up to a certain optimal point of divergence, after which it decreases. It has also been shown, in several different ways, that an extreme deviant exerts either a very great, or very little influence, while a "moderate" deviant has a more uniform effect throughout the population. This is probably why so many revolutionary parties and churches water down their wine in order to become more respectable and increase their following while awaiting the end of history or the day of the last judgement.

This relationship between the type of message and the type of receiver has also been observed in studies on the impact of communications.

During World War II, the men in an army training camp were exposed to one-sided versus two-sided arguments regarding the estimated length of the war with Japan. The results indicated that, for men who were already convinced of the point of view presented, the one-sided arguments were more effective in changing attitudes than the two-sided arguments. For those who were initially opposed to the point of view, the two-sided arguments were more effective (Hovland *et al.*, 1949). Today we have more precise knowledge about these phenomena, and we know that they are contingent upon certain aspects of the behavioural style in which they are presented, and not merely on the degree of difference and the number of alternatives present in a message.

All these findings are in accord with one notion: by behaving dogmatically, a minority affects the opinions of those who were already more or less convinced of its point of view, but it confirms the others in their initial positions. On the other hand, a "fair" minority modifies not only the opinions of those who were already well disposed towards it, but also the opinions of those who were initially opposed to it.

As the laboratory sometimes forgets wider realities, we will now attempt to forget the laboratory for a moment and consider some wider realities. Instead of talking in terms of "condition (R)" and "condition (F)", we will talk in terms of "leftists" and communists. The most innocent spectator of contemporary history, in Europe at least, knows that these two Marxist currents have more or less the same intellectual ancestry and the same language, but they differ in their methods and in their relations with the rest of society. Leftist groups see themselves as very radical and revolutionary, and are wary of anything which might be interpreted as compliance or compromise on their part. "Compliance" and "compromise" are seen as bad tendencies on the part of communists, whom they consider to be reformists. The communists, on the other hand, make a distinction between what they call tactics and strategy. They are willing to delay temporarily some of their political aims for the sake of being able to enter into alliances, agreements, and so on, which they believe will ultimately make their position stronger.

Mugny's findings tend to suggest that the leftist groups will have just as much, if not more, influence on people already sympathetic to Marxist ideas, as the communists will. But the other side of the coin is that, even within this fraction of the population, they will have aroused hostility because of their dogmatism, and their unwillingness to acknowledge the possibility of different opinions. Beyond the fraction of people already sympathetic to the left, the methods of the communists are undeniably more effective. These methods were originated by Lenin, at the beginning of this century, and were in fact designed to counter the "leftists" of that time. In particular, he ordered support of and solidarity with the peasant class in their struggle against tsarism, to be followed by the equal distribution of the land among the peasants. This latter measure, of course, went contrary to the orthodox tenet of immediate collectivization. Lenin wrote: "To the peasant bourgeoisie who want democracy, to the city proletariat who want socialism, and to the miserable rural poor, this order will be better understood than the brilliant but empty phrases of the populist socialist-revolutionaries."

It is not for me, or anyone, to decide between different political groups or methods. Everyone chooses his own path, and the ability to win converts is not the only criterion of historical truth. I have attempted to limit myself to exploring, with the findings of experimental studies, the reasons why some groups are more immediately influential than others. I would like to take this exploration a little further, in order to better understand the significance of these experimental findings.

Mugny has frequently indicated that the two styles of behaviour, "rigid" and "fair", exhibit the same degree of consistency, and that this is perceived by the subject. It is the dynamic of the styles, only, which distinguishes them, gives them distinct meanings, and brings about different relationships with the majority audience. Extrapolating further, one could say that, within one's own group, if it is a minority, the dogmatic style of behaviour is adequate. The "fair" style becomes important only when there are contacts between majority and minority, or with another group. Or, the first style is compatible with intra-group relations, the second style is compatible with inter-group relations. In brief, within a group, rigidity is effective: apart from a few exceptions, the more rigid the style, the more influence it will exert. In external relations, however, the "fair" style, equally firm and consistent, must be used in order to affect the social environment.

In other words, one cannot behave in the same way on the inside and on the outside of a group. This is something which the students, and sometimes the participants, of social interaction have not always thought about. But, in order for "internal" and "external" behaviour to be different, there must be a distinction made between internal and external environments at the level of organization and capacities. In this necessity, a group resembles a living organism. The relations between groups are largely determined by the success or otherwise with which this distinction is made, and by whether the groups concerned have, or do not have, an internal environment.

This speculation can be illustrated with the same historical example that was used before—that of leftists and communists. Leftist groups address the external world as though it were their own, internal world. They behave towards outsiders in the same way as they behave towards insiders. Their success with a certain segment of society stems precisely from this. At the same time, their rigidity gives rise to latent hostility. Too strong coercion and rhetoric create pockets of opposition.

Here, for example, is the way in which a reader of the radical publication *Science for the People* (July 1973, p. 13) reacted to its style:

> ... I have been feeling out the reactions of my colleagues (and reflecting on my own) to *SftP*. I think there's unanimous agreement that the publication is informative and thought-provoking (argument-provoking, too—and that's good). However, everyone I've given the mags to has commented upon the stale radical rhetoric. I'm afraid I must concur. I served my time in SDS as an undergraduate (1965–1969) and gradually broke away from the group (noble though their motives and gripes were) because I got tired of listening to their crappy over-stated way of delivering their message. I'm afraid I react the same way to *SftP*. I wish you had a quelch editor—someone who would reread all the stuff to be printed and get rid of all the emotionally-loaded words which the radical left has (unfortunately) polluted for evermore for many of the very people *SftP* is trying to reach. For example, it doesn't matter that genocide is the exact word you want—confirmed by the dictionary and by the writings of the U.N. The word is polluted. When I see genocide on a title, I get nauseated—not because of the presumed *act* of genocide, but because 9 times out of 10 when that word is used, it is misapplied by knee-jerk radicals. The word evokes strong responses, in me anyway, toward the writer, not the perpetrator of the act. Maybe I'm not alone ... The content of your magazine is so super; the emotional gilding is spoiling it.
>
> Regardless—I shall continue to support your group in any way I can.

The editor's response to this is no less interesting. Where the reader calls for a change of rhetoric, the editor sees an intellectual gap which must be filled:

> ... Because the charge of "rhetoric" mongering is frequently made against radicals, often with some basis, we think a comment is in order. The rulers

of America and most of the world are conscious architects of crime against the people—for which no rhetoric could overstate the case. Furthermore, many politicians justify these activities with such words as "freedom" and "democracy". The problem with rhetoric arises when people, attempting to share their perception of reality, fail to substantiate it for others, or fail to show that there are real alternatives: that outrageous situations are not simply inevitable features of an inherently corrupt world. If some words have become "polluted", it is usually because we haven't done the homework justifying them. This allows people who haven't encountered the full impact of the evidence on which a "radical analysis" is based, to back away from the otherwise jolting conclusions. We must not let this happen. Many of us will have to contribute through struggle, speaking and writing, to remove rhetoric from truth . . .

Who is right? I shall not try to decide. It is clear enough, however, that these two are missing each other's point. They see the problem on different levels. The reader agrees with the content of the publication, and with the aims of the "radical" movement, while wishing for a change, a re-adaptation of the rhetoric. The behavioural style is judged to be exaggerated and rigid by this reader, who is reacting in opposition to the coercion which this style represents. But the editor stands by this rhetoric, justifies it, and sees no valid reason to change it. He does, however, believe that an improvement in the content and a move to place the ideas on a more solid factual basis will remove any negative, and thereby arbitrary and coercive, aspects.

In fact, when the reader asks the editor to adapt the emitter to the receiver, the editor asks the reader to adapt the receiver to the emitter; the reader considers the rhetoric to be both important and changeable, the editor considers it to be both secondary and immutable. This controversy reflects the processes observed in the laboratory, and also gives insight into the subjective factors which may prevent a rigid behavioural style from exerting influence, even when there is already a large degree of sympathy for the content of the message being conveyed.

This specific example also throws light on a wider phenomenon. We see that this type of group absolutely refuses to "open up", and any moves towards this within the group are interpreted as betrayal, abandonment, or apostasy, even if the moves concern inessential matters. This is bound to mean that such groups do not have the means to penetrate sectors of society which are opposed to them, however slight that opposition may be.

Why is "opening up" seen as such a threat, why is flexibility such an

s.i.s.c.—6

impossibility? It could be said that the main reason for this is that such groups lack an internal environment; "closedness" is their only guarantee of unity, the only protection against dissolution and the dangers of the external environment. Their competitors and adversaries, the communists, have adopted two styles of behaviour. One functions to maintain the cohesion and stability of the group itself; the other is directed towards other groups and social classes. The one is adapted to the internal environment, the other to the external environment.

We see also that political and economic concessions often go together with a reinforcement of ideological discipline, and that the notion of coexistence, even unity of different social groups, tends to occur simultaneously with an insistence on group solidarity and fidelity to traditional policies and ideology. This may seem paradoxical from the outside, and yet, from another point of view, this duality conforms exactly to the psycho-sociological exigencies revealed by the experiments we have described. Going a step further, we can discern something like a developmental pattern: at its inception, a deviant minority group manifests rigid behaviour, which permits it to consolidate itself within the shelter of a closed unity and internal environment. This is the phase of separation and constitution. After a certain stage of evolution, it is ready to develop a different style of behaviour, derived from its now elaborated internal base with the addition of some necessary appendages. This new, "fair" style allows it to retain consistency while at the same time making alliances and widening its sphere of influence.

The genetics of social groups is still in its infancy. Why is this? Perhaps these conjectures will contribute something to the impetus it now lacks. It is my view that the analysis of behavioural styles is one way of approaching the genetics of social groups, which provides some very interesting clues. However, for the present, the experimental evidence available permits only the modest conclusion that "fair" behaviour is an effective way of exerting social influence.

The functions and determining factors of behavioural styles have only recently begun to be looked at. For the moment, we must be content with merely describing the styles and their effects. Which is the best style? Which is the most effective? Such questions betray a magical, not scientific, approach to the problem. There is no ultimate weapon, no foolproof method of influence. Everything depends on circumstances, the internal states of the minority or the majority, and their relations with their social environment. The decision and the ability to use one or other of these behavioural styles depends on these internal states and on the external circumstances, just as much as on the reason for wishing to influence.

However, I would like to stress once more one important consequence of taking behavioural style into account as a source of influence. Common sense attributes influence effects to social status, leadership, majority pressure, and many other forms of dependence. It is my contention here that these different forms of dependence—i.e. power dependence and institutional dependence—are not decisive factors in social influence. A minority can modify the opinions and norms of a majority, irrespective of their relative power or social status, as long as, all other things being equal, the organization of its actions and the expression of its opinions and objectives obey the conditions I have outlined of consistency, autonomy, investment, or fairness.

One is on even firmer ground in stating that the almost exclusive preoccupation with "external" variables—status, leadership, competence, and so on—has obscured the real problems posed by social influence processes, and resulted in concentration on the most self-evident features; those, precisely, which needed no explanation. By insisting on power and influence as interchangeable concepts, focusing on dependence and neglecting behavioural styles, many social psychologists have worked hard to build scientific knowledge around phenomena which, as far as we know, raise no problems and require no explanation. Or, at least, they took as their starting-point a perspective that was unproblematic, and therefore raised questions which needed no answers.

7

Social Norms and Social Influence

Proposition 5

The course of the influence process is determined by objectivity norms, preference norms, and originality norms

Imagine showing the same picture to three different people. One of them may comment on its realism, another may express simply a liking for it, while the third may see exciting qualities in it. The first person is expressing appreciation of the accuracy with which the subject of the picture is portrayed; the second is expressing a spontaneous reaction of taste; and the third person is expressing an evaluation of the quality of this picture as compared to others. Suppose that we wished these three people to reach agreement about the picture. We would first of all have to decide on the aspect of the picture about which agreement should be reached—its realism, the reaction of taste it evokes, or its technical and aesthetic qualities. It is easy to see that the outcome may be very different, according to which one of these three aspects is chosen. The outcome may be different, not necessarily in terms of the degree of agreement reached, but in terms of the manner in which agreement is sought and arrived at. Why should this be so?

Generally speaking, consensus has two psycho-sociological functions. These functions are, on the one hand, to validate opinions and judgements, and on the other hand to provide self-enhancement, re-affirmation of identity, for the person expressing opinions and judgements. There can be no doubt that social importance is attached to being "correct", to being on the side of objective accuracy. But it **is** just as important to be "right", to have one's judgements and opinions accepted by others, and hence to have one's individuality endorsed. In the first case, it is a question of a person wishing to confirm that personal perception and understanding of reality corresponds to the socially endorsed reality. The second case is a question of justifying and advocating one's own perception of reality, a private reality, in other words, and of attempting to share this private reality so that it may become a public reality. That which *we* think is true, must also be seen to be true by others; we want others to like what *we* like. Both of these functions of consensus enter into the influence process, but whichever is dominant, and therefore shapes social interactions and influence exchanges, is determined by social norms.

What are these norms? There is, first of all, the *objectivity* norm. This concerns the need to test opinions and judgements according to the criterion of objective accuracy, so that decisions can be made on whether they may be universally accepted. Secondly, there is the *preference* norm. This norm presumes the existence of more, or less, desirable opinions, reflecting different tastes. It views consensus as the result of a series of comparisons between these opinions. Finally, there is the *originality* norm, which selects judgements and opinions according to the degree of novelty which they represent, and the degree of surprise they are capable of inducing. Consensus, according to this norm, selects the judgement or opinion considered to be both the most appropriate, and the most unusual. Realism, liking, and excitement, in our imaginary experiment, each correspond to one of these three norms; and if the three people had been required to reach an agreement, they would have obeyed one of these norms, unconsciously, quite as closely as if the norm had been translated into explicit experimental instructions.

It can be seen that, at one extreme, the objectivity norm gives priority to the validation function of consensus; while at the other extreme, the preference norm gives priority to the self-enhancement function, which allows scope for individual variations and choices. Mid-way between these two, the originality norm both demands respect for objective correctness, and facilitates self-enhancement, since it is the least commonplace possibility which is most carefully considered. At the same time, this norm demands the avoidance of the trivial, the familiar, and the ordinary.

What are the effects of these norms on interpersonal relations, and relations between individuals and groups? The objectivity norm quite definitely entails conformity pressure, since by definition there can only be one correct response, and every deviant response is necessarily false.

Deviations are intolerable, and must be resolved in order for agreement to take place. Furthermore, exchanges governed by the objectivity norm are centred on the object, since it is the properties and dimensions of the object which decide the value of any arguments put forward. In gross terms, a photograph either represents or does not represent an object, and whether it does or not can be verified by placing the photograph and the object side by side.

In contrast, the preference norm presupposes, in the limiting case, the absence of pressure and a tendency towards uniqueness of the individual opinion, assuming of course that everyone is permitted to respond. Judgement is in terms of individual, personal scales of values. If individuals or groups have occasion to compare their responses, the point of departure is the subjective scale of values, and it is on this basis that everything is considered and decided. In this case, consensus represents a convergence of tastes—the fact that everyone happens to have similar reactions and tastes.

Once again, the originality norm falls between the other two. It creates a centrifugal pressure, each member of the group being induced to take up a unique position and to avoid imitating the responses of the others, while justifying this position with reference to an external object, or to an area of professional, artistic, or scientific activity. The possibility of a consensus is raised by the exceptional interest or novelty of a particular position, but consensus is only reached by the demonstration of both its heuristic power and its congruence with reality. It is the *object*—an observed phenomenon, a work of art, a colour—which is at the centre of discussion. Nevertheless, it is as the "object of a subject" that it is seen and recognized, and it is in this capacity that it provokes controversy. When, for example, we speak of a Cartier Bresson photograph, the Zeigarnik effect, Picasso blue, or de Broglie waves, we are referring to objects or phenomena which are "marked" by someone by virtue of the fact that that person discovered, invented or created the object, and that it represents personal idiosyncrasies. At a more familiar level, in every day life it is equally true that certain colours, arrangements of furniture, ideas, scenery, may be associated with the actions and opinions of a particular friend, colleague, or with a particular social class. In fact, the object is one which is marked by a particular person, and yet is also independent of personalities. A photograph by Cartier Bresson is also simply a photograph; Picasso blue is just another blue, and so on.

In the final analysis, the objectivity norm requires that, in the course of social interaction, every person thinks and behaves with reference to the public reality—that reality which is open to inspection by all, which is the same for all, and which is easily interpreted by all who have eyes to see and ears to hear. Three straight lines can be nothing but three straight lines, blue can be nothing but blue, a house is nothing but a house, and these things are inescapable. Sane men cannot be mistaken in these matters; they are "obvious", "self-evident", "immediate". If a man sees three curved lines where others see three straight ones, if he sees green where others see blue, of if he sees a pink elephant where others see a house, then there is something wrong with him—he is, as we say, out of touch with reality.

The preference norm, in contrast, organizes all exchanges in the sphere of the private realities of individuals and groups. Divergences in this sphere become apparent with differences of point of view and of taste with regard to photographs, landscapes, works of art, cuisine, and so on—they are not concerned with judgements of veridicality. Justification of such divergences is made in terms of the experience, motivation, culture, and choices which make up the history of the individual or group concerned. Of course, consensus is sought in this sphere also, and this is why influence can take place. But it would be hard to find anything more than a common denominator to many different private realities, such as is represented by stock-market attitudes and voting behaviour, for instance, which do not imply that a person has abandoned a private point of view or preference. If, however, the sought-after consensus in this sphere does result in the same taste being expressed towards the same object, in the same degree, for the same reasons, and in the same circumstances, then it is no longer a question of a common scale of preferences, but has become a matter of conformity of opinion and choice.

The originality norm combines both public and private reality. It presupposes the existence of, or it demands the creation of, a private reality in an individual or a group. Everything in art, science, technology, culture, began with the emergence of a vision or an activity which was unique to one artist, scientist, engineer, or a people. This "one" may have remained in isolation for a long time, but this will have insulated and strengthened the private reality. Despite social isolation, the norm still affects each individual, but it is through interaction with others that the private reality becomes transformed into a viable public reality, for others. Paradoxically, it is only when this transformation succeeds that the singularity of an idea, style, belief, theory, or whatever, becomes apparent. If the originator, in however humdrum a sphere, does not see his or her creation evaluated by others, then self-doubt creeps in.

The emergence of a "style" in such a situation provides a provisional defence against doubt, and also clears the way for the conversion of several private realities into public ones. Thus the Bauhaus, which at first simply permitted original artists and designers to meet, work, and transmit their ideas through students, later attempted to shape all visual objects in the environment—thereby affecting the daily reality of millions. The search for originality is, even more, the desire to change the reality of others.

These remarks are largely speculative. However, they should not be dismissed before being subjected to a thorough theoretical and experimental examination. One thing is certain: up to now, the influence process has been analysed exclusively in terms of its validation function, as required by the objectivity norm. As if we did not know how closely influence is related to the self-enhancement of a person, a social class, a school of thought, or a state! Innovation in general appeals to a different norm than that governing conformity—it appeals to the originality norm. People do not only want conventional objects, true and accurate judgements; they also want novel objects and judgements. In science, in art, and in the economic sphere, there is constant striving after novelty and originality. Nothing could be more damaging to the reputation of an artist or scientist than to be accused of banality or imitation. It is my intention to show that the originality norm, and also the preference norm, play a part in the influence process. This will be done in broad outline, setting aside for the moment the detailed conceptual work which also needs to be done.

I have already mentioned Crutchfield's finding that no conformity was observed when subjects were asked to express a preference. This had been interpreted as evidence that preferences are not subject to social pressure. However, this interpretation must now be rejected. Allen and Levine (1971) asked subjects under majority pressure to make judgements about twenty stimuli of three types: names of famous characters (e.g. Whitman, Twain), personality traits (e.g. impulsive, deliberate), and straight lines. In one of the experimental conditions, it was stressed that there were no correct answers, and subjects were urged to express their personal preferences. These subjects, when exposed to group pressure, modified their responses to a greater extent than when they made their decisions in private. This justifies these authors' conclusion that "preference judgements are not immune to group pressure" (p. 124).

What happens when a minority tries to exert influence in a social setting where originality is at a premium? Without hoping to deal exhaustively with this question, I would like to put forward some suggestions in answer to it. The first suggestion is that, since pressure towards conformity is usually very strong (the objectivity norm being most frequently in force), the originality norm has many obstacles to overcome before it can create the pressure to differentiate. Secondly, when the "novelty" criterion has been recognized by the group, the behavioural consistency required in the response is not as great as would be required if the objectivity norm were governing. The third suggestion is at the same time very obvious, and rather complex. If the minority response seems "novel", "surprising", "exciting", it will surely arouse a certain amount of interest. At the same time, it acts as an example, objectifying the demands of the norm. The norm demands an original response from each individual, and therefore demands, in the first place, a *response*. The minority provide the example for at least this initial requirement. But as soon as a person imitates the minority response, that person is differentiated from the others only by virtue of having validated the minority response. Self-enhancement is forfeited, and the demands of the norm have not been met, since this second response is imitative, not original. New responses must therefore be generated. We would expect, then, that in a group insisting on originality, the effect of a minority will be, first, to produce imitations of the minority response, and second, to produce original responses in the group. The fourth and final suggestion is related to the fact that, while a minority in an originality-demanding situation is deviant, its behaviour nevertheless conforms to the norm in force. It therefore demonstrates excellence in a field which is important to the group, and evokes favourable attitudes, perhaps even winning the right to a leadership role.

A series of experiments carried out by Moscovici and Lage used the following experimental paradigm in order to explore these four possibilities. Subjects in groups of six were asked to judge the colour and luminosity of a series of thirty-six slides. All the slides were identical in colour (blue), but their luminosity varied. A minority made up of two confederates judged the slides as "green". Such a judgement could either be considered as "original", or as "incorrect". The experimenters stressed originality in their instructions. There were five experimental conditions. In condition 1, which was called "simple originality instructions", the task was described in a very objective way. The only manipulation concerned the aim of the experiment as it was represented to the subjects; they were told that the experiment was concerned with the originality of colour perception.

Condition 2 was a "discussion condition", in which, before the experiment proper took place, subjects discussed the definition and meaning of originality. Such a discussion could reveal not only the subjects' view of original behaviour, but also any resistance they might have towards it. The notion of originality is, in fact, ambiguous. On the one hand, an individual who distinguishes himself from others by inventive, interesting behaviour is classified as "original". But, on the other hand, the word can also denote bizarre, incomprehensible, pathological behaviour, and it can denote simple incorrectness of judgement as well. The discussion oscillated about these two interpretations without reaching a consensus.

Condition 3 was a "normative condition", in which the originality norm was stressed, and the positive aspect of original behaviour was enhanced in the subjects' eyes. The instructions pointed out the new ways of seeing, the new uses of form, colour and line which have changed contemporary painting, architecture, design, and so on. The subjects were told that we wished to study the genesis of art as related to such innovations in a simplified situation, in which originality of colour perception would be investigated. The task itself, of course, was otherwise presented exactly as before. The instructions in this condition, more than in the previous ones, encouraged subjects to seek original responses, and made the minority response appear as conforming to the norm.

Condition 4 was a "self-enhancement condition", which attempted to reinforce the subjects' belief in their own originality, in their ability to generate and to communicate "different" responses. Before the experiment proper, subjects were given a fictitious "creativity test". The "test" was individually administered, and afterwards each subject was given a "score", described as being higher than average. The experiment proper followed immediately, with a different experimenter. The "simple originality" instructions were used, as in the first condition.

The rather intense emotions aroused by this situation made it necessary to have a special debriefing and discussion session, in which the subjects were told the real purpose of the experiment.

Condition 5, the "norm-resistance condition", was included because subjects accustomed to the objectivity norm have difficulty in accepting the originality norm. These difficulties are manifested by the tacit pressures towards uniformity which the subjects apply to each other, and by the tendency to revert back to objectively "correct" responses immediately after giving a "different" response. These pressures and tendencies were revealed by the final discussion, and also by other indices such as tone of voice, gesture, and so on. In the previous experiment (condition 3), the originality norm was imposed immediately before the interaction situation. This does not allow subjects to accustom themselves to the norm, nor to distance themselves from the experimental stimuli, which in themselves strongly evoked objective judgements. We therefore decided to include in condition 5 a time-lag which would enable subjects to accustom themselves to the originality norm, by visualizing themselves in the new situation. The subjects were asked to come *one day* before the experiment, in order to familiarize themselves with the procedure. They were given a résumé of the experimental instructions to read, from which they learned that the original responses which would be looked for concerned the perception of colours.

The different conditions were therefore as follows:

Condition 1: simple originality instructions
Condition 2: discussion between subjects on the meaning of originality
Condition 3: reinforcement of the originality norm
Condition 4: self-enhancement of subjects ("creativity test")
Condition 5: overcoming norm-resistance (time-lag)

The first two conditions introduced originality only as an alternative criterion in colour perception; objectivity was still the dominant norm. The third condition insisted upon the originality norm. The fourth condition laid stress on subjectivity, and on the ability of the subject to experience the stimuli in a novel manner. The fifth condition, by making the originality norm still more dominant, weakened the objectivity norm and the resistance to subject differentiation.

In discussing the results, these conditions will be compared with the degree of influence exerted by a minority in a condition in which subjects were asked to make objectively correct judgements. The following items are relevant:

— percentage of "green" responses;

— percentage of original responses (topaz, grey, including the green ones), in the total number of responses;

— number of groups in which these two types of response occurred, as a percentage of the total number of groups (groups giving simply "green" original responses were distinguished from groups giving other kinds of original responses);

— percentage of subjects giving original responses in the total number of subjects.

The following table shows the distribution of the responses.

TABLE 13

Influence of a consistent minority in a situation demanding originality of judgement

	Condition I 6 groups	Condition II 6 groups	Condition III 6 groups	Condition IV 7 groups	Condition V 6 groups
% of all original responses	8,10	13,08	17,59	21,63	28,58
% of "green" responses	7,87	11,69	10,76	13,19	15,04
% of influenced groups (all original responses)	67	83	100	100	100
% of groups responding "green"	67	83	100	100	100
% of influenced individuals (all original responses)	37,50	62,50	67	86	92
% of individuals responding "green"	37,50	46	42	68	62,50

Among the five conditions, only three (conditions 3, 4 and 5) produced a high level of original responses. The percentage varied between 17·59% and 28·58%, and a large proportion of subjects (67% to 92%) gave such responses. All the groups were affected.

As can be seen, the nature of the minority influence differs according to experimental conditions. In the first two conditions, the introduction of the originality norm does not produce any particular effect, as compared with the objectivity norm. However, in the remaining three conditions one notices a marked effect since a high level of original responses is maintained. Therefore, the consistent minority undeniably has a greater impact when the requirements of originality are clearly reinforced.

More specifically, it can be seen that in the "normative condition", of the 17·59% of original responses, 6·37% named shades of green as turquoise, blue-green, etc. These "shade responses" allowed subjects to take up a position of compromise, of acknowledging the presence of green in the slides without making a conspicuously unconventional response. What does such a result mean? We had invited subjects to give original judgements without at the same time structuring the situation in any particular way. What they did was to adopt a solution which permitted them to distinguish themselves from others through small differences in the names they gave to the slides. This solution allowed them to escape conflict while retaining the "illusion" of being original.

In contrast, the "self-enhancement condition" was a much more structured condition, putting more pressure on subjects to take up an original attitude. We obtained 21·63% of original responses, comprising 13·19% responses of "green", 3·67% of "shade" responses, and 4·76% designating other colours (grey, yellow, etc.). Three attitudes were therefore observed: convergence to the minority response, complete originality and compromise. In the control condition in which subjects took the creativity test only, without being subjected to influence, the same three attitudes appear, but in a lesser degree: there were 2·94% "green" responses, 2·45% "shade" responses and 3·27% responses designating other colours. It is clear that the minority accentuates considerably the tendencies which already exist, and leads the subjects at the same time to prefer the "green" responses, since this response was given more frequently in the experimental than in the control condition. Examining these results more closely, we see that the three types of response do not come from different subjects, but *from the same subjects.* We consider that this indicates a certain destructing of perception and uncertainty probably due to the emotional effects of the creativity test. Furthermore, the test was immediately followed by the influence situation, and the subjects, while strongly constrained to abandon objective responses, had nevertheless not had sufficient time to consolidate a new attitude.

In the "norm-resistance condition", there were no attempted manipulations at the personality level. Subjects were simply allowed a period of time in which to familiarize themselves with the originality demands of the experiment, and to adopt a corresponding strategy of behaviour. 28·58% of the responses in this condition were original. Among these were 15·04% "green" responses, 0·69% "shade" responses and 12·84% other colour responses (grey, yellow, white, etc.). It was in this condition that the emergence of completely new responses was strongest. Close examination of data shows that, this time, the different effects of influence are evidenced by *different* individuals. In other words, certain individuals responded "green", essentially, while other individuals responded mainly "green". What criteria were adopted for the choice of original responses? The response "yellow", which is the only one amongst the responses which truly names a colour, could have had some rational justification. The fact that some subjects responded "blue" and others "green" indicated the possible existence of yellow somewhere in between. Subjects responding "yellow" therefore chose a response which was implied by two other conflicting responses. But it was "grey" which overwhelmingly dominated this category of response, expressing mainly the *luminosity* of the slides. The search for originality has therefore led some of the subjects to change the *response dimension* in face of the constraining aspect of the stimulus and under the pressure of influence. The stimuli had two dimensions (colour and luminosity), and while some innovated with respect to colour, others chose the dimension of luminosity, the only other alternative.

A similar effect has been obtained by Lemaine (1966), who has studied the creativity of groups when one of the groups is handicapped. The handicapped group chose a new criterion for the evaluation of responses which makes it non-comparable with the other group. As these two pieces of research show, the constraints facing the subjects in originality situations lead them to an analogous reaction: to base their responses on the dimension ignored by the others. More specifically, in our experiment, this means an *opposition to the minority*. It can therefore be asked whether we are not dealing here with the creation of a counternorm in a group being pressed to innovate, with a sub-group consistently proposing a novel response.* It seems therefore that the reinforcement of the norm of originality leads to a diversification of opinions within

---

* The results discussed here are due to the norms and not to a time-lag. In a control condition (six groups of six subjects each) we used the same experimental procedure, but we appealed to the objectivity norm. The results were as follows:

"green" responses: 8·21%
"influenced" groups: 50%
"influenced" individuals: 12·50%

groups. But this research, while giving some indications, is not able to carry them to their further implications. New research will be necessary to make this possible.

From previous studies, we already know that the normative context determines the behaviour of individuals and groups. An objectivity norm, insisting on the validity of opinions and judgements, is inherent in social control. As long as interest is focused on conformity, the problem of different norms does not arise. Social psychologists have, in fact, looked at the influence processes as though norms did not exist, or were of no importance. But as soon as innovation enters into the picture, norms command our attention. Their study, and particularly that of the originality norm, related to the existence of a minority and of deviance, must become a priority.

This led to a predominant concern with this norm in our research. In all the experiments just described, the minority functioned like a trigger, initiating the process of change which led to the adoption of the new judgements. Subjects were more willing to abandon the "obvious" judgement than they would have been if objectivity had been at a premium. Not only did they adopt for their own use the minority judgement, they also generated new ones. In addition, their responses often indicated a tendency to avoid the conflict aroused by influence, that is to opt for a "shade" response which is truly original, and which, furthermore, the experimental instructions had not encouraged. It therefore seems that these subjects, in spite of the originality norm, were having difficulty in freeing themselves from that of objectivity.*

In general, the original response, whether put forward by a minority or a majority, had the same effect: on the one hand, subjects adopted the response of the influencing agent ("green"), and on the other hand they put forward completely new, original responses themselves. In addition, their responses often indicated a tendency to avoid the conflict aroused by influence, that is, to opt for a "shade" response which is not

---

* The majority is not influential in the context of originality. Conditions of norm resistance seem the most appropriate to show this. There were six groups, and the subjects had been brought individually to the laboratory a day in advance of the experiment in order to be given instructions. Confronted with a majority of four peers who gave the response "green" consistently throughout the interaction, the naive subjects this time occupy positions 3 and 6. Here are the results:
original responses: 28·70%
"green" responses within the category of original responses: 17·36%
"influenced" groups: 67·00%
"influenced" individuals: 80·00%

truly original, and which, furthermore, the experimental instructions had not encouraged. It therefore seems that these subjects, in spite of the originality norm, were having difficulty in freeing themselves from majority pressure.

Why is it that, the greater the influence exerted by the minority in an originality-demanding situation, i.e. the greater the number of "green" responses adopted by the majority, the greater also the variation of "individual" or "different" responses? In situations governed by the objectivity norm, subjects have to choose only between "minority" and "majority" responses (in our experiments, "green" or "blue"). But, as we have already been at pains to point out, when the notion of originality is introduced, several different things happen. If originality is introduced only as a *criterion* for judging the properties, particularly physical properties, of a stimulus or object, it has no effect. In contrast, if it is introduced as a *norm*, it seems to authorize the members of the majority to adopt more readily the minority response. This, in itself, does not make the majority active or innovative. It is only when the subjective, personal aspect of behaviour is reinforced that the pressure towards conformity is effectively resisted, and that activity and innovation take place. In other words, each individual of the majority behaves like the deviant minority, and becomes deviant himself. This is the result of the conflict which is set up by the norm. After all, to adopt the minority response is not being original. In order to avoid this conflict (as in condition 4), the subjects vacillate, trying to dissociate themselves from both minority and majority responses. They take the path of compromise, and resort to responding in terms of "shades", not colours. If the conflict is even greater than this (as in condition 5) subjects systematically generate responses along a different dimension, which allows them to appear original and different from the minority. It may be noted in passing that, in this condition, there were no flight reactions or random responding; subjects clearly intended to give responses which were relatively closely tied to the objective stimuli. Self-enhancement, as I pointed out at the beginning of this chapter, is not sought at the expense of validation of judgement.

The effect of the minority, then, is to force subjects to strengthen their singularity; the minority also frees them to some extent from the physical constraints of the stimulus, but it does not lead them to abandon objective reality altogether.

Does the consistency of the minority matter in an originality-demanding situation? In an experiment quite similar to the one just reported, the confederate gave "green" responses on 67% of trials, and "blue" responses on 33% of trials. The percentage of "green" responses in the subjects, revealing the minority influence, was 8·45%. But when the objectivity norm was in force, and objectively correct responses were sought, the inconsistent minority had no effect. Therefore, it seems that, in a situation demanding originality, the existence of a strong minority response, even a less consistent one, is sufficient to exert influence.

The results I have been discussing are necessarily provisional. They do suggest, however, that the mechanism of influence is quite different when an *objectively* correct judgement is sought from when a correct but *original* judgement is sought. The theoretical and experimental framework changes, and the problems to be solved become more complex when this mechanism is taken into account. There is another point. We have tended to think of norms as being exclusively the product of the influence processes. However, it now seems that the norms themselves play a part in the course of these processes by determining the nature of the consensus that is set as a goal, and the validating and self-enhancement functions that it fulfils. I have pointed out three of these functions which seem to me to be both distinct and essential: these are objectivity, preference, and originality. I am not excluding the possibility that there are others, or that the three functions may be reducible to a single one. I very much doubt, however, that without taking them into account it is possible to attain a coherent concept of opinion change and group behaviour.

8

Conformity, Normalization and Innovation

Proposition 6

The modalities of influence include normalization and innovation, in addition to conformity

It can be stated without reservation that the influence process extends far beyond the limits within which theory has confined it up to now. The study of conformity alone cannot do justice to the influence process as a whole, which includes two other social influence modalities: *normalization* and *innovation*. The existence of these influence modalities must be attributed to the particular forms taken by social conflict, and to the particular forms taken by the norms which are the outcome of, or which canalize, these conflicts.

CONFORMITY

Conformity is at work when the individual, confronted with a group from which his opinion diverges, is anxious to know: "How can I avoid disagreeing with the group? Should I continue to defend my view when the group or its leaders do not agree with it?" The very fact that these questions are occurring to the person indicates the impossibility of maintaining the position—that yielding is inevitable. Remaining isolated or ignored seems too high a price to pay, once the certainty of being right has been lost and initial confidence in personal views cannot be recovered.

In this case, a majority representing the group confronts a minority, subgroup or individual who find themselves in an isolated position. The majority represents both the norm and reality, while the minority represents the exception, the abnormal, and a certain unreality. This is, of course, a very convenient way of dividing human beings into those who belong, and those who do not. However, there are some problems attached to this way of stating alternatives and organizing relations. It is difficult, for instance, to know whether the majority is objectively entitled to identify itself with the norm. We would all agree that theft is forbidden by moral, as well as by criminal, law; but this does not prevent large numbers of our fellow citizens from stealing without the least compunction—furthermore, students cheat in examinations, tradesmen weight their scales, and taxpayers falsify their incomes, without anybody being much concerned. Notwithstanding these numerous infringements, everyone thinks and acts as though the rules proclaimed by society were strictly enforced. This convention is essential for influence to be possible. Within the framework of such a convention, conformity defines the behaviour of an individual or subgroup, when this behaviour is determined by legitimate group norms and expectations—a situation which leads the individual or subgroup to assimilate into its own judgements and opinions the judgements and opinions of the real or ideal group, regardless of any original discrepancy. The function of conformity is to eliminate deviance, which permanently threatens the integrity of the whole social entity. This function is fully and successfully in operation when (a) the majority of the group is in complete agreement on attitudes and judgements, i.e. when it has a clear-cut and well-defined set of responses, norms, etc.; (b) social pressure is exerted on an individual or subgroup which is "confined" within the group culture, or which lacks (at least theoretically) any alternative culture, articulated set of responses, norms, etc., as well as any means of enforcing them.

In the phenomenology of conformity, it is customary, and useful, to distinguish between external, or behavioural, consent, and internal consent, which implies acceptance of values and beliefs. In spite of its practical importance, such a distinction modifies only slightly the basic features of this particular influence modality. Let us take a closer look at this game of conformity. In the very nature of things, one of the participants, the majority, has its own code, its own set of definitions of the social and material environment. It decides what is in keeping with common sense and human nature, and what is correct in the way of opinions and judgements. The attraction or cohesion of the group induces everyone to respect previously learned rules or norms. Unity, unanimity, the joyful celebration of reassuring cultural truisms, all serve to confirm the soundness of tradition and the wisdom of previous choices and decisions. They also preclude the possibility of adopting other rules or norms, which will usually be labelled as "barbaric", "primitive", "foreign", "odd", "unrealistic", and so on.

The other participant, the minority individual or subgroup, has no possibility of finding any alternative normative or cognitive support within the group, regardless of whether he himself chooses to move away from the group in order to challenge it, or whether it is the group that has identified him as "different", "incomprehensible", "delinquent", etc. He has no way of procuring moral reward from the group for his behaviour, nor can he hope to bring about a consensus favourable to his opinions and judgements. In the absence of such possibilities, of course, the minority suffers from internal uncertainty, which is produced by the apparent "misunderstanding" which separates it from the majority. When discrepancy between majority and minority becomes more marked, and when "normal" individuals are differentiated from "deviant" individuals with reference to a code that was previously accepted by all, the majority is forced to canalize or eliminate the conflict if it wishes to act to keep the situation under control. The minority is also forced to act. Its uncertainty concerning a pre-existing norm places it in a difficult psychological position. Neither side can avoid conflict. The group cannot, because it must attempt to re-establish consensus and stable relations between its members and the external world. The individual cannot avoid conflict, because internal consistency has been lost; this makes it impossible to cope with the situation, or even to survive socially. It is obvious that, of the two participants, the majority has only a very narrow margin for deviating from its customary position, and it has no motivation to make concessions; while the minority, for its part, has no choice but to submit or to leave the group altogether, which is a difficult choice. The nearer to unanimity is the majority, and the greater its consistency, the more firmly it will deal with its "opponent" by excluding or pretending to exclude any compromise or dialogue in its attempt to maintain its own point of view. The minority realizes that it may be forced into isolation with a concomitant loss of a common reality, and that it will be placed in the position of an outlaw, or else be subject to an internal conflict which will break down its resistance and compel it to rejoin the majority. The minority yields when it cedes its own position, either temporarily or permanently, in order to adopt fully the group's position, or when it abandons the attempt to dissent, either by surrender or by internal splitting (of the sub-group, or of the personality in the case of an individual).

Such a description is, of course, more accurate for a "closed group" confronted with a life-and-death issue. Most situations are not so dramatic, and the course of the conflict is both less poignant and more subtle. But this does not in the least invalidate what has been said, firstly because reality provides many closed groups and many life-and-death issues, and secondly because the conceptual representation of a concrete phenomenon should formulate an "ideal" type in the sense of Max Weber, and avoid simply reflecting the infinite variety of reality. The point being made here, however, is that conformity pressures have as their objective the reduction or absorption of conflict aroused in a group by a minority or an individual who is deviant by virtue of either proposing a new norm, or of simply disregarding the existing norm. The entire dynamic of interaction and communication is shaped accordingly.

NORMALIZATION

How does the interaction of individuals or sub-groups result in compromise, the averaging out of their respective positions? And why do compromises occur? When reciprocal influence in groups induces group members to formulate or accept compromises, we speak of normalization. This concept makes explicit, in effect, the pressure exerted reciprocally during exchanges that are aimed at establishing a standard of judgement or opinion acceptable to everybody. Sherif, who has done the most careful work on this phenomenon, has emphasized that we are not dealing here with conformity or a prior group position; there is neither majority nor minority, neither real nor potential deviation. It is a question of *plurality* of norms, judgements, and responses which are all considered equivalent. Why is the outcome in this situation a process of averaging, a compromise? Firstly, because the persons interacting all have equal capacities and competence, and their opinions therefore carry equal weight in everyone's eyes. No one can legitimately impose an opinion on the others (French, 1956). Secondly, because the individuals involved all have the same behavioural style; they have no particular self-assurance, and have no particular motive for refusing concessions. Finally, because the commitment of the individual is very slight, since the individual's response has received no reinforcement one way or the other.

Mausner (1954) has carried out a very convincing experiment on this. He asked subjects to estimate the length of lines, first individually and then in pairs. Each group consists of two subjects who have given very different responses individually. Half the subjects are told that their individual estimates are likely to be inaccurate in the new situation. Consequently, there are three kinds of subject pairs: those in which both subjects have received positive reinforcement, those in which one subject has been positively reinforced and the other has been negatively reinforced, and those in which both subjects have been negatively reinforced. The results indicate that only the pairs in which both subjects have been negatively reinforced tend to converge towards an average position when they are in a group situation. It is obvious that the giving up of the individual norm is related to a lack of firmness and certainty on the part of the subject. Under such circumstances, there is no motivation for maintaining one's own judgement, or for running the risk of making a different judgement in order to get the better of the partner, since the partner is also in the same position. The most appropriate behaviour therefore seems to be to avoid extreme responses and to select those that come closest to one's own. If this were not so, the chances are much smaller that an agreement would be reached, and the likelihood that the state of tension would be maintained would be much greater.

Furthermore, since the reduction of intrapersonal response conflict (i.e. the maintenance of intrapersonal consistency) depends on the reduction of interpersonal response conflict, it is undesirable or dangerous to allow divergences of judgement. The existence of a plurality of individual norms with respect to an identical stimulus results in the obliteration of each norm in turn, so that uncertainty and anxiety remain at a high level. There is an urge to coordinate responses, and a tacit negotiation takes place in order to avoid a conflict in which there can be no winner. The need for concessions makes itself felt also, and the outcome is a convergence of judgement or opinion with a consequent disappearance and levelling of differences. This explains why, in experiments on the autokinetic phenomenon, individual judgements are at first very dissimilar, but after a few trials begin to converge towards a common value. These, in effect, mutual concessions allow each person to have the validity of personal judgement confirmed to a certain extent, without having to submit totally to a different point of view. Consensus is arrived at by blurring extreme, sharply defined judgements and by avoiding situations in which choices would have to be made; this is simply achieved by adopting the least controversial position. The golden rule of bargaining, that truth lies in the middle road, is effectively applied here, and thus impasse is avoided.

Kelley and Thibaut's (1968) observation that "while reacting *with* other persons, the person reacts to them by tempering his judgement so as to avoid the possibility of being extremely different from others" (p. 749) is thus confirmed. We have already observed that the responses given are of such a nature that they can serve as a rallying point for everyone, and they therefore reduce the risk of the individual's or subgroup's opinion being contradicted by others. Individuals are sometimes guided by the wish to avoid possible clashes of opinion, without settling the question of whether this is in fact the ethical line of behaviour, or the correct answer. As Riecken (1952) observes: "The consensus that is reached in many cases is nothing but an agreement not to disagree" (p. 252).

To summarize, the group product (opinion, norm, etc.) expresses the double inacceptability of provoking a divergence, even a justified one, and of resolving any divergence in favour of one of the social partners. The only alternative would be to continue the conflict, and therefore *the influence which is exerted, normalization, is tinged by the necessity of avoiding conflict, and of preventing disagreement in terms of the frame of reference.* The partners seek to discover what is "reasonable", rather than what is true; no one wishes to dominate, but no one wishes to be left in the wrong. Such a situation not only induces a positive movement towards cooperation and mutual understanding, but also offers an escape from choices between incompatible terms. The process essentially consists of the suppression of differences and the acceptance of the lowest common denominator. Many of our daily transactions, in law courts, politics, trade unions, etc., are founded on this doctrine, which is deeply embedded in our social and ideological system.

INNOVATION

There are many ways in which transformations in a group or society may occur. These transformations may be important and dramatic at some times, and secondary and almost unnoticed at others. We do not, as yet, have any good theoretical description of these changes, nor have there been any reliable investigations of their effects. I will therefore limit myself to a few special cases. One could, for instance, start out by distinguishing between innovation "from above" and innovation "from below". The former involves changes introduced by leaders, i.e. persons with the necessary authority to impose new behaviours on their followers, or to induce their followers to accept deviant behaviours. Hollander (1964) has outlined the study of such innovation from above. I shall concentrate here on the process of change and innovation "from below", in which change results from the action of a minority lacking privileged status either in terms of social position or competence. More specifically, I will examine the case of an active and consistent minority. Two typical situations which this minority will have to cope with can be visualized:

the majority lacks *a priori* norms or well-defined approaches to a specific problem;

the majority does have such norms or approaches, around which it has established an implicit consensus.

In the first case, innovation is analogous to the creation of new attitudes, and in the second case it implies a change in existing attitudes or judgement. We will now examine these two cases and their psychological implications.

First case: *Avoiding the avoidance of conflict*
When a group of individuals is confronted with a set of objects or stimuli about which they must make a judgement, and there are no norms or rules to guide their responses, individuals tend to be hesitant and relatively inconsistent. As soon as they start emitting judgements, they become aware of the divergence between their own judgements and those of others. Because there is no motivation for increasing uncertainty or engaging in conflict, i.e. differentiating themselves from each other, they will tend spontaneously to compromise. Such compromise is reflected in the setting up of an average wherever values are placed on a single dimension, or by equal or near-equal frequencies, when there is a choice between dimensions. The normalization process is at work. However, this process, this set of mutual concessions, will be blocked if one of the individuals expresses a personal point of view, refuses to follow the group compromise and shows determination to make well-defined choices. In so doing, the individual not only challenges any norm that would be an average of individual judgements, but also undermines its value. At the same time, before the others have had time to constitute properly the compromise norm, this individual exerts in-

fluence on the outcome by means of a coherent response, adding to the weight of certain responses in the group, and influencing the definition of the object. Besides this negative aspect, which consists of obstructing compromise, the individual plays a positive role by offering a solution that is theoretically as valid as any of the others which have been put before the group. Moreover, since the behaviour of the individual is more consistent than that of the other members of the group, it offers a more assured focus for consensus. For all these reasons, a resolute and consistent minority channels majority responses and leaves its mark on the common norm. Despite their apparent simplicity, these observations should be carefully scrutinized. The empirical evidence at our disposal tends, on the whole, to corroborate them.

Gurnee (1937) drew attention to a phenomenon which is probably familiar to everyone. Often, when a group of people have to solve a problem, the individual members hesitate and fluctuate before reaching a judgement or making a decision. But occasionally there is one person with faster reactions who, from the very start, proposes an appropriate hypothesis. Gurnee pointed out that this is the individual who often takes the lead during the whole ensuing decision-making process.

Shaw (1963) has provided some research data on this phenomenon. Shaw wished to study the effect of the quality of information available to a group on its behaviour and performance. In his experiment, each group of three subjects was asked to discuss two cases. In one experimental condition, a selected member of the group was given two options; in the second condition he was given four options; and in the third condition he was given six options. The other two members of the group had no information at all about the options. Shaw found that, the fewer the number of options made available to the informed member, the faster he entered into the discussion compared with the non-informed members. Shaw also pointed out that the fewer the options given to the individual, and the faster he entered into discussion, the more rapidly his solutions were accepted, and the more his contribution was valued. This individual was also more likely to be chosen as leader. These findings indicate that the subject who presents fewer solutions appears to be correspondingly more systematic and capable of offering clear choices. He is the most effective, and the one most likely to be chosen as leader. Carrying the logic of this argument a little further, it might be supposed that one individual would be more consistent than three individuals (unless the three have previously reached a preliminary agreement). A single person may be better able to concentrate the attention of the group on one proposition.

There is some evidence to support this supposition. Torrance (1959) observed the impact of an individual's testimony before a group. The groups were composed of six to twelve individuals who had been asked to taste a food item characterized as "pemmican". Some of the witnesses giving testimony had been favourably impressed by the food, while others had not. One of the results emerging from this study was that when a *single* individual testified to an unfavourable impression, the group was more influenced in the same direction than when the unfavourable impression was expressed by two or more witnesses. It is clear that the testimony of a single subject who, in the very nature of things, is unanimous with himself, is more effective than a number of individuals, who are bound to have a lesser degree of unanimity among themselves. By virtue of being very consistent in his judgement, the single individual becomes the focus of attention. Torrance explains this as follows:

> Apparently, if an individual is the only member of a group who has experienced the object, he alone is the "star". Everyone looks to him for his judgment and he can speak without fear of contradiction. If there are others who have experienced the attitude object, he is reduced at least to a co-starring role. Even though he may be in agreement in his judgment with the other experienced members, he probably does not feel as free from freedom of contradiction as he does when he alone has experienced the object. Of course, should the experienced members choose to form a coalition to consolidate their "stories", their influence may be sharpened thereby (p. 255).

What this suggests is that an individual, by expressing a position consistently and resolutely, may focus attention on himself. This may enable him to induce the other members of the majority to rally to his position as the focal point for consensus. Where the minority has more than one member, they must consolidate their positions in order to present a "united front".

Second case: *Accept the challenge and create a conflict*
We will now consider the case of influence by a minority which is consciously acting to modify established rules, traditions, etc. To clarify our ideas, let us first consider how social interaction takes place. The presence of a norm is revealed by the spontaneous conformity of all those who share it. This norm induces each member of a group or

"culture" to accept unhesitatingly a certain way of dressing or speaking, to agree on what is useful, and so on. As long as there is a table of categories showing what is permitted and what is forbidden, the "good citizen", the "good father", can quickly sort out the right from the wrong behaviour, what is good from what is bad. When an isolated individual or sub-group moves away from this line of agreement, from this generally accepted classification, the convergence of individual responses towards the same norm is interrupted, and an exception becomes apparent to the otherwise ever-present conformity pressure. Moreover, this minority casts doubt on the infallibility of the majority's judgement by entertaining a different model for the purpose of achieving the same goals and explaining the same phenomena. This substitution of diversity for uniformity increases group uncertainty in two ways. In the first place, it affects the consistency of social pressure on each member of the social system, and is a threat to unanimous social consensus. Where previously only one "culture" held sway, there are now two "cultures" face to face, the new one offering an alternative to that presented by the old culture. Secondly, by introducing totally new dimensions, or by recombining the old dimensions and establishing differences or overlaps where previously there were none, internal (intra-individual) consistency is disturbed. For example, at the time of the 1968 student revolt in France, many people saw their standards of judgement and their scale of values thrown into confusion because students took up the workers' cause. The fact that two groups which up to then had been considered to symbolize two mutually exclusive classes—the middle class and the proletariat—should be associated in a single group gave rise to considerable tension because of the incompatibility of these responses with previously appropriate responses. The confused and uncertain reactions on the part of the police and political organizations resulted from this new combination of social dimensions.

Recombination of existing dimensions explains change in art, science, and economic life which occurs unexpectedly. From the point of view of both social (external) and individual (internal) consistency, the majority is confronted with an increasing number of competing solutions and is compelled to interpret as a mere option, preference or arbitrary convention what was previously thought to be a certainty, an absolute, a necessity almost decreed by nature. Before the publication of Copernicus' work on the heliocentric system, astronomers and theologians believed that the universe was as Ptolemy had described it, with the earth at the centre and the planets circling round the earth. After Copernicus' work, they tried to maintain that both hypotheses were equally likely. The solidity of the universe was dissolved to make way for human arbitrariness. In Lewin's terminology, a "thaw" of norms and cognitions took place. Furthermore, these norms became mutually contradictory. A genuine thaw could only take place when a minority displayed coherent views and firm convictions, exerted constant pressure, and finally made its own views as persuasive as the currently accepted ones.

One can easily understand why minorities, such as Copernicus in the example above, or outstanding artists, writers, and so on, are loth to accept any compromise, and tend to express their views in the most categorical manner. In doing this, their vision of reality becomes more sharply defined and its most enduring features are enhanced. The group is then compelled to choose between terms which are nearly equally valuable and powerful as alternatives. At the same time, the demand for the recognition of truth and objectivity affects the course of the conflict by making it more and more difficult to disregard the minority.

If a response must be "objective", disagreement is unusual, and any conflict which does occur between two contradictory evaluations of the same object cannot be solved by a compromise. One of the reasons why minorities appeal to higher entities, classes or categories such as truth, beauty, history, and so on, is at least in part due to their wish to represent their alternative as indispensable, and to increase the tension which led to the formulation of their alternative. What, otherwise, is the meaning of such an appeal to a higher entity? In looking exclusively at intra- or inter-personal relations, and at intra- or inter-group relations, we usually forget that there is always, in the background, a "third party" which is concretized in institutions, frames of reference, and norms. "What emerges" writes the sociologist Cicourel (1973) "is that status relationships are based upon norms (external to immediate interaction) that have a broad consensus among 'third parties' in social networks related to 'ego' and 'alter', in some larger community" (pp 13–14).

In the preceding chapter, we have seen how effective norms are when they are supported, in experiments, by a "third party" representing science, or the university, or some such authority. Usually, majorities consider this "third party" as a natural ally, and speak in the name, often, of the invisible partner. By appealing equally confidently to the higher authority, minorities legitimize their choices, positions, images of the world and of society. At the same time, they cast doubt on the legitimacy of the choices, positions, and images of the world and of society of the majority. Even more, they reveal flagrant contradictions. Have we not seen, in the past few years, student movements underlining the gap between the ideas taught by the universities and by the adult world in general, and the compromises which characterize actual practice? When the legitimacy of the minority's viewpoint is thus affirmed, while that of the majority's is called into question, a sort of equivalence between the two parties is brought about. They can no longer be defined as "majority" and "minority" with reference to the higher moral authority they have both invoked, and so the impression of a plurality is created. It is on the basis of this antagonistic plurality that a choice becomes possible.

In this way, the minority achieves its aim of obtaining recognition for an original social identity or truth, in place of the established uniformity. This means that they assume the psychology of a person or a group who is different and willing to be different, able to accept disapproval, impervious to physical and psychological hostility as well as to continuous tension. Instead of stressing uniformity, which is the business of the majority, the deviant minority stresses individuality, insisting on that which divides rather than that which unites. They transform what can be seen only as a negation of the law from the point of view of the majority, or of the traditional conception of reality, into a new law or conception of reality which offers an alternative solution.

The Reformation was thus judged, and continues to be judged, by a part of the Roman Catholic world as a sort of non-religion, or heretic, inferior, religion. It became another religion, as everyone knows, by dint of numerous conflicts and changes in society. Individuals and groups act according to the assumption that a person who is not like the self is a non-person. It is only gradually that we realize that the non-ego is an alter-ego. This is how relations between parents and children, and even between classes and nations, frequently develop. This intensification of divergences is an indispensable condition for moving from one social order, one point of view, or one truth, to another. In this sense, one might say that the innovating group or individual is a creator of conflicts; that the negotiation taking place between the majority and the minority with respect to innovation revolves around the creation of a conflict where none existed before. Here we can grasp the characteristic property of this influence modality. *It centres on the creation of conflicts, just as normalization centres on the avoidance, and conformity on the control or resolution, of conflicts.*

In such a framework, consistent social pressure exerted by a minority is one of the preconditions of success, most importantly because it brings about a blockage or breakdown in group institutions and in the application of the norms upheld by the majority. This emerges even in a relatively indirectly related experiment like that of Rosenthal and Cofer (1948). They were studying the question of whether symptoms of indifference in some group members would have measurable effects on the attitudes of other group members with regard to group goals and their levels of aspiration regarding group success. No noticeable effect could be detected at the level of aspiration, but the attitudes of group members shifted significantly with respect to the likelihood of attaining the group goal, and with respect to the sincerity of the other group members in this undertaking.

Another factor is that when a minority deviates substantially from the accepted point of view, and simultaneously represents its own positions in a systematic way, it will redirect the field of forces and communications in the group, creating a pole of persuasion of its own. Research by Festinger and his associates provides ample evidence that being a deviate, and at the same time asserting this position, results in attracting most of the communications attempting to restore social cohesion. By making use of this communication channel, the minority, instead of being passive, can itself become active and direct counter-pressure along this channel towards the group, compelling it to choose between the minority solution and the group solution. Having become the centre of group attraction, its arguments and actions gain much more attention than the arguments and actions of the conformist members of the group. Unquestionably, just as the group relies on the pressure caused by divergence to absorb deviation and resolve conflict, so an active minority will emphasize divergence and conflict in order to obtain the maximum leverage from the messages channelled in its direction. This tactic of polarizing attention is often used to initiate the influence process. Moreover, the tactic has a disruptive effect on the majority, which relies on uniformity and may temporarily reinforce the minority, which needs to be reassured that it is really different. In any case, this opening up of communication channels, and the diversion of the communication channels in the direction of the deviant minority, increases the minority's chances of changing the majority.

This emerges very clearly in Emerson's (1954) replication of Schachter's experiment (1951). In line with Festinger's theory of informal communication, Schachter had predicted that an increase in the relevance of the task, and in group cohesion, would lead to a corresponding increase in efforts to lead the deviant individual back into the fold by increasing the number of communications in his direction. If the deviate persisted in ignoring these pressures, a tendency would arise to redraw the boundaries of the group, reject the deviate, and reduce the number of communications addressed to him and, the more coherent the group and the more relevant the task, the greater this tendency would be. These predictions were confirmed on the whole. However, Emerson's secondary school students became less certain of their opinions, and were influenced by the deviate and the slider. Consequently, there were few cases of rejection of the deviate, and the number of communications addressed to him stayed constant to the end. As the author concludes, this means that "pressures towards uniformity took the direction of changing self . . ." (p. 693) that is, they led to a change in majority opinion. The subjects seemed to have no other way of avoiding the conflict of responses forced on them by the minority than by yielding to the minority. It must be realized that the minority has a great asset in negotiating under these circumstances, since the group is generally hesitant to set in motion a genuine separation or rejection process. A minority of this type, by resisting or challenging the existing rules, demonstrates that one can liberate oneself from social constraints.

Usually, in social life, people believe that there is no other possible way of behaving than the customary one. Even if they are dissatisfied or actively unhappy with the established way of life, they do not believe in the possibility of inducing change, of any alternative, or at least of being able to bring about some change without risk to themselves. At the same time, they are often in a position of pluralistic ignorance, that is, they are unaware that the other members of the same community share their ideas and desires. When a minority is brave enough to reject the established order, or to propose something previously thought "forbidden" or "illegal", it proves that there are other acceptable ways of acting or living, and that they do not necessarily have direct consequences. The minority thereby strips the norms and institutions of their authority by proving that refusal is possible, and that the minority is able to bear the full weight of this refusal, even if it includes such consequences as rejection, hostility, etc.

There are not many experimental findings in support of these assertions but those that do exist are quite promising, and lend some support to what has just been said. We have already mentioned the results of experiments carried out by Faucheux and Moscovici (1967), Nemeth and Wachtler (1973), and Biener *et al.* (1974). Moscovici *et al.* (1969) set out to determine the influence of a minority where there is a conflict between alternative possibilities. They used an experimental paradigm in which (a) this conflict is intensified by minority consistency and consensus; (b) objectivity is implicitly demanded by the judgement; (c) the minority and majority responses are mutually exclusive, though one is not the negation of the other, as when two equal lines are said to be unequal; (d) differences in judgement cannot be attributed to differences in individual traits; (e) the judgement of the laboratory majority corresponds exactly to that of any normal person outside the laboratory, whereas the judgement of the minority is exactly the opposite of what one would normally expect. A series of experiments were carried out, each one involving a different localization of influence. In the first experiment, an attempt was made to induce change in the response only, i.e. in the way that subjects characterized the stimulus. In the second experiment, the objective was to bring about a change in perceptual code. In this case, it was hypothesized that a subject who has undergone minority influence will show the effects of this in perceptual discriminations carried out after the influence situation.

The subjects were students in the humanities, law, and social science. Because of the nature of the experimental materials, which were colour slides, it was considered preferable to use female students as subjects, since females are generally more interested in colour than males. The stimuli were slides on which two different types of filters had been placed: (1) photo filters allowing the passage of light rays of the dominant wave length ($\lambda = 483 \cdot 5$) in the blue range, and (2) neutral filters which reduced light intensity. In the complete set of six slides, three were brighter than the rest. This variation in light intensity had been introduced in order to make the task more realistic and less tedious. Its effect was controlled.

Each experimental group consisted of four naive subjects and two confederates. As soon as the subjects had been seated in a row facing the screen onto which the slides were to be projected, they were told that the experiment was concerned with colour perception. They were also told that they would be asked to judge the colour and variation in light intensity of a set of slides, and were given a brief explanation of the meaning of light intensity. Before making their judgements, they were asked to take the Palack test collectively, ostensibly to make sure that each participant's "chromatic discrimination" was normal.

In fact, the administration of this test had a double purpose; first of all, to eliminate subjects that might happen to have visual abnormalities, and secondly to stress the fact to the subjects that all group members had normal vision, so that the confederates' responses could not be attributed to visual abnormalities.

After the results of the test were known, and it had been confirmed that everyone had normal vision, the subjects were informed about what sort of responses to give, and how the experiment would be carried out. They were asked to respond aloud by naming the colour of the slide, and assessing the light intensity of the slide on a 5-point numerical scale (from 0 for the darkest to 5 for the brightest intensity). They were also told that there would be a practice trial, in which they were to judge the light intensity only. After this preliminary practice trial, the set of six different slides was shown six times, the order of presentation being varied systematically each time. This procedure resulted in a total of 36 trials lasting 15 seconds each and separated by about 5 seconds of darkness. In each trial, the confederates exerted influence by calling every slide "green". They were both internally consistent, and consistent with each other.

At the end of the experiment, the subjects filled in a questionnaire about the stimuli and about the other members of the group. As usual, the real purpose of the experiment was revealed to the subjects before they departed.

It seemed reasonable to ask whether the subjects in this experiment might have undergone some change in their perceptual code, even though there might not have been any change in their overt responses during the course of the experiment. It was hypothesized that there would be a shift in the blue-green perception threshold, which might reveal reactions repressed during actual social interaction. Some subjects were perhaps unwilling to openly adopt the minority response, and felt obliged to remain loyal towards the general norm, while nevertheless beginning to question its validity. One might expect that a latent influence would come into play, and express itself by an extension of the term "green" to stimuli located in a zone that a control group would call "blue". The opposite reaction (extension of the blue concept to stimuli in the green zone) would be the result of polarization.

The first part of the second experiment was identical with the first experiment, that is, the majority was submitted to minority influence. At the end of this phase, the experimenter thanked the subjects and told them that another scientist in the department was also interested in vision phenomena, and would like to ask them to take part in another research project, unrelated to the one in which they had just participated. The experimenter then left the room, and the second experimenter entered immediately and repeated the request. Having obtained the subjects' consent, the experimenter explained to them that the experiment concerned the effect of exercise on vision phenomena. He then described the experimental materials, isolated the subjects by means of cardboard screens, and asked them to write down their responses individually on a sheet of paper. The experimental materials consisted of 16 discs in the blue-green zone of the Farnworth 100-hue set perception test. Three discs, at each end of the blue and green scales, were absolutely unambiguous, but the other ten stimuli were potentially ambiguous. Having made sure that the subjects understood the instructions, the experimenter announced that the test would begin. Each disc was presented against a neutral background for about 5 seconds, on the middle of a table which was within sight of all the subjects. The set of 16 discs was shown 10 times without a pause, the order of presentation being random. After this test, the first experimenter returned and asked the subjects to complete the post-experimental questionnaire, and the experiment was concluded in the same way as the preceding one.

The third experiment was designed to test the hypothesis that a minority which does not express its view in a firm, consistent manner will not exert significant influence. The procedure was identical to that in the previous experiments, except that the confederates sometimes responded "green", and sometimes "blue", in the proportions 1/3 and 2/3 respectively. In one condition, one of the confederates would respond "green" when the other was responding "blue" (diachronic inconsistency), and in the other condition they would respond "green" or "blue" according to the predetermined proportions, but independently of each other (diachronic and synchronic inconsistency). The same control group was used for all three experiments.

The results of these experiments were as follows. The "green" response (which indicates the extent of influence exerted by the minority) represents 8·42% of the responses of the 128 subjects in the first two experiments. There is no significant difference between the two sets of groups. In the third experiment, in contrast, there are only 1·25% "green" responses. Among the 22 control group subjects, only one person gave "green" responses (two in all), which constituted 0·25% of the non-influenced responses. This means that the control group perceive the stimuli as blue, and that this norm is firmly rooted socially. This difference between the control groups and the experimental groups is significant by the Mann-Whitney U test ($z = 2·10$, one-tailed $p = 0·019$). 43·75% of subjects in the experimental groups made four or more "green" responses. (It was found that there were actually 14 to 18 such responses in these groups.) This means that at least one individual made more than two "green" responses. 32% of the subjects in all groups yielded. There were thus two types of group, those where none of the subjects was influenced, and those where some of the subjects were influenced. In the latter groups, 57% of the subjects, or two per group, on average, made the same response as the confederates. In these groups, 18·75% of the responses were "green".

The number of "green" responses was due not so much to isolated individuals who totally yielded to the confederates, as to an overall modification of judgement within the group.

The results of the third experiment indicate that the minority did not exert any influence on the majority:

	Condition I (Diachronic inconsistency)	Condition II (Diachronic and synchronic inconsistency)
"green" responses	0·35%	1·25%
influenced groups	17·0%	40·0%
influenced individuals	4·0%	20·0%

In every case, the percentage of "green" responses is very close to that in the control group.

To what extent was the underlying hypothesis, that a minority may be as effective as a majority, borne out? In an experiment carried out by Elizabeth Lage and myself, a minority of two naive subjects were confronted with a majority of four confederates who maintained that blue slides were green. Compared to the control group they were, of course, very influential, but they were not significantly more so than a minority, as the results tabulated below demonstrate.

	Minority	Majority
"green" responses	10·07%	12·07%
influenced groups	50·0%	30·77%
influenced individuals	42·50%	34·61%

We can say that the influence of a minority is as important as the influence of a majority of confederates. The numerical size of an influence source is therefore not in direct proportion to the degree of influence exerted.

Considering now the discrimination test results, the aim of this test was to determine whether those subjects who changed their responses under the influence of the consistent minority also changed their perceptual code. The other hypothesis under test was that subjects who did not change their social response may yet have changed to some extent their perceptual code, *even in groups where the effect of the minority on the overt responses of the majority was nil.* The measure used was the frequency with which the "green" concept was carried over into the "blue" zone in the discrimination test responses.

Comparison of threshold figures provides the best check on this hypothesis. For each experimental condition, there was a mean threshold value, obtained from individual data on the following: the 50% threshold stimulus (the stimulus judged "blue" as often as "green"); the lower threshold stimulus (the stimulus evoking 75% "green" responses and 25% "blue" responses); and the upper limit stimulus (the stimulus evoking 75% "blue" responses and 25% "green" responses). The effect of influence is inferred by comparing the experimental group threshold figure with that of the control group's (the control group not having been submitted to influence during the first phase of the experiment).

We will evaluate (a) the displacement of these three thresholds in the experimental groups as compared to the control groups; (b) the dispersion of responses in each type of group; and the responses made during social interaction by influenced as compared to non-influenced subjects.

The first of these comparisons shows whether the influence experienced during the social interaction phase modified the experimental subjects' perceptual code. This will provide the answer to the question posed by this chapter.

The second comparison will show the direction and extent of threshold displacement in the same experimental condition. A wide dispersion of responses could indicate one of two possible response effects: either the extension of the "green" response to stimuli considered blue by the control group, or the extension of the "blue" response to stimuli considered green by the control group. Whatever the specific direction of response, such a threshold displacement indicates a response conflict persisting after the social interaction phase.

The aim of the third comparison is to determine whether subjects react differently in this discrimination test according to the specific responses they have made during the influence phase. In other words, does the perceptual threshold displacement take place only in subjects who have been influenced in their overt responses during the social interaction phase, or does it occur in all subjects, regardless of their previous responses? Most important of all, from a general point of view this comparison provides information on the persisting effects of influence at a covert level.

As was expected, the experimental subjects had their perceptual code modified under the effect of influence. The three measures (differential threshold, lower threshold, and upper threshold) differ significantly between the experimental and control groups, as the following table shows:

lower threshold $t = 1.68, p < 0.05*$
differential threshold $t = 1.78, p < 0.04*$
upper threshold $t = 2.33, p < 0.01*$

* one-tailed p

The influence of the minority therefore had an effect not only on manifest judgements, but also on the covert processes underlying them. In a general manner, the judgement "green" was extended to cover stimuli judged to be blue by the control group.

This reaction was not unique to the subjects who were overtly influenced during the social interaction phase. It occurred as much in subjects who held to the response "blue" as in those who made "green" responses—there was no significant difference in this respect between these two sub-groups. It therefore becomes apparent that the analysis of latent effects reveals a more important aspect of influence than the analysis of overt effects alone would show. In other words, it is possible to determine that the subjects were in fact influenced by the minority, regardless of the particular responses they may have made during the social interaction phase.

This aspect of the results seems to us particularly important, in so far as it clearly demonstrates that the overt response is not the totality of influenced behaviour. However, the degree of dispersion in the results indicates that the extent of threshold displacement varies considerably between subjects (differential threshold: $t = 1.88$, two-tailed $p < 0.10$, one-tailed $p < 0.05$; upper limit stimulus: $t = 1.71$, $p < 0.10$).

Does the same phenomenon occur when the deviant minority is inconsistent? We already know that such a minority, incoherent and unclear about its position, has no effect on the manifest judgements of the majority. It is not able to create the conflict required to induce the majority to revise its opinions. Our data from the post-experimental discrimination test show that the inconsistent minority has no effect on latent judgement either. There is no difference between the experimental and control groups, either in the displacement of differential thresholds, or in the dispersion of responses. The inconsistent minority therefore seems incapable of exerting influence at any level.

These findings provide additional evidence pertaining to the importance of a consistent behavioural style for the source of influence. It would seem that a consistent minority is more effective on the level of covert responses than on the level of overt responses, whereas an inconsistent minority is ineffective on both levels.

But what happens when the source of influence is a majority? Do the responses made in the course of social interaction represent a surface agreement or do they indicate a genuine adherence to the majority view? If the first alternative is the correct one, we would not expect a change on the discrimination test after the influence situation, but if it is the second possibility which prevails, then we should expect to see such a change.

In fact, there is no effect on the perceptual code. We observe no shift in the differential thresholds of the experimental subjects as compared with control group subjects, although there is a wider range of responses in the experimental group. This result seems to be due to the fact that some subjects persisted in responding "blue" to stimuli which were judged to be green by the control group. Unfortunately, it is not possible to analyse this tendency in any systematic way; it seems to indicate a polarization of judgements. The discrimination test results of the subjects who were influenced during the social interaction phase do not differ from those subjects who were not influenced. Therefore, a non-unanimous majority has no major effect on the covert judgement of the minority. Majority influence seems to lead to a surface agreement only, while minority influence has an effect which is both apparent on the surface and which extends to a more profound change in judgement. These differences are probably due to variations in the intensity of the conflict which is subjectively experienced. In fact, conflict arising out of attempts at influence is not the same when minorities are involved as when it is a question of a majority. The deviant character of a judgement is much more apparent when it is shared by only a few individuals. If it is also presented in a coherent and consistent manner, and with conviction, then the other members of the group cannot avoid taking it into consideration. The resulting conflict seems to herald the restructuring of the perceptual-cognitive system which is the source of the judgement. The minority point of view thus becomes an integral part of majority subjects' apprehension of reality, even though they had previously accepted the contradictory majority norm as being self-evident.

But these differences seem to depend on another related phenomenon. We may rightly believe that it is easier for a minority to change the perceptual code, that is, the covert responses of the majority, than their social responses, whereas majorities will have more influence on the open social responses than on the perceptual codes, the covert responses of individuals. This hypothesis, which was formulated *a posteriori* some years ago (Moscovici and Nève, 1971), has recently been confirmed, at least in part, by Mugny (1974). In his experiment, Mugny used an apparatus designed to create the Müller-Lyer optical illusion. This well-known illusion consists in making two lines which are objectively of equal length appear to be unequal by placing them in different contexts of perception: at the ends of one of the horizontal lines the two-pronged fork seems to extend the line, while at the ends of the other line the fork turns back, making the horizontal segment appear shorter.

The procedure that Mugny used is simple. The situation is presented to the subjects as a scientific study of perception. Once this explanation is given, the experiment itself begins by a measurement of the perceptual code, "operationalized" by evaluating the point at which the two lines appeared to be subjectively equal. In other words, the subjects judged at what point the two segments of the lines were equal. The experiment continues with three phases: measurement before the social response, influence phase, measurement after the social, or verbal, response. Each phase was conducted in the following manner: the experimenter himself manipulated the mobile line segments according to a programme that was the same for each phase. The subjects were to say whether the left-hand line was longer, shorter, or equal to the right-hand line. In addition, subjects were to evaluate the difference between the two lines in centimetres for each trial. Each phase consisted of five trials. The real differences between the lines for each trial were the following (the + sign indicates that the left-hand segment is longer by so many centimetres): item 1: +5; item 2: 0; item 3: +3; item 4: +7; item 5: −1. The total of the differences for the five items is +14. Subjects were given 3·5 seconds in which to view the apparatus for each trial.

After the subjects responded to the five trials individually, they were exposed to social influence. The subjects were told that the experimenter was interested in knowing whether information about others' responses helped them or not in evaluating the differences. In the two experimental conditions subjects were told that twenty-five people had previously been asked to do "the same thing as you".

In the majority condition, the experimenter went on to say, "I have decided to give you the responses of some of the twenty-five people that I just mentioned. I shall give you the responses of twenty people who systematically answered in the same way, but I shall not give you the answers of the five others.

In the minority condition, the same protocol was used, except that the numbers "twenty" and "five" were inverted: ". . . I shall give you the responses of five people who systematically answered in the same way, but I shall not give you the answers of the twenty others."

The subjects were first shown the apparatus, then were given the responses of the twenty or the five people, and after this they gave their own evaluation of the two lines. The responses of the experimenter's "confederates" were systematically four units larger than the real difference. The total for the five items was +34 (item 1: +9; item 2: +4; item 3: +7; item 4: +11; item 5: +3).

After this influence phase, there was a measurement "after" the verbal response. The experiment was terminated by an "after"-evaluation of the subjective impression of equality.

The following measurements were analysed as results:

(a) verbal response: the measure consisted in adding each subject's responses on the five items for each phase of the experiment. Two indices of influence were used: the difference between the measurements of the pre-test and the collective phase, and between the pre-test and the post-test.

(b) "perceptual code": the "before" and "after" measurements of the differences between the real point of equality and the subjective point of equality of the two lines were taken. The difference between these two measurements constituted the index of influence pertaining to the "code".

Does the majority have more influence on the verbal level and the minority more influence on the perceptual level? The results obtained here seem to indicate that this is indeed the case. From the statistical analyses in Table 14 we can see that the difference in the changes appearing in the evaluations before the interaction and during the influence phase is highly significant $(t = 3.32, p < 0.005)$. The majority had more influence on the social response than the minority, although the latter also had some effect $(t = 1.992, p < 0.05)$.

TABLE 14

Averages of the evaluations on the level of verbal response*

Condition:	individual "before"	Phases: interaction "during"	individual "after"
Majority	6·73	24·86	17·06
Minority	7·20	12·60	8·13

* The averages correspond to the total of the five items.
The real differences come to a total of +14, and the differences attributed to the source of influence comes to +34. n = 15 for each square.

Does this influence in both conditions of the experiment maintain itself without information on the responses of the source of influence? A comparison of the differences before and after the interaction shows that the influence continues to be high for the subjects who were opposed to the majority $(t = 2.041, p < 0.03)$. In the minority condition, this difference is not significant: subjects cease to respond according to the minority system. Thus it is abundantly clear that the majority exercises a much greater influence than the minority on the verbal level. But does the minority have a greater influence on the perceptual code than the majority? The statistical analysis (see Table 15) of the differences between the point of subjective equality obtained before and after the interaction phase indicates that the minority influences the perceptual code more than the majority ($t = 1\cdot882$, $p < 0\cdot05$). We can observe that while the changes obtained in the minority condition are significant, they are not significant in the majority condition. In spite of all the difficulties in operationalizing the perceptual code, it nevertheless remains that, on the whole, there are powerful reasons to believe that the hypothesis concerning this inversion of the effectiveness of the minority as compared with the majority contains a great deal of truth.

TABLE 15

Average of the differences between the points of subjective equality and the real point of equality (perceptual code level)*

Condition:	Phases:	
	Before the interaction	After the interaction
Majority	$+1\cdot80$	$+1\cdot70$
Minority	$+1\cdot83$	$+2\cdot63$

* The averages correspond to the differences of both trials. n = 15 for each square.

All of the foregoing remarks concern the effect of minority-majority relations in the modification of the perceptual code. One set of data is, however, particularly interesting in this respect. The displacement of the blue-green boundary in the Moscovici *et al.* (1971) experiment was more marked in groups where the majority of naive subjects had *not* adopted the "green" response, than it was in groups where the majority *were* overtly influenced ($t = 1\cdot50$, which is close to the value of $1\cdot68$ which is significant at $0\cdot01$ by a two-tailed test). It had been expected that in groups where there had been no overt influence, or where it might be assumed that the "green" response had been in some way repressed, there would be a greater number of "green" responses in the post-experimental discrimination test. This was indeed the case. The difference between the groups in which the majority was not overtly influenced, and the groups in which the majority was overtly influenced, is significant ($X^2 = 14\cdot94$; $p < 0\cdot002$). We can conclude that a consistent minority has an even greater influence on the perceptual code of the majority than it has on the overt response. Subjects who respond spontaneously in accordance with a colour designation norm change their perceptual code after experiencing minority pressure, regardless of whether or not their verbal responses change.

What has happened is that subjects presumably sharing a universal norm (for perceiving and/or naming colours) have, under minority pressure, either changed their responses and characterized as "green" what most people would call "blue", or they have continued to respond "blue" to a stimulus which the minority pressure has induced them to begin seeing as "green". In either case, the change seems to be the result of an intensive cognitive activity on the part of the individuals. Confronted with a minority which vigorously maintains a different point of view to their own, the majority subjects, who have no compelling reason to reject the minority position, attempt to understand this position and to see through the eyes of the minority. They do not remain passive, nor are they content merely to accept or reject blindly a norm that is opposed to their own. It is this cognitive effort, triggered by individuals apparently convinced of the validity of their own responses (our confederates) which is the probable explanation of the perceptual shift.

If these data are reliable and their interpretations are correct, then there are some more general implications to consider. The notion of "perceptual code" is difficult to define. We shall assume, however, that it designates a content that we can actually see and touch, in contrast to the "linguistic code" that deals with the manner in which we classify and label objects. We can see, then, that a deviant minority can bring about significant modifications in the perceptual code more easily than in the linguistic code, in what is seen and thought more easily than in how it is named and expressed. Conversely, a majority seems to affect the linguistic code more than the perceptual code. If this is truly the case, then we may suppose that minorities change responses and ways of seeing things on a covert level before their actual responses change, and sometimes even without knowing it. Research on conformity has accustomed us to the opposite phenomenon: individuals *apparently* adopt the judgements and opinions of the group or authority while continuing to hold onto their previous judgements and opinions in private. Where there is innovation, influence is more effective on the private level than on the public level. The contrast between public and private judgements and opinions is a feature of both phenomena, but they move in opposite directions. In one case, we witness *compliance*, and in the other *conversion*.

Let us try to examine these contrasts more closely. In a situation of conformity, the pressure on the individual to respond in a certain way, defined by the majority, and to accept the common frame of reference, is always explicit. The change that is thus induced is, at least for a certain amount of time, purely external. The individual is placed in a state of *forced compliance* in which he is obliged to say what he does not want to say, to do what he does not want to do, either out of indifference or for fear of being isolated and rejected from the group. The collectivity initially accepts this type of submission, for it dislikes deviancy and it knows from experience that, with time, it is possible to believe what one says and to desire what one does. Pascal captured this three centuries ago by advising Christians to pray whether or not they believed, and advocating that faith would eventually win out. What are the reasons for such transformations? It is simply the existence of a conflict between private opinions and judgements and public ones. Since the latter cannot be modified, in order to resolve the conflict, the private side is changed, which allows the individual to justify his having submitted to the pressures of the majority for no special reason.

In a situation of innovation, where the pressure to change remains implicit, the new response appears as an alternative to the existing response, and adopting the new is not the result of constraint. If a member of the majority is interested in or attracted to this response, if he changes in that direction, the change is often indirect or unconscious, or, in a word, private. Since people do and say certain things for purely ritual reasons, its effect is often to empty the judgements and usual behaviours of their content. When it becomes apparent that they no longer have any real meaning, the conflict which emerges is an external one, between what one is beginning to believe, the newly adopted ideas, and the beliefs and ideas of "the others" which one still pretends to share. For minorities it is a problem of capitalizing on the modifications that it has induced, and to lead the movement they have initiated. History teaches us that they can succeed in one of two ways. Minorities can become more flexible, by making their points of view more widely acceptable, and by turning overt behaviours to their own advantage; or they can commit people to certain actions—petitions, strikes, votes on certain issues, etc.—by emphasizing the break with the previous structure of social relations, and by forcing people to harmonize

CONFORMITY, NORMALIZATION AND INNOVATION

what they say with what they think, and what they do with what they want.

It is obvious that deviant minorities will have to invent many more ways and means of taking advantage of the influence which they exert. When they fail, or are provoked to failure, the majority reaps the benefits in their stead. This is a phenomenon that, for the last few years, has been called "recuperation". The criticisms, the examples and the actions of a great many marginal groups and minorities have produced important changes in values, language, habits of dress, as well as in the political and social spheres. But these groups were not able to legitimize those new languages and behaviours, nor were they in a position to do so. But a new social and psychological space had been created, which was taken over by other financial, intellectual and political groups who were able to legitimize these novelties. Suddenly, long hair, the demands of students and racial minorities, the sexual mores which were previously unspeakable and stigmatized, were incorporated into the programmes of highly conservative parties, adopted by social circles to which they were repugnant, and became objects for industry and commercialization. Minorities were at the root of these changes, the goals of which were now modified, but the minorities were not able to capitalize on them, to obtain a transformation.

This, of course, is not always the case. Instances such as the Reformation or the socialist parties should be enough to convince us of the opposite. Successful conversions are more common than we tend to believe.

In summary, in situations of innovation we always ask ourselves, "Why do people resist once they have been convinced by the minority?" In situations of conformity, as we know, the opposite question is always asked, "Why do people not resist since they are not convinced by the majority?" It is obvious that the minority does make converts, but these converts encounter external obstacles to expressing their true affiliations. The majority makes compliers, obtains the acquiescence of many, who conceal their reservations under explicit demonstrations of unreserved adherence. The practical problems which arise in the two cases are correspondingly different. Minorities attempt to change private attitudes and beliefs into public behaviour, while majorities concentrate their energies on attempting to change public behaviour and declarations into private attitudes and beliefs. But in both cases, the split between the group and the person, between what one says and what one thinks, between what one does and what one wants, is a possible solution to which we are all indebted for the schizophrenic world and divided personalities in which we live.

The fact that a majority of individuals may label "blue" what they began by seeing as "green" also has other implications. This phenomenon was worth demonstrating experimentally, for the sake of more precise description, but the demonstration has a value beyond this. It reveals the character of a change which, literally, cannot be given a name. Objective facts are no longer the same; the deviant minority has had its effect, and the innovation has taken place. But no linguistic accommodation has taken place; words and formulae referring to the objective facts remain unchanged, as though the minority had had no effect, and no innovation had occurred. People believe that, in continuing to use the same language and continuing to perform the same acts, they are dealing with a reality which has also remained the same. Their belief is mistaken. Take the example of an Englishman who votes for the Conservative party. This party of the centre-right, glanced at briefly, appears as the representative of private property, of *laissez-faire* economic policies, and of the interests of the bourgeoisie. In voting for this party for thirty years, the Englishman has expressed his adherence to its values, social and political philosophy, and its interests. However, if the Conservative party is looked at more closely, it is seen that it has in fact adopted and assimilated a whole series of economic and legal policies which are frankly socialist (social security, nationalization, and so on), and which are contrary to its supposed doctrine and tradition. This is explained by history, the force of circumstances, and the evolution of class relations. The person who continues to call himself "Conservative" denotes by this word a political content which is quite different from what it was, much as our subjects continued to call "blue" what they had begun to see as "green". We are observing here the creation of a social illusion: the illusion of stability when all the facts are changing. The opposite effect is not uncommon: words and linguistic forms change, while acts and their content remain the same. The significance of these phenomena is clear: they show the difference between the two types of influence as mechanisms producing social illusions. The most powerful of these mechanisms are those which cause innovations to appear as the outcome of conformity. Proverbs illustrate this effect—"New wine in old bottles", "nothing new under the sun", *plus ça change, plus c'est la même chose*, and so on. Conversely, innovation may be rapidly transformed into conformity, as salon revolutions, radical chic, and imitation in the arts and sciences amply demonstrate.

Every scientist is aware that, sooner or later, the methods and the ideas he has learned and thought important will become obsolete and forgotten. Scientists even contribute actively to this cycle of obsolescence and innovation, because of an enduring curiosity about the truth. This is the only justification they could have for such bizarre behaviour. But ideas presented here are not only relevant on an individual or interindividual level. Every kind of conformity shares the features I have referred to. Every organization, every society seeks to create an impression of unanimity. When politicians speak in defence of law and order against anarchy and disorder, they claim to be speaking on behalf of a silent majority. That is the impression, at least, that they wish to convey. By doing so, they imply that people who are *not* silent are deviant; they are the ones who make "noise" in the midst of a quiet, serious collectivity who only want to be left alone to follow their pursuits in decent peace. The collectivity, in any case, has no profound motivation to change: at most, it will make corrections here and there for errors or excesses. All this is an obvious feature of conformity—the total society attempts to maintain control over the diverse parts which make it up by means of appeals to the much-invoked concept "law and order".

Normalization is a common feature of institutions. Take the example of parliamentary commissions. They are composed of representatives of all parties, who often have opposed ideologies and different opinions with regard to the matter in hand. Their work consists of hearing the opinions of experts who, themselves, are far from agreement, and considering the views presented by delegates of different groups whose interests are in conflict: management and labour, industry and agriculture, and so on. All the participants—the delegates of interest groups, the representatives of political parties, and, to a lesser degree, the experts, try to get their own point of view accepted and to bring off a decision which will be favourable to them. Even so, all are agreed on one point—that the conflict which is the reason for the commission should not erupt into open confrontation. All influence attempts are directed to this end, as well as to attaining a "fair" compromise. The reports produced by these commissions clearly show the extent to which interactions during the proceedings are dominated by these two motives: the attenuation of conflict, and the search for a compromise which will be at an optimal proximity to the position of each group involved. I suppose that those scholars who have studied political systems must have arrived at a major distinction between systems which are founded on normalization as the influence mode and compromise as the norm of relations between political groups—the Anglo-Saxon system, for example—and systems founded on conformity and the pressure to choose between orthodoxy and heterodox alternatives, such as the French system. This is not to imply that conformity and choice are absent from the one, and normalization and compromise from the other, but that they are not distinctive features of the system. If parliamentary commissions are accepted as an index of normalization, as an influence mode, then their existence in England and the United States is in contrast to their absence in France. I am not suggesting that this provides the measure for invidious political comparisons, or that one or other of the systems produces a greater democracy. I have pointed out this distinction because it corresponds, at the level of social groups, to the phenomena observed in small groups and individuals in the laboratory.

I do not intend to say more about innovation at this point. I have repeatedly stressed the parallelism between the processes revealed by experimentation and those observed in the real world. Can it be said that behavioural styles are purely individual, or do they only have effect in inter-individual situations? I hope the day will come when, with the necessary time perspective, histories are written of the movements against the Algerian war in France, and against the Vietnam war in America. Whether as a close or distant observer of one or the other, one cannot help being struck by the similarity of attitudes of the members of these two movements, and by the moral and physical courage they have shown. In reply to those who invoked motives of opportunity or strategy, they refused absolutely to compromise on the issues of democracy, torture, and genocide. Beyond the will to face squarely the evidence, the courage to endure sanctions, ostracism and isolation from their social and professional groups, there was a consistency and autonomy of behaviour clearly demonstrated by hundreds and thousands of men and women. From teach-ins and sit-ins in the United States, clandestine meetings and clubs and "demonstrations of intellectuals" in France, to marches and mass demonstrations, the odd and isolated little currents of dissent merged to become floods of protest. Once the opportunity for expression was provided, these movements grew at a constant rate and increased their pressure on the respective governments. This is not to say that such movements were responsible for the ending of the wars in Algeria and Vietnam. But their contribution, certainly a decisive one, is difficult to over-estimate. In the creation of these movements, as well as in their effect on society, some of the phenomena studied by social psychologists have been at work, even though the science could not, of course, reproduce them on such a large scale. This is why it is necessary to consider large-scale social movements in the world as natural experiments. Otherwise, there will be many arguments to limit the generality of statements in social psychology, and many arguments to limit the power of its concepts and theories to interpret the reality in which we live.

I have taken a broad view in this chapter, drawing attention to some facts and relationships which are familiar, and others which are less so. I have attempted to knit together ideas and data which are scattered through my own research and that of others. Starting from the position that our understanding of social influence must include an appreciation of the role of conflict, I defined conformity, normalization and innovation as influence modalities contingent upon the reduction, avoidance, and creation of conflict. This was the only appropriate starting-point for the elucidation of the specific nature of these modalities, which may allow an investigation of their mechanisms. At that point, we would have the tools to propose a truly general theory of social influence. But agreement must first be reached on the idea that I have put forward in this chapter, namely, that each of the influence modalities represents (a) a type of behaviour contingent upon the development of conflict; and (b) a specific way of establishing social norms and codes. It is important to remember that norms and codes differ not only in their aim and content, but also in the way in which they have been established.

9

Majorities' Reactions To Deviant Minorities

> Although you are different from me,
> my brother, far from harming me,
> your existence enriches mine.
>
> *Saint-Exupéry*

The handicap of being different

We have examined so far how deviant, but active, minorities may be in a position enabling them to exert an influence on majorities. How are these minorities perceived by others? What attitudes do those who have been subjected to their influence adopt towards them? Contemporary social psychology provides an answer to these questions, which is based on the notion of *attraction*. It is widely accepted that the reason why, and the ways in which people become, dependent on each other are related to the dynamic of attraction. Specifically, social and interpersonal bonds are shaped while mutual choices are being decided according to feelings and opinions concerning the intellectual and subjective qualities of each person involved. Amongst the factors which create and strengthen such bonds, there is the basic need for social approval, causing the individual to avoid those who reject him and to seek out other people who will accept and reward his way of thinking and behaving. The need for social comparison also comes into play urging the individual to try and gain some information about himself and others so as to pass a correct judgement on his own capacities and opinions.

Through his endeavour to satisfy such needs, the individual finds his proper position in a suitable social network and succeeds in defining his social identity. But what characteristics must other people possess, in order to give social approval and provide a basis for social comparison? It appears that, in order to play a reassuring and beneficial role and make the subject's self-understanding easier, they must be on similar, or at least on familiar, grounds with him. Too wide a gap between "self" and "others" is likely to increase the already existent tensions and uncertainties and, by the way, renders the expected reward all the more problematic. Therefore, it is only between persons who are close to one another, belonging to the same group, sharing a common background and a similar view of reality, that interpersonal bonds happen to be shaped. Should any misunderstanding occur or the hitherto maintained balance be upset, the individual is ready to shift his opinions and change his behaviour in order to restore the level of social approval reached up to then, as well as the existing means of social comparison. That is why he allows himself to be influenced, and why he feels attracted towards the very source of this influence. In fact, he wants to keep in contact with those who are like him and avoid becoming estranged or different. In this respect, the search for that which is like the "self" can be viewed as the essential feature of most relationships between individuals as between group members.

We are attracted towards those who are similar to us; such is, in a nutshell, the wisdom underlying all existing theories and experiments.

Interpersonal attraction and social influence [assert Walster and Abrahams, 1972] are so intimately related that if one understands each process, he can probably intuit the relationships between them. Thus many readers may already feel that they can guess at many of the ways in which attraction and influence are related. Nearly all the theorists agree that a likeable person will be more effective in exerting social influence than will be a less likeable person (p. 223).

Therefore the span of likes and dislikes provides a powerful dimension on which one can assess people's modes of perception and the ways in which they judge and affect each other.

This dimension also provides an answer to the two questions we have put forward. A minority, because of its distinctiveness, cannot be either a criterion for comparison or a provider of social approval; it is devoid of power of attraction. On the other hand, "liking" is correlated with attractiveness. Consequently, a minority is bound to be rejected and disliked. Any potential deviant knows that, as an experiment by Allen (1974) shows. The material used in the group discussion was the now classical case history of the juvenile delinquent, Johnny Rocco. Each subject in the group was led to believe that his judgement concerning the treatment of Johnny Rocco differed from the group's. The experiment had been scheduled so as to require that a ballot be taken in order to eliminate one of the subjects in the next phase of the discussion. As expected, 69% of the college student subjects thought that they would be rejected for being, in each case, the single element disagreeing with the group. An early study by Schachter (1951) completes the picture by clearly showing that a minority has good cause for being apprehensive: it is actually rejected and disliked. During this experiment, groups of subjects discussed Johnny Rocco's case story after each subject had read it individually. A typical group consisted of nine participants, six of whom were naive subjects and three who were confederates of the experimenter. The confederates each played one of three roles; the *modal* person, who takes a position identical to that of the average naive subject; the *deviate*, who takes a position opposed to the general opinion of the group; and the *slider*, who begins by agreeing with the deviate, but who, during the course of the interaction, gradually shifts to a conforming, modal position. There was therefore one consistent, and one inconsistent deviate. The results of the experiment clearly showed that the modal person was liked most, and the consistent deviate was liked least. These findings have been repeated many times, and there is no reason to doubt them, particularly as they correspond to what is already known of such processes in general. We are therefore sure to find similar results in other experiments in the course of which a deviant minority attempts to exert its influence on the majority. But it is precisely this predicted and expected outcome which raises new problems. How is it that a minority, in spite of being disliked, or not particularly liked, can exert some influence? What is the nature of its relationships with the majority? What does the minority seek and obtain from the majority besides its agreement? In trying to clarify these problems, we are led to discover a sphere of interpersonal and social relations which is wider than the sphere of interpersonal and social attraction.

The disliked and the admired

The empirical evidence pertaining to the ways in which deviant minorities are perceived and the attitude they evoke has been obtained largely from experiments in which naive subjects were exposed to one or two confederates, and afterwards responded individually to post-experimental questionnaires. The procedure is well-known and need not be described in detail. There are various types of questionnaires in use, but all of them include questions aiming to assess, on the one hand, whether and how much the majority subjects like the deviant minority and, on the other hand, how they evaluate the behaviour and qualities of this minority. We shall now outline systematically the results which have been obtained from those questionnaires.

The "green-blue" experiment (Moscovici *et al.* 1969)
In this experiment, the deviant minority consisted of two individuals, who consistently maintained that objectively blue slides were green. The intention was to demonstrate that subjects attribute neither competence nor power to a consistent minority. The only significant attribution was, in fact, the perceived certainty of the minority's judgements. If this perceived certainty is inferred from consistent behaviour, then one would expect that a minority behaving inconsistently would be perceived as being uncertain. Such a result would conclusively demonstrate that behavioural style is a factor determining the success of innovation. In order to study the way in which subjects perceive the agent of influence in different experimental conditions, both in terms of the resources and the conviction attributed to the agent, we focused our questions on three features: competence, conviction, and leadership.

We therefore asked subjects to evaluate the competence of each member of the group in judging luminosity and colour, on an eleven-point scale. After this, they categorized each member according to the degree of confidence he showed in making his responses. The categorization was made on a four- or six-point scale, according to the number of subjects. Finally, the subjects collectively made decisions on whether to accept or reject nominated leaders, and who they would designate as the leader in a future experiment.

We found that the minority was judged incompetent in colour judgement. The naive subjects judged themselves to be more competent than the confederates, whether or not they had responded "green" during the course of interaction.

There were also differences in the attribution of competence to each confederate. The confederate who was the first to respond was judged less competent than the other confederate. It was as if the first confederate to respond was held responsible for the surprising judgement, even though the same judgement was made by both confederates. We will come back to this point later.

All of these results clearly show that the influence of a minority cannot be due to an attribution of superior competence in colour designation. However, although subjects do not recognize any particular competence on the part of the consistent minority, we would at least expect them to attribute greater conviction to the minority.

We found that the naive subject does attribute greater assurance to the minority than he does to himself. The two minority individuals were not judged to be equally confident. The first to respond was judged to be the most confident. He is thus judged to be less competent but more assured. Both judgements indicate that the first confederate is believed to be the initiator of the response. The assurance attributed to the confederate is closely linked with the consistency of his behaviour. In fact, a change from consistent to inconsistent behaviour is sufficient for the confederate to be no longer judged as particularly confident. The influence of the minority is therefore essentially due to its consistency of behaviour; to the assurance which subjects attribute to the minority as an inference from this consistent behaviour. While it is true that influence is a function of consistency of the confederates, is it also true that subjects confer on them a privileged sociometric status? Not necessarily. We have already pointed out that the influence of a consistent minority is not due to any particular power. Consequently, we would not necessarily expect an influential minority individual to be given the position of a leader. Our results show that minority individuals score no differently than naive subjects on this measure. They are neither accepted, rejected, nor nominated as leaders more frequently than naive subjects. Thus there is no superior status associated with their influence. On the other hand, when minority members are inconsistent, they are rejected as leaders significantly more often than the other members of the group.

What emerges from these results is that the consistent minority exerts influence to the extent that naive subjects attribute superior assurance to them. If minority members are consistent, they are not rejected as leaders, but neither are they particularly sought after as leaders.

Why were the perceptions of the two confederates so different? Each seemed to have a different role in the dynamic of the conflict between majority and minority. The one to respond "green" first took the role of innovator, while the second in subscribing to the same view appeared as a follower. But while the initiative for change belongs to the presumed innovator, it is the follower who makes this influence possible. The follower's behaviour gives a social dimension to the minority response.

These observations offer some insights into the conflicts over influence in situations of innovation, and into the interpersonal relations which arise in these situations. They allow us to understand better how a consistent minority can influence a majority even when this majority shares an explicit and objective norm. Above all, it appears that minority individuals force the majority to take their point of view into account, not by virtue of any particular expertise, but because they put forward their point of view with coherence and firmness. Such qualities do not necessarily make the minority attractive; yet, if they are lacking, the minority is definitely rejected.

The "patterning/repetition" experiment

In this experiment, Nemeth *et al.* (1973) carried out two sets of comparisons. On the one hand, they compared the influence of an individual responding randomly (Random Condition) to that of an individual who responded consistently. On the other hand, they compared the influence of a confederate who always repeated the same response ("green" or "blue-green") with the influence of a confederate whose responses followed a certain pattern. The stimuli presented to the subjects were blue.

As would be expected from the results of the experiment described above, the confidence attributed to the confederates was higher in the patterned (consistent) condition than it was in the random (inconsistent) condition. The confederates were also judged to be more organized in the patterned condition. Naive subjects said that they would trust the confederates in the patterned condition more than in the random condition.

The contrast observed between the two types of consistent minority— the patterned and the repetitive—is equally instructive. In this experiment, the minority was not influential when it simply kept responding "green". When it responded exclusively "blue-green", it was only marginally influential. The post-experimental questionnaire showed that those confederates whose responses were patterned were seen in a particularly favourable light. They were perceived as being more sure of their judgements and "better" in colour perception than naive subjects. In the case of exclusively "blue-green" responses, there was no significant difference between patterned and repetitive responses on these items. But confederates responding "green-blue" were more admired, liked and trusted when their responses were patterned rather than repetitive. When the responses were exclusively "green", there was no such difference between patterned and repetitive responses.

This completes our picture. The consistent minority, through its behaviour and apparent attitude, is not only admired, considered sure of itself and trustworthy, which indicates a certain social recognition of its position in the group; it is also liked, and, in a way, considered more worthy of social approval than other members of the group. This is true regardless of the degree of influence actually exerted. In order for the consistent minority to acquire this positive image, it is sufficient for it merely to be active and to make its existence known.

The "painting" experiment (Nemeth and Wachtler, 1973)
In this experiment, which has been described in detail earlier, four naive subjects were grouped with one confederate, who was introduced as being of German, Italian, or unknown ethnic origin. On each trial, subjects were asked to express a preference for one of two paintings, which were labelled "Italian" or "German". The results showed that the presence of a confederate who took a consistent position, whether it was pro-Italian or pro-German, had the effect of making naive subjects more pro-German than the control group. The confederates, of course, were biased. How were they perceived?

In general, naive subjects rated the confederate more "certain of his decision" than the other members of the group. An analysis of variance showed an interaction between the alleged nationality of the confederate and his rating relative to others on the certainty measure. When the confederate was presented as Italian (Angelo) or as being of unknown ethnic origin (Bob), he was rated as considerably more certain than when he was presented as German (Fritz). Moreover, Angelo and Bob were judged more certain than the naive subjects in their own groups, whereas Fritz was not. When subjects were asked to rate each other on bias in painting selection, the confederate was judged to be more biased than the other naive subjects. Finally, subjects reported that they had felt more influenced by Fritz, Angelo or Bob than by the other subjects.

These results were entirely as predicted, and are consistent with those we have already discussed. The minority individual is seen as more assured and more consistent than the other group members. The fact that he was biased did not prevent him from being influential. On the contrary, in such circumstances, his bias becomes understandable to the other subjects. It is seen as something positive, expressing the strong preference which is expected from such an individual. But it also expresses a certain amount of courage. It certainly required courage, particularly in Angelo's case, to demonstrate partiality. But it required even more courage for Fritz to oppose the pro-Italian norm of his group. His persistent pro-German stance was probably interpreted as a sign of honesty. This experiment shows that the minority individual becomes, in many ways, a central figure of the group.

The "jury trial" experiment

Nemeth and Wachtler (1973a) similated a jury trial in the laboratory. In one condition, the confederate taking a deviant position was made to appear to choose the head chair. In another condition, he was assigned to this chair. In the first condition, he was influential; in the second condition, he was not. The naive subjects were asked to express their opinions of the other members of the group in a post-experimental questionnaire, so that the way in which the confederate was perceived could be assessed. He was judged to be more consistent, more independent, more strong-willed, to have induced them to think more and reassess their own positions more than the other subjects. At the same time, the confederate was considered less perceptive, less warm, less liked, less reasonable, fair, etc., than the naive subjects. Statistically, all these differences are significant. We see, here again, a series of positive traits being attributed to the minority group or individual, in terms of activity, independence and capacity to stimulate, for making other subjects aware of possibilities of change and renewal. He therefore contributes definitely to the group's resources. But we also see, more clearly than in the other experiments discussed, a set of negative evaluations. Thus, attitudes which are positive at the objective level are counteracted by rather negative ones at the subjective level. As Heider once pointed out: "One has a cool admiration for a person when one admires him but does not like him very much" (1958, p. 236).

The originality experiment

The experimental paradigm in this case was identical to that used in the "green/blue" experiment. The subjects were constrained to give original responses. We found that the minority was very influential in this case. In general, in all five experimental conditions, the two deviant confederates were considered to be less competent than the naive subjects themselves. On the other hand, they were judged as being more certain of their responses, particularly the confederate who responded first. The roles of the deviant minority, therefore, are differentiated in the context of originality as well. The initiative behind the original response is attributed to the first confederate in a way which is more or less pronounced according to the conditions.

An interesting difference is revealed when this experiment is compared with the earlier one (the "green/blue" experiment) in which the group norm was an objective one. In the originality experiment, the confederates were perceived as being more attractive. In several of the experimental conditions, they received more sociometric choices than the naive subjects. The naive subjects seemed, therefore, to have a more positive image of the minority. The confederate was more trusted in the groups which had the task of finding something novel than in the groups whose task it was to find something which was objectively correct. In this way, the confederate gained access to leadership.

We are now in a position to take stock of all these findings. Our discussion so far has been based on evidence from the responses of about fifteen hundred people, a number which is not negligible. The fact that similar reactions have been observed in France and the United States assures us of a certain degree of generality. (This generality, admittedly, has some limit: the subjects in these experiments being all students.) The findings oblige us to say that most social psychologists have been right in affirming that a deviant minority is likely to be rejected, disliked, or at least regarded with indifference by the majority. But they have been wrong in inferring that "the non-conformist may be praised by historians or idealized in films, but he is usually not held in high esteem, at the time, by the people to whose demands he refuses to conform" (Aronson, 1972, p. 15). These two aspects are quite independent of one another, and sometimes they represent a real choice for the minority. Whether to please others or to speak the truth and risk ill-favour is often the alternative which an individual or a group must face, and this is also true for a large number of artists and even scientists until they gain acceptance from the public or their peers. In all of these cases, respect and esteem are often won at the expense of "liking", affection and warmth.

The results obtained thus far need to be elaborated and refined. But already a simple trend emerges from them: the relationship of a majority with a minority is ambivalent. The positive aspect is that the deviant individual or subgroup is one of the poles of the group and of social change. The negative aspect is that deviants are kept at a distance, forced to remain on the fringe of society; their qualities, merits, and contributions are recognized without being overtly acknowledged and approved. It is as if society accepted them and disapproved of them at the same time. Clear-cut ambivalence is observed not only in the laboratory; there are many societies in which some individuals or professions are both sacred and segregated. Jews, in Western society, occupy a position, both real and symbolic, which is out of all proportion to their number. They are considered to be one of the founding races of this civilization. Yet despite the abilities which are attributed to them, great care is often taken to exclude them, in a more or less explicit manner, from many important functions, and particularly from the narrow circle of national government. Scientists and artists are respected, praised, even revered for their various contributions. No one is ashamed to know them personally or to be associated with them. And yet, the same qualities of intelligence, sensitivity and curiosity are often associated with judgements of absent-mindedness, lack of practicality, childishness, and irresponsibility which are all ways of setting them apart. Above all, there is a reluctance to entrust responsible social and political positions to them; such positions are reserved for businessmen, civil servants, clergy, and military men. The Romans expressed the underlying attitude in clear terms: admire the work, beware the artist. Since then, the formula may have worn thin, but the mentality underlying it has not disappeared. It can even be appropriately extended: admire the act or idea which is deviant, dislike the person who produced it. This ambivalence, or *double-think*, is a constant in social attitudes towards minorities.

In search of social recognition

The outlook is not all that bleak for a minority. To be apart is not necessarily a disadvantage, even if it is not always a comfortable situation. To be disliked is not even an obstacle to influence. But this is not the most important. What is important is to know the forces which push the minority to take the risk of being disliked, rejected, and what it gains in so doing. In order to find the answer, one must consider once again the nature of social relations. The first point is that, to be liked one had to "exist" and be perceived as existing. Getting one's existence acknowledged is a serious problem for many people. Ethnic and social groups, nations, creative individuals, children, and so on, all desire and expect to be identified for what they are or for what they deserve. No doubt, we are surrounded by people who are striving to be liked and to be given approval, and we consider them attractive or unattractive. But those people after whom we model and define ourselves, and whose judgements matter to us, are all "visible" persons. Elsewhere there looms a zone inhabited by "invisible" creatures and groups who rarely cross the threshold of our vision and whose feelings and commitments we totally disregard. They have little existence in our eyes, except occasionally and at most for the impersonal, instrumental use we can make of them. We do not see them, do not hear them, do not talk to them. The old in the eyes of many youngsters, the poor in the eyes of the rich, the Blacks for the Whites, the savage for the civilized, the beginner for the well-established scientist or artist: so many individuals or groups who, in so many ways, are reduced to invisibility in the eyes of other individuals or groups. There are always two aspects to any interpersonal and social relationship, *visibility* and *attraction*, the former being a prerequisite for the latter. Whoever seeks to be liked, to be chosen as a standard for social comparison, or to rank among those who provide social approval, must, in the eyes of the individuals or groups who command the selection join the ranks of those who are visible. As a matter of fact, people expend a tremendous amount of energy to become parties to social comparison and providers of social approval. This is not a vital necessity for the marginal, deviant but active minorities. Whatever the sacrifice, their primary concern is, in fact, to gain visibility and, therefore, the acknowledgement of their full existence in the eyes and the minds of the majority. The results of our experiments indicate precisely this striving which aims at the majority, taking the qualities of a deviant individual or subgroup into consideration.

Thus we are led to explore, from a social psychological point of view, what "visibility" really means and what it encompasses here. What are the social and psychological processes which relate to the search for visibility? Let us imagine, to start with, this process from the point of view of some hypothetical individual or subgroup in a peripheral position who would represent those previously described as being consistent. He is confident in his own opinions and beliefs, he feels he is right, he is a human being like all others, he has produced something worthwhile in the political, scientific or social fields, and he defends certain definite positions. In his own eyes it is as if he were hoarding a surplus of personal or collective resources (whether intellectual or material). This attitude on the part of people who are "committed and convinced" that they benefit from "excess profits" is noticed whenever a discrepancy (either objective or subjective) arises between their own and other people's evaluations of the same resources. Most often such a gap is the consequence of the fact that, owing to people's uprooted prejudices and inertia, and individual or collective rights, new achievements go unheeded with respect to evaluating others, and new realizations are judged by means of outdated criteria. Invisibility then follows, and at the same time the need to overcome it. Actually, parents are always astounded when they have to face the fact that their children are grown up; a teacher is invariably amazed when some student who he had underestimated meets with success on social and professional grounds; majorities are startled whenever ethnic minorities come into prominence in a sphere they were supposed not to be qualified for. Surprises of this sort are not purely accidental: on the contrary, they appear to be the culmination of long efforts, obstinately pursued to the point of bringing them about, making them noticeable for those who refused to notice them until then. These efforts are particularly marked in those who think they possess the above-mentioned resources, and whose only opportunity for preserving them lies in the possibility of interacting with other individuals or groups and affecting their behaviours, their beliefs, and their ways of thinking. One's own value and the value of whatever one has produced is thus certified and corroborated by one's ability *to act* and *to do* something to someone else; in a nutshell, to "count for" and be "counted upon". In this way a common goal is achieved: that of being identified, listened to and individualized.

It is in the interpersonal and social domains that one becomes visible and acknowledged. The need which corresponds to this process of assessing one's resources or one's right to act and initiate change in one's social and material environment, is the need for *social recognition*.

The minorities in our experiment gained just this recognition. Most economic, social, political and scientific struggles also aim, as we know, at obtaining it. The first concern of any emerging nation, of a class awakening to consciousness, a scientist just making a discovery, or an artist polishing off a sculpture, is not to exist *de facto*, but to be recognized with their own specific qualities by other nations, classes, scientists or artists, and even beyond. Any representative of these groups has the feeling of having been recognized when, and only when, he has grounds for noticing that he and those like him were the originators of some change occurring in other nations or classes, and, for a scientist or an artist, when his work exerts some impact on the work of other scientists or artists. Many of the rituals, symbols, honours, titles, ceremonies, and greetings of all styles, are mainly intended, in most societies, to facilitate the assessment of such an impact.

To sum up, the need for social recognition originates from an individual or collective presumption of a surplus of intellectual or material resources, and is expressed by the subjectively experienced feeling of certainty and legitimacy about the individual or the subgroup's *capacity to affect other people according to its own tendencies and longings*. This need reaches its highest point among minorities; their behaviour and strategies are mainly intended to fulfil it. Obtaining, maintaining, or heightening visibility is therefore an index of the change produced. A few simple propositions concerning the dynamics of interpersonal and social relations can be derived, by way of example, from this hypothetical analysis. We may suppose that the need for social recognition will lead to:

(a) Raising the general level of all activities and initiatives intended to affect other people's beliefs or opinions. Such will especially be the case for nomic groups and individuals, specifically, subjects who are self-assured, who hold definite stands and/or are committed to them.

Bass (1961) observed that the frequency of attempts at leadership is related to self-esteem and self-attributed status as well as to the ability to cope with the group problems. Fouriezos, Hutt and Gruetzkow (1950) noticed greater participation in goal achievement by those who are confident in their own views. Veroff (1957) measured motivation for power and recognition on a projective test and found that individuals whose scores were high were judged by their teachers as being high in argumentation and in attempts to affect the behaviour of others. Strickland (1965) found that persons who are internal-control oriented are more likely to commit themselves to civil rights actions than persons who are external-control oriented. In an interesting experiment, Levinger (1959) brought together pairs of subjects who were not acquainted with one another to engage in a task requiring a series of common decisions. Prior to the decision-making, one of each pair of subjects was induced to believe that his information about the task was either inferior or superior to that of his partner. Those subjects with the belief of superior information were more assertive and made more attempts at influence. Other studies by Lindskold and Tedeschi (1970), Gore and Rotter (1963), Lippit, Polansky, Redl and Rosen (1952) point towards the same tendency of individuals who are confident in their abilities, worth or knowledge, to initiate action and to try more frequently to influence other individuals in the group.

Conversely, a person or group who does not feel capable of affecting others or of producing a change, and who, for this very reason may want to avoid being affected or changed, will seek contacts with a person or a group who is like him, both to feel reassured and to protect himself. Byrne and Close (1967) showed that as the general feeling of uncertainty about oneself increased, at least up to a certain point, the tendency to like persons with similar attitudes also increased. In a study by Shrauger and Jones (1968), subjects were clearly more attracted to others who agreed with them than to others who disagreed with them when they were unable to obtain information about the correctness of their own opinions. When expert opinion was available, there was no such differential preference for others. Furthermore, Singer and Schokley (1965) found that subjects were more likely to associate with peers in order to evaluate accurately their abilities when objective norms about ability were absent than when these norms were available.

(b) Seeking contact with persons who are different from oneself: this will take place to the extent to which the acquiescence or conversion of others to one's own ideas and conceptions of reality are the only possible ways of acknowledging them favourably.

(c) Preferring contact with groups and individuals from which one is most distant or with whom one is in disagreement: several experiments have shown that this is often the case. Hare and Bales (1965), and Cohen (cited in Strodtbeck and Hook, 1961) have shown that if a group of five subjects, assigned to a task requiring common agreement, are seated around a rectangular table in the arrangement 1–3–1–0 (with one side for the experimenter), subjects are more likely to address persons who are most distant from them. During pauses between experimental sessions, however, subjects are more likely to address their immediate neighbours. More to the point, Sigall (1970) has shown that individuals who are deeply involved in an issue prefer to talk to a "disagreer" than to an "agreer". With the "disagreer" there is a chance of converting him to one's own point of view. Another way of putting it is that one prefers converts to loyal members of one's own group.

(d) Willingness to measure oneself against others, particularly when difficult problems arise, demanding scarce resources or original solutions: where problems are such that they can be solved by anyone, the resources being easily available and the possible courses of action being well charted, there is no opportunity for demonstrating one's abilities and therefore no way of gaining recognition. This is why scientists try to make original predictions, artists strive towards exceptional performances, minority groups carry out startling and outrageous acts, and the founders of religions base themselves on miracles which "become" less and less frequent as the religion becomes more established.

(e) Seeking more extreme conflict in order to demonstrate one's merits and one's viewpoint, and ultimately to achieve one's ends.

(f) Perceiving social interaction in a long-term perspective.

These propositions can, and no doubt will, be enlarged upon and added to by future work. They explain, to a large extent, why minorities in search of social recognition for their existence and capabilities are prepared to take risks, to persist for long periods in uncomfortable situations, and to endure unpopularity.

Let us now consider the point of view of the person who gives recognition to others who seek it. No doubt this person is aware of being the object of strong solicitation, and is also aware that the agent who is soliciting is very different from himself. Whether the agent is an individual or a group, their behaviour will be carefully scrutinized, particularly with regard to the investment they place in their work and their willingness to sacrifice in order to be integrated into, or to change, the social field from which they had been previously excluded. They are therefore watched and evaluated from afar, as objects of interest rather than of sympathy, and it's only with the passage of time that it becomes possible for them to be seen as being like the self, even though still different in some ways. The distant respect and interest which they evoke at first will later be increased by a positive evaluation of their capabilities and opinions, an appreciation of the difficulties of their position as deviants, and of their courage in defending it. Thus, admiration for the deviants slowly builds up. Throughout this sequence, the minority behaves in a firm and consistent way, and is seen as being self-assured and confident. This in turn engenders confidence in the host group, and eventually social recognition is granted. This does not necessarily mean that they are granted social approval. As we have seen, sometimes they will continue to be regarded as being in some sense less competent, less fair (more biased), or less wanted. Even if one follows the minority, one may not wish to see them in positions of leadership. This means that a minority which actively tries to win influence is more likely to gain social recognition (eventually) than social approval. Its influence is more likely to be associated with the former than with the latter.

In this way, one is led to view the relations between people in a somewhat different light, or at least those relations which, arising from reciprocal interaction, lead to the discovery of a person or a group which was previously unknown or ignored; these relations give a new visibility and identity to the person or group which sets out to be discovered, and eventually is discovered. Similarities or dissimilarities appear, then, to be subordinate to the activity or the passivity of the partners involved. To see this more clearly, it is worthwhile to take as a starting point a general principle which was clearly expressed by Tajfel (1972), namely, that "the function and purpose of social categorization is to order and systematize the social environment: it is a *guide* to action" (p. 298). The categories "similar" and "dissimilar" are no exceptions to the rule; they do not float along by themselves, or serve as replicas for an individual or a group. They stand where they are in order to point out the relationship between the "same" and the "other", that is, reciprocal behaviours in the terms of social agents. If we isolate the categories from their contexts, they no longer appear as "guides to action"; they become terribly misleading and unreliable. What is important is not at all the similar or dissimilar character of a person or a group, but the way in which the other is involved in an on-going or a possible interaction. This means, for example, that psychosociological phenomena can be intensified when, instead of their being the *reflection* of what we *are*, the outcome of our reaction to the desires and judgements of others, we take them to be the *effect* of what we *do*, the outcome of our action on the desires and judgements of others. In other words, we are much more sensitive to our work, requiring a corresponding effort on the part of a social partner, than to what is presented to us or present in us as a given, requiring no modification on anyone's part and the investments of no one.

True, it is nice to be admired and loved by someone who is similar.

But it is even better to be loved and admired by someone who is different. Everyone knows intuitively that what a person loves and is attracted to in someone who is similar is really himself, through the mirror that he also reflects in the other person. Neither partner is responsable for, and neither has invested in their encounter. One is simply loved, and is simply attractive; one does not need to make oneself loved or make oneself attractive. On the contrary, when it is a person who is different, if he has positive feelings, then one knows intuitively that it is for oneself, for the impression that one was able to make on him. His love, his attraction towards you are considered as the effects of a specific action, of a change for which you are responsible, and the results of an effort which that person had to make in order to overcome the internal resistances and external distance which kept you apart. It is therefore right to feel even more sensitive and to respond even more favourably than in ordinary circumstances. This is even the case in the laboratory. Jones *et al.* (1971) invited pairs of college women to have a brief conversation. During the conversation, each subject was either in agreement or in disagreement with her partner on a number of issues. Subsequently the subjects were given the opportunity of eavesdropping on a conversation that another college woman (a confederate) was having with a third person, during which the confederate was heard to express her feelings about the subject: in one condition she seemed to like her; in another condition she seemed to dislike her. What impact did this have on the subjects' feelings about the person with whom they had first exchanged their opinions? The subjects showed a preference for the persons with whom they had disagreed and who, in spite of this, liked them. Thus, liking increased when it corresponded to the liking of a person with dissimilar attitudes. This is probably why the subjects in this experiment are inclined to think, like the rest of us, that there must be something special and unique about them, since someone found them attractive even though they had nothing or very little in common.

Other experiments, notably that of Aronson and Linder (1965), show that a person whose liking for us increases gradually will be preferred to someone who has always liked us. Conversely, a person whose liking for us decreases gradually will be more strongly disliked than someone who has always disliked us. Needless to say, in both cases, when the liking or disliking develops over time, one has to face up to the consequences of what one has done, to the effects one has produced on the other, which explains the intensified feelings.

Here we must develop another aspect of the associative bonds between persons. We do not necessarily avoid some degree of distance from another person, as an index of affective and intellectual autonomy, individuality, and mutual esteem, which can perfectly well coexist with great intimacy of thought, action, and interest. Thus, in relationships, the difference which permits such a distance would be preferred, in opposition to what one might think, to the similarity which may, and often does, erase it. It is not a hypothesis that can be discarded without further reflection. After all, the possibility of living closely with other individuals or groups—families, communities, are good examples—without losing one's self is not only one of the greatest difficulties in personal and social relationships, but also one of the important requirements for their survival. The possibility seems to exist when reciprocal respect and recognition are established, and the development of one partner is seen as an asset to the other, not as an obstacle to his own development. Similarly, it is only when deviants and eccentrics are accepted for what they are, as having a potential contribution to make, rather than being regarded as threats, that relatively harmonious, though still distant, relationships are viable. To be able to be admired and to admire in return, without embarrassment or resentment, is a very great asset, just as it is to be able to be loved and to love in return without jealousy. This ability has been lost or ignored by our frantically competitive and propriety-minded society. Other societies have developed it and have fared and endured as well as ours; we are sometimes tempted to see in the rag-bag of their traditional wisdom a paradise out of which we have been cheated.

One-standard and two-standard relations

Visibility and attraction, admiring and liking are at the root of many social relations, and they must be considered together. This is so because of the two basic paradoxes of social relations.

Although we take a great interest in competent, creative, eccentric, courageous, independent, persons and groups, they make us feel ill at ease, and as a consequence we keep our distance from them and avoid them. Often this avoidance is justified by our saying that they are unapproachable, aloof, inhuman or superhuman. If they ever become liked, it is only after they have revealed some weakness or vulnerability, thereby showing that they do, after all, share the common lot. The surrounding people are then able to detect in these marginal elements some reassuring similarity with themselves, and the eventuality of some kind of contact can be examined.

At the opposite end of the scale, uncertain, tense, troubled individuals or groups usually avoid to change or to be changed, to judge or to be judged, and to evaluate their true resources in a task-defined or task-oriented situation. They try to establish affiliative and emotional bonds exclusively with those people whose sensibility is similar to their own. "Liking" and attraction are their main concerns and criteria of exchanges with others. It is as if "liking" and attraction, though highly regarded, served as defence mechanisms against other dimensions of social exchange which seem to be fraught with threats. It is only after they have succeeded in being reassured that individuals of that type can become involved in social exchanges based on a larger set of criteria and pertaining to more objective and "cool" dimensions as, for instance, cleverness, competence, skill, courage and aptitude to take risks, and so on. These observations are corroborated by many experiments in social psychology.

From these paradoxes we first of all learn the following: there is an inverse relation between attraction and visibility, liking and admiring. We also learn that there exist two types of social bonds. The first type can be described as a one-standard relation. In such a relationship the individual or group subjected to pressures to change their point of view, have a feeling of unity with those who initiate this pressure. If they consider that the pressuring persons are attractive, powerful, likeable, they will attribute sureness of judgement to them, and give them access to leadership. Nothing is negotiated, neither authority, nor participation, nor the wish to conserve links with those who are influential. Religions and political parties provide so many examples of this kind of relationship that it is hardly necessary to mention any specific instances. In the experiments discussed, we have seen the same kind of relations, in the cases where a consistent minority adopted behaviour which was patterned, and therefore flexible, or when the group task was defined in terms of originality. I call this type of relationship "one-standard", because only one set of criteria is needed in order to define it. Social recognition goes along with social approval, the one being derived from and reinforcing the other.

The second type of relationship is two-standard. In order to describe it, one can recapitulate some remarks made concerning the responses to post-experimental questionnaires. There is one striking characteristic of the experiments which were discussed: the naive subjects found themselves in the presence of a minority which appeared to be sure of its stance, and would not compromise. It came close, without actually breaking out into, conflict with the other group members. The appeals of the others for the minority to join them, to accept some compromise, to allow itself to be influenced, and to "be reasonable", were doomed to failure. By behaving in this way, the minority won the respect and confidence of the others. It succeeded in placing a real choice before the group, in imposing its views, and in being appreciated for doing this. Most of the naive subjects were conscious of this, and remarked on it. They were even pleased to have been able to discover the difference, and to have had their view of things changed. At the same time, however, they were aware of a kind of constraint. They were forced to change, to engage in conflict, to adopt the opinions and judgements of the minority without having been able to change the minority in any way. This is why, although they were well-disposed towards the minority, they did not wish to be like them, nor did they judge them to be superior or socially preferable.

When one agrees with other persons, is willing to accept their point of view, and admire them, it does not necessarily follow that one wishes to live with them, or identify with them. On the contrary, one will be inclined to avoid them, to resist their influence, and to set up certain barriers. The fact that one admires a man for his work does not mean that one wishes to sit at his table, or be his friend. Such a prospect may even be terrifying, and one may do much to avoid encountering him too often. Among contemporary great figures, de Gaulle, for instance, evoked a great deal of admiration for his acuity of judgement, courage, and stubbornness. But there were not many who sought to be his personal friends. He called forth as much, if not more, hatred and disapproval as love and approval. If one is concerned with great questions while most other people are worried about smaller matters, and if one judges by absolute principles where others can only operate with relative ones, one is accepted by everyone, but from afar. Above all, if one wishes to be right when others seem to be wrong, ill-feeling will be aroused.

All this is not only true of individuals. We see analogous attitudes and feelings among groups. Consider youth movements, for instance. Today, no one denies that they have succeeded in putting much into question, and in overturning many established values. They have obliged adults, parents, teachers, political leaders, to concern themselves with problems such as colonial wars and racism, and to reduce the dissonance between what they say and what they do. It is an understatement to say that, despite their successes, these movements have not won the support or the attachment of adults. On the contrary, they have been condemned. People have tried vigorously to dissociate themselves from their ideas and methods, while borrowing their vocabulary, style of dress, and their authors. The "racist" attitude towards the young, who are so much discussed in France, is an expression of this coldness, even hatred, towards them. On the one hand, one may submit to the influence of an individual or a group, and change. On the other hand, one may be influenced, and in addition feel resentment because of it, avoiding and denying any affinity with the influencing person or group.

In the language used in this book, one would reformulate this by saying that a positive increase in social recognition does not imply a correlative increase in social approval. Rather, it is compensated in a negative sense, by social disapproval. Therefore, there are two standards being applied. One concerns the interaction leading to influence; the other concerns the association between the sender and the receiver of influence. The link is quite as often one of resentment and distance as of identification. This should not surprise us. Every change, every innovation, implies a certain violence, a break with something to which one has been attached or habituated. The group or individual responsible for the break will suffer for its audacity, even if the audacity is judged by everyone to have been salutary and necessary. Whoever discovers a truth, or breaks an unjust law, is hailed for having corrected the error, or for having striven to deliver us from injustice. At the same time, there is an irresistible urge to reprimand him, for having disregarded another truth, or for breaking the law. The ancient practice of executing messengers who brought bad news was not uninformed by a similar urge to scapegoat. The hero, too, quickly finds that he is assumed to have certain responsibilities. Soon after executing the arch-enemies, the revolution will dispose of its own leaders. The double-standard relation is precisely this; on the one hand to recognize and admire the novel and exceptional, and on the other hand to disapprove and deny it, and to re-admit the ordinary and normal.

This description is extreme, because it deals with reactions to minorities who conduct themselves in an extremist manner. There are varying degrees of the phenomenon, and in some situations—in fact, in many situations—more reciprocity can be expected. In all cases, however, the individual or group capable of entering into this second type of relationship must be ready to relinquish the central position, and live in a differentiated social field. The first type of social relation, in contrast, requires a good dose of egocentrism and a uniform social field. "Thus", observes Heider (1958), "at first liking and admiring are closely connected. The more differentiated and the more egocentric a person is, the less liking will be distinguished from admiring, but with greater sophistication the distinction between the two reactions becomes more clearly defined" (p. 237).

To put it briefly, one can summarize the whole argument in two propositions:

(a) attraction represents the passive aspect, and visibility the active aspect of interpersonal and social relations;

(b) social comparison (approval) expresses the need of minorities or groups which are or feel themselves to be dependent, while social recognition expresses the need of minorities or groups which are or feel themselves to be independent.

In the eyes of those for whom society is purely passive adaptation and dependence, everything is a matter of attraction and social comparison (approval). In contrast, in the eyes of those for whom society is active growth and a means of asserting one's independence, everything is a matter of visibility and social recognition. But society is a mixture of both, of imposed growth and growth which is sought after, of the affirmation and negation of the independence of each. For this reason, attraction and visibility, social comparison and social recognition either appear together or separately according to the structure of social relations and the position one occupies in that structure.

In most of the experiments described earlier, the minority is both disliked and esteemed at the same time. In some, especially when the norm of originality is emphasized, the minority is both liked and esteemed. Thus, at times we observed the minority to impose itself in the eyes of the majority as one of the distant terms of the social relation, and at other times as a close and familiar term of the relation. The complexity of the data and the processes involved are just barely perceptible through the results which are still simple and uncertain. The ideas which have been developed from these results are also both simple and uncertain. But there is still one problem which the experiments and ideas discussed here have not yet touched upon.

As has been pointed out several times, the deviant minority becomes one of the poles of the group. It may be judged as a resource by the rest of the group. There is, therefore, some potential for positive attitudes towards them. Is it possible that such positive attitudes, at the level of social recognition, could be translated to other levels, particularly those of affect or social approval? And if so, in what circumstances? We sense that this must be so, but we do not know how, or why. This knowledge would be of the greatest importance in understanding the mechanism of the transformation of social relations between minorities and majorities. The process of innovation in our society would then not only be better understood, but better managed. Collectively we seriously underestimate the power of knowledge, and fail to see that, when science reveals profound truths, it affects the thinking of those who, in turn, shape the world in which we live.

10

Conclusions

There is still a great deal to learn in the psychological field of social influence. The fundamental idea put forward in this work is a simple one: the resolution of conflict will be in favour of the party (individual or subgroup) able to shape its own development, is the most active and is seen to adopt the "proper" behaviour. For this reason, psychology of social influence is one of conflict and difference, both in terms of their production and of their management. The dynamic of this psychology is a subjective, not an objective, one: it consists of an interplay between subjects in a chosen environment and not merely of some manipulation of objects in order to play against one or several subjects in a given environment. The function of influence, in this respect, far from being to eliminate the "errors" produced by deviant minorities is rather to incorporate these "errors" into the social system. As a result, the social system undergoes some changes, becomes more differentiated and complex, adopts new ramifications—in a word, it grows. The importance of minorities lies precisely in their being factors, and often originators, of social change in societies where social change is taking place so rapidly. In these societies, the boundaries of the majority are not clearly marked, and more often than not, the majority is "silent". It is the active individuals and groups who, being profuse in ideas and initiatives, express or create new trends. This may be regretted, but it is surely desirable that innovations and initiatives should question and challenge the bases of "law and order". Hence, it is inevitable that problems will arise, and that new social actors, setting up new schemes and modalities of action, will emerge to vindicate their right to a full existence. This is dealt with from a positive point of view in this book, as should be evident from the choice of the phenomena studied and in the formulation of theory.

In accordance with general practice, I began with a detailed account of the prevailing functionalist model of social interaction and influence. I then pointed out the limitations of this model, which affect its basic assumptions and its ability to explain adequately certain problems. Finally, I outlined the basic assumptions of the genetic model. The genetic model not only avoids the limitations of the functionalist model, but also opens up new approaches in this area of social psychology. The contrasts between the two models are clear, and can be summed up by Fig. 3.

	Functionalist model	Genetic model
Nature of Relations between Source and Target	Asymmetrical	Symmetrical
Goals of Interaction	Social Control	Social Change
Interaction Factor	Uncertainty and Reduction of Uncertainty	Conflict and Negociation of Conflict
Type of Independent Variables	Dependency	Behavioural Styles
Norm determining Interaction	Objectivity	Objectivity, Preference, Originality
Influence Modalities	Conformity	Conformity, Normalization, Innovation

Fig. 3. Social influence from the point of view of the Functionalist and Genetic models.

In spite of these contrasts, it is possible to interpret existing notions and data, particularly those concerning deviance and conformity, in this new framework. The fact that this can be done shows the generality of the model. In addition, new problems which have hardly yet been looked at can be satisfactorily approached using the model, and there is every indication that we can look forward to their solution. This can be achieved once the confounding of power with influence has been corrected, change has been seen as a group goal, and the active character of individuals and sub-groups has been recognized. Theories which, in their original formulations, ignored influence phenomena, should now be made to contribute towards this end. The theory of cognitive dissonance, for instance, can help us to understand the dynamic of conflicts, while hypotheses about attribution can help us to analyse the effects of behavioural style.

The genetic model also reveals some new problems. One of these is that the influence process may have several phases. People who have carried out experiments on the influence exerted by a minority have noted, for example, that individuals belonging to a minority may be admired and positively perceived, without necessarily being seen as attractive or arousing favourable affective reactions. It has also been observed that when members of a majority are influenced by a minority, they are not necessarily prepared to acknowledge publicly the change that has taken place in them. As far as minorities are concerned, there is the problem of conversion, and the progress of an opinion from private to public acceptance. Up to now, our conjectures about these problems have depended on our reasoning and our methods, determined by the functionalist model, and have only dealt with a single phase of the processes involved. They have neglected the later phases in which, perhaps, positive perception may facilitate the development of favourable feeling, and genuine liking, just as private acceptance eventually becomes public acceptance, and compliance under pressure, as dissonance theory suggests, finally leads to authentic change.

There is another challenge, whose importance must be stressed, which concerns methodology. The experimental procedures used are closely bound to the functionalist model. The relationships between subjects are supposed to be asymmetrical and hierarchical, and the assumption of power relations is obvious in the instructions and the experimenter's interventions. If, in line with the assumptions of the genetic model, one wants to observe phenomena deriving from the symmetrical relations between partners, that is, reciprocal influence, and consequently to minimize interference based on status, it will be necessary to devise a corresponding experimental design which will be far removed from current methods. Some experiments which have been carried out on group decisions have shown what can be done in this direction.

It must be admitted that no new set of experimental designs have been developed in this book; but a new methodology must certainly be created. A model alone, notwithstanding the effort required in elaborating it, cannot lead very far. It may guide research in directions which could be interesting, raise questions, and outline answers. But it gives no information about the conditions in which a particular effect will occur, offers no detailed predictions, and does not even offer rigorously defined concepts. Only if theories spring from the model can these gaps be filled, and the fruitfulness of the model demonstrated.

I hope to have given sufficiently specific descriptions and analyses to make this possible. I also hope to have drawn attention to a sufficient number of relationships between hitherto neglected phenomena to make the undertaking appear interesting and worthwhile. Above all, however, I hope that I have managed to convey a new perception of, and a new sensitivity to, some aspects of human and social reality. Only when ideas and facts are based on continually renewed perception and sensitivity can they lead to true understanding, and to the enhancement of knowledge and life. Therein lies the justification for the ambitiousness of this work.

References

Abelson, R. P. and Lesser, G. S. (1964). *In* Cohen, A. R. (ed.) *Attitudes Change and Social Influence*. Basic Books, New York.

Allen, V. L. (1974). *Social Support for Non-conformity*, (Mimeo) Madison.

Allen, V. L. and Levine, J. M. (1968). Social support, dissent and conformity, *Sociometry*, **31**, 138–149.

Allen, V. L. and Levine, J. M. (1971). Social pressure and personal preference, *Journal of Experimental Social Psychology*, **7**, 122–124.

Archer, J. (1968). *The Unpopular Ones*, Crowell-Collier Press, New York.

Aronson, E. (1972). *The Social Animal*. Freeman and Co, San Francisco.

Aronson, E. and Linder, D. (1965). Gain and loss of esteem as determinants of interpersonal attractiveness, *Journal of Experimental Social Psychology*, **1**, 156–171.

Asch, S. E. (1952). *Social Psychology*, Prentice-Hall, New York.

Asch, S. E. (1955). Opinions and social pressure. *Scientific American*, **193**, 31–35.

Asch, S. E. (1956). Studies on independence and conformity: a minority of one against a unanimous majority, *Psychological Monographs*, **70** (416).

Asch, S. E. (1959). A perspective on social psychology. *In* S. Koch (ed.), *Psychology: A study of a science*, Vol. 3., pp 363–384. McGraw-Hill, New York.

Back, K. W. and Davis, K. E. (1965). Some personal and situational factors relevant to the consistency and prediction of conforming behaviors. *Sociometry*, **28**, 227–240.

Bandura, A. and Walters, R. H. (1963). *Social Learning and Personality Development*. Holt, Rinehart and Winston, New York.

Bass, B. M. (1961). Some observations about a general theory of leadership and interpersonal behavior. *In* Petrullo, L. and Bass, B. M. (eds), *Leadership and Interpersonal Behavior*. Holt, Rinehart and Winston, New York.

Biener, L. (1971). The effect of message repetition on attitudes change: a model of informational social influence, Ph.D. Thesis, Columbia University.

Biener, L., Stewens, L. Barrett, D. and Gleason, J. (1974). *The Effect of Minority Status on the Power to Influence*. (Mimeo) Los Angeles.

Bramel, D. (1972). Attrait et hostilité interpersonnels. *In* Moscovici, S. (ed.), *Introduction à la psychologie sociale*. I, pp 193–236. Larousse, Paris.

Brehm, J. W. and Cohen, A. R. (1962). *Explorations in Cognitive Dissonance*. Wiley, New York.

Brehm, J. and Lipsher, D. (1959). Communicator-communicatee discrepancy and perceived communicator trustworthiness, *Journal of Personality*, **27**, 352–361.

Brodbeck, M. (1956). The role of small groups in mediating the effects of propaganda, *Journal of Abnormal and Social Psychology*, **52**, 166–170.

Burdick, H. A. and Burnes, A. Y. (1958). A test of "strain toward symmetry" theories, *Journal of Abnormal and Social Psychology*, **57**, 367–370.

Byrne, D. and Close, G. L. (1967). Effective arousal and attraction, *Journal of Personality and Social Psychology*, **6**, No. 638.

Churchman, C. W. (1961). *Predictions and Optimal Decisions*. Englewood Cliffs, Prentice-Hall, New York.

Cicourel, A. V. (1973). *Cognitive Sociology: Language and Meaning in Social Interaction*. Penguin Education, London.

Coch, L. and French, J. R. P. Jr. (1948). Overcoming resistance to change. *Human Relations*, **1**, 512–532.

Cohen, A. R. (1964). *Attitude Change and Social Influence*. Basic Books, New York.

Crutchfield, R. S. (1955). Conformity and character, *American Psychologist*, 195–198, **10**.

De Monchaux, C. and Shimmin, S. (1955). Some problems of method in experimental group psychology, *Human Relations*, **8**, 58–60.

Deutsch, M. and Gerard, H. B. (1955). A study of normative and informational social influence upon individual judgment, *Journal of Abnormal and Social Psychology*, **51**, 629–636.

Dittes, J. E. (1959). Effect of changes in self-esteem upon impulsiveness and deliberation in making judgments, *Journal of Abnormal and Social Psychology*, **58**, 348–356.

Di Vesta, F. J. Effect of confidence and motivation on susceptibility to informational social influence. *Journal of Abnormal and Social Psychology*, **59**, 204–209.

Di Vesta, F. J. and Cox, L. (1960). Some dispositional correlates of conformity behavior, *Journal of Social Psychology*, **52**, 259–268.

Eisinger, R. and Mills, J. (1968). Perception of the sincerity and competence of a communicator as a function of the extremity of his position, *Journal of Experimental Social Psychology*, **4**, 224–232.

Emerson, R. (1954). Deviation and rejection: an experimental replication, *American Sociological Review*, **19**, 688–693.

Faucheux, C. and Moscovici, S. (1967). Le style de comportement d'une minorité et son influence sur les réponses d'une majorité, *Bulletin du C.E.R.P.*, **16**, 337–360.

Festinger, L. (1950). Informal social communication, *Psychological Review*, **57**, 217–282.

Festinger, L. (1954). A theory of social comparison processes, *Human Relations*, **7**, 117–140.

Festinger, L. (1957). *Theory of Cognitive Dissonance*. Evanston, Row, Peterson.

Festinger, L., Gerard, H. B., Hymovitch, B., Kelley, H. H., and Raven, B. H. (1952). The influence process in the presence of extreme deviates, *Human Relations*, **5**, 327–346.

Fouriezos, N. T., Hutt, M. L. and Guetzkow, H. (1950). Measurement of self-oriented needs in discussion groups, *Journal of Abnormal and Social Psychology*, **45**, 682–690.

Freedman, J. L., and Doob, A. N. (1968). *Deviancy: the Psychology of Being Different*, Academic Press, New York and London.

French, J. R. P. (1956). A formal theory of social power, *Psychological Review*, **63**, 181–194.

French, J. R. P. and Raven, B. H. (1959). The bases of social power. *In* Cartwright, D. (ed.), *Studies in Social Power*, pp. 118–149. University of Michigan Press, Ann Arbor.

Gerard, H. B. and Greenbaum, C. W. (1962). Attitudes toward an agent of uncertainty reduction, *Journal of Personality*, **30**, 485–495.

Goldberg, L. R. and Rorer, L. G. (1966). Use of two different response modes and repeated testings to predict social conformity, *Journal of Abnormal and Social Psychology*, **3**, 28–37.

Gordon, B. F. (1966). Influence and social comparison as motives for affiliation, *Journal of Experimental Social Psychology*, **1**, 55–65.

Gore, P. M. and Rotter, J. B. (1963). A personality correlate of social action, *Journal of Personality*, **31**, 58–64.

Graham, D. (1962). Experimental studies of social influence in simple judgment situations, *Journal of Social Psychology*, **56**, 245–269.

Gurnee, E. (1937). A comparison of collective and individual judgment of fact, *Journal of Experimental Psychology*, **21**, 106–112.

Hain, J. D., Graham, R. N. Jr., Mouton, J. S. and Blake, R. R. (1956). Stimulus and background factors in petition signing, *Southwest Social Science Quarterly*, **36**, 385–390.

Hardy, K. R. (1957). Determinants of conformity and attitude change, *Journal of Abnormal and Social Psychology*, **54**, 287–294.

Hare, A. P. (1965). *Handbook of Small Group Research*. Free Press of Glencoe, New York.

Hare, A. P. and Bales, R. F. (1965). Seating position and small group interaction, *Sociometry*, **28**, 480–486.

Harvey, O. J. and Consalvi, C. (1960). Status and conformity to pressure in informal groups, *Journal of Abnormal and Social Psychology*, **60**, 182–187.

Heider, F. (1958). *The Psychology of Interpersonal Relations*. John Wiley, New York.

Hewgill, M. A. and Miller, G. R. (1965). Source credibility and response to fear-arousing communication, *Speech Monographs*, **32**, 95–101.

Hirschman, A. O. (1970). *Exit Voice and Loyalty*. Harvard University Press, Cambridge.

Hochbaum, G. H. (1954). The relation between the group member's self-confidence and their reaction to group pressure to uniformity. *American Sociological Review*, **19**, 678–687.

Hollander, E. P. (1960). Competence and conformity in the acceptance of influence. *Journal of Abnormal and Social Psychology*, **61**, 360–365.

Hollander, E. P. (1958). Conformity, status and idiosyncrasy credit, *Psychological Review*, **65**, 117, 127.

Hollander, E. P. (1964). *Leaders, Groups, and Influence*. Oxford University Press, New York.

Hollander, E. P. (1967). *Principles and Methods of Social Psychology*. Oxford University Press, New York.

Homans, G. G. (1961). *Social Behavior, its Elementary Forms*. Harcourt, Brace, and World, New York.

Hovland, C. I., Janis, I. L. and Kelley, H. H. (1953). *Communication and Persuasion*. Yale University Press, New Haven.

Hovland, C., Lumsdaine, A. A. and Sheffield, F. D. (1949). *Experiments on Mass Communication*. Princeton University Press, Princeton.

Jackson, J. M. and Saltzenstein, M. D. (1958). The effect of person-group relationships on conformity processes, *Journal of Abnormal and Social Psychology*, **57**, 17–24.

Jones, E. (1961). *The Life and Work of Sigmund Freud*. Basic Books, New York.

Jones, E. E. (1965). Conformity as a tactic of ingratiation, *Science*, **149**, 144–150.

Jones, E. E., Bell, L. and Aronson, E. (1971). The reciprocation of attraction from similar and dissimilar others: a study in person perception and evaluation. *In* McClintock, C. G. (ed.), *Experimental Social Psychology*, pp 142–183. Holt, Rinehart and Winston, New York.

Jones, E. E. and Gerard, H. B. (1967). *Foundations of Social Psychology*. John Wiley, New York.

Kelley, H. H. (1967). Attribution theory in social psychology. *In* Levine, L. (ed.), *Nebraska Symposium Motivation*. University of Nebraska Press, Lincoln.

Kelley, H. H. and Lamb, T. W. (1957). Certainty of judgment and resistance to social influence, *Journal of Abnormal and Social Psychology*, **55**, 137–139.

Kelley, H. H. and Shapiro, M. M. (1954). An experiment on conformity to group norms where conformity is detrimental to group achievement, *American Sociological Review*, **19**, 667–677.

Kelley, H. H. and Thibaut, J. W. (1968). Group problem-solving. *In* Lindzey, G. and Aronson, E. (eds), *Handbook of Social Psychology*. Addison-Wesley, Reading, Mass.

Kiesler, C. A. (1969). Group pressure and conformity. *In* Mills, J. (ed.), *Experimental Social Psychology*, pp. 235–306. Macmillan, New York.

Kiesler, C. A. and Kiesler, S. B. (1969). *Conformity*. Addison-Wesley, Reading, Mass.

Kiesler, C. A. and Pallak, M. S. (1975). Minority influence: the effect of majority reactionaries and defectors, and minority and majority compromisers, upon majority opinion and attraction. *European Journal of Social Psychology*, **5**(2), 237–256.

Kuhn, T. (1962). *The Structure of Scientific Revolutions*. University of Chicago, Chicago.

Lage, E. (1973). *Innovation et influence minoritaire*. Thèse de 3ème cycle, Université de Paris VII (Miméo).

Lemaine, G. (1966). Inégalité, comparaison, incomparabilité: esquisse d'une théorie de l'originalité sociale. *Bulletin de Psychologie*, **20**, 24–32.

Lemaine, G. (1974). Social differentiation and social originality. *European Journal of Social Psychology*, **4**(1), 17–52.

Levinger, G. (1959). The development of perceptions and behavior in newly formed social power relationships. *In* Carthwright, D. (ed.), *Studies in Social Power*, pp. 83–98. University of Michigan, Ann Arbor.

Lewin, K. (1948). *Resolving Social Conflicts*. Harper, New York.

Lindskold, S. and Tedeschi, J. T. (1970). Threatening and conciliatory influence attempts as a function of source's perception of own competence in conflict situation. Mimeographed manuscript, State University of New York at Albany.

Linton, H. and Graham, E. (1959). Personality correlates of persuasibility. *In* Hovland, E. and Janis, I., (eds), *Personality and Persuasibility*. Yale University Press, New Haven.

Lippit, R., Polansky, N., Redl, F. and Rosen, S. (1952). The dynamics of power, *Human Relations*, **5**, 37–64.

McGinnies, E. (1970). *Social Behavior, Functional Analysis*. Houghton-Mifflin, New York.

Mann, R. D. (1959). A review of the relationships between personality and performance in small groups, *Psychological Bulletin*, **56**, 241–270.

Mausner, B. (1954). The effect of prior reinforcement on the interaction of observer pairs, *Journal of Abnormal and Social Psychology*, **49**, 65–68.

Meunier, C. and Rule, B. G. (1967). Anxiety, confidence and conformity. *Journal of Personality*, **35**, 498–504.

Milgram, S. (1956). Group pressure and action against a person, *Journal of Abnormal and Social Psychology*, **25**, 115–129.

Milgram, S. (1965). Liberation effects of group pressure, *Journal of Personality and Social Psychology*, **1**, 127–134.

Milgram, S. *Obedience to Authority*. Harper and Row, New York.

Millman, S. (1968). Anxiety, comprehension and susceptibility to social influence. *Journal of Personality and Social Psychology*, **9**, 251–256.

Mills, J., and Jellison, J. M. (1967). Effect of opinion change of how desirable the communication is to the audience the communicator addressed. *Journal of Personality and Social Psychology*, **6**, 98–101.

Moeller, G. and Applezweig, M. M. (1957). A motivational factor in conformity, *Journal of Abnormal and Social Psychology*, **55**, 114–120.

Moscovici, S. (1968). *Essai sur l'histoire humaine de la nature*. Flammarion, Paris.

Moscovici, S. and Faucheux, C. (1972). Social influence, conformity bias, and the study of active minorities. *In* Berkowitz, L. (ed.), *Advances in Experimental Social Psychology*, Vol. 6, pp. 149–202. Academic Press, New York and London.

Moscovici, S. and Lage, E. (1975). Comparaison de l'influence majoritaire et de l'influence minoritaire dans un groupe. *European Journal of Social Psychology* (in press).

Moscovici, S., Lage, E. and Naffrechoux, M. (1969). Influence of a consistent minority on the responses of a majority in a color perception task, *Sociometry*, **32**, 365–379.

Moscovici, S. and Lage, E. (1975). L'influence minoritaire dans un contexte d'originalité des jugements(in press).

Moscovici, S. and Nemeth, C. (1974). Social influence II: Minority influence. *In* Nemeth C. (ed.), *Social Psychology: classic and contemporary integrations*, pp 217–250. Rand McNally College Publishing Company, Chicago.

Moscovici, S. and Neve P. (1971). Studies in social influence: I. Those absent are in the right: convergence and polarization of answers in the course of a social interaction. *European Journal of Social Psychology*, **1**(2), 201–213.

Mouton, J. S., Blake, R. R. and Olmstead, J. A. (1956). The relationship between frequency of yielding and the disclosure of personal identity, *Journal of Personality*, **24**(3), 339–347.

Mugny, G. (1973). *Négociation et influence minoritaire*. (Miméo) E.P.S.E. Université de Genève.

Mugny, G. (1974a). Importance de la consistance dans l'influence de communications minoritaires "congruentes" et "incongruentés" sur des jugements opinions. Genève (Miméo).

Mugny, G. (1974b). Notes sur le style de comportement rigide. (Miméo) Genève.

Mugny, G. (1974c). Majorité et minorité: le niveau de leur influence (Miméo) Genève.

Mugny, G., Humbert, B. and Zubel, R. (1973). Le style d'interaction comme facteur de l'influence sociale, *Bulletin de Psychologie*, **26**, 789–793.

Mulder, M. (1960). The power variable in communication experiments, *Human Relations*, **13**, 241–257.

Myers, M. T. and Goldberg, A. A. (1970). Group credibility and opinion change. *Journal of Communication*, **20**, 174–179.

Nemeth, C. and Endicott, J. (1974). The midpoint as an anchor: another look at discrepancy of position and attitude change (Miméo).

Nemeth, C. and Swedlund, M. and Kanki, B. (1974). Patterning of the minority's responses and their influence on the majority. *European Journal of Social Psychology*, **(4–I)**, 53–64.

Nemeth, C. and Wachtler, J. (1973). Consistency and modification of judgment. *Journal of Experimental Social Psychology*, **9**, 65–79.

Nemeth, C. and Wachtler, J. (1973a). Five angry men: the deviate as a source of influence in a simulated jury trial (Miméo).

Newcomb, T. M., Turner, R. H. and Converse, P. E. (1964). *Social Psychology*. Holt, Rinehert and Winston, New York.

Nord, W. R. (1969). Social exchange theory: an integrative approach to social conformity, *Psychological Bulletin*, **71**, 174–208.

Nunnally, J. and Hussek, T. R. (1958). The phony language examination: an approach to the measurement of response bias. *Educational and Psychological Measurement*, **18**, 275–282.

Paicheler, G. *Normes et changement d'attitudes: de la modification des attitudes envers les femmes* (Miméo). Thèse de 3ème cycle, Université de Paris VII, 1974.

Paicheler, G. and Bouchet, Y. (1973). Attitude polarisation, familiarisation, and group process. *European Journal of Social Psychology*, **3** (1), 83–90.

Powell, F. A. and Miller, G. R. (1967). Social approval and disapproval cues in anxiety—arousing communications, *Speech Monographs*, **34**, 152–159.

Raven, B. H. (1959). Social influence on opinions and the communication of related content, *Journal of Abnormal and Social Psychology*, **58**, 119–128.

Ricateau, P. (1971). Processus de catégorisation d'autrui et les mécanismes d'influence. *Bulletin de Psychologie*, **24**, 909–919.

Riecken, H. W. (1952). Some problems of consensus and development. *Rural Sociology*, **17**, 245–252.

Rommetweit, R. (1954). *Social Norms and Roles*. Oslo University Press, Oslo.

Rosenberg, L. A. (1963). Conformity as a function of confidence in self and confidence in partner. *Human Relations*, **16**, 131–141.

Rosenthal, D. and Cofer, C. N. (1948). The effect on group performance of an indifferent and neglectful attitude shown by one group member, *Journal of Experiment Psychology*, **38**, 568–577.

Rosner, S. (1957). Consistency in response to group pressures. *Journal of Abnormal and Social Psychology*, **55**, 145–146.

Samelson, F. (1957). Conforming behavior under two conditions of conflict in the cognitive field, *Journal of Abnormal and Social Psychology*, **55**, 181–187.

Schachter, S. (1951). Deviation, rejection, and communication, *Journal of Abnormal and Social Psychology*, **46**, 190–207.

Schank, R. L. (1932). A study of a community and its groups and institutions conceived of as behaviors of individuals, *Psychological Monographs*, **43** (2).

Science for the People, 1973, July.

Secord, P. F. and Backman, C. W. (1964). *Social Psychology*. McGraw-Hill, New York.

Shaw, M. E. (1963). Some effects of varying amounts of information exclusively possessed by a group member upon his behavior to the group, *Journal of Genetic Psychology*, **68**, 71–79.

Sherif, M. and Hovland, C. I. (1961). *Social Judgment*. Yale University Press, New Haven.

Sherif, M. and Sherif, C. (1969). *Social Psychology*. Harper and Row, New York.

Shrauger, J. S. and Jones, S. C. (1968). Social validation and interpersonal evaluations, *Journal of Experimental Social Psychology*, **4**, 315–323.

Sigall, H. (1970). The effect of competition and consensual validation on a communicator's liking for the audience. *Journal of Personality and Social Psychology*, **16**, 251–258.

Singer, J. E. and Schokley, V. C. (1965). Ability and affiliation, *Journal of Personality and Social Psychology*, **1**, 95–100.

Smith, C. E. (1936). A study of the automatic excitation resulting from the interaction of individual opinions and group opinion, *Journal of Abnormal and Social Psychology*, **30**, 138–164.

Smith, K. H. and Richards, B. (1967). Effects of a rational appeal and of anxiety on conformity behavior. *Journal of Personality and Social Psychology*, **5**, 122–126.

Smith, R. J. (1967). Exploration in non-conformity. *Journal of Social Psychology*, **71**, 133–150.

Sperling, H. G. (1952). *In* Asch, S. E. *Social Psychology*. Prentice Hall, New York.

Steiner, I. D. (1966). Personality and the resolution of inter-personal disagreements. *In* Maher, B. A. (ed.), *Progress in Experimental Personality Research*, Vol. 3, Academic Press, New York and London.

Strickland, B. R. (1965). The prediction of social action from a dimension of internal-external control. *Journal of Social Psychology*, **66**, 353–358.

Strickland, B. R., and Crowne, D. P. (1962). Conformity under conditions of simulated group pressure as a function of the need for social approval, *Journal of Social Psychology*, **58**, 171–181.

Strodtbeck, F. L. and Hook, L. H. (1961). The social dimensions of a twelve-man jury table. *Sociometry*, **24**, 397–415.

Tajfel, H. (1972). "La catégorisation sociale", *In* Moscovici, S. (ed.), *Introduction à la psychologie sociale*, Vol. 1, pp 272–303. Larousse, Paris.

Taylor, H. F. (1969). *Balance in Small Groups*. Van Nostrand-Reinhold Company, New York.

Thibaut, J. and Strickland, L. M. (1956). Psychological set and social conformity, *Journal of Personality*, **25**, 115–129.

Torrance, E. P. (1959). The influence of experienced members of small groups on the behavior of the inexperienced, *Journal of Social Psychology*, **49**, 249–257.

Veroff, J. (1957). Development and validation of a projective measure of power motivation. *Journal of Abnormal and Social Psychology*, **54**, 1–8.

Wahrman, R. and Pugh, M. D. (1972). Competence and conformity: Another Look at Hollander's Study. *Sociometry*, **35**, 376–386.

Walster, E. and Abrahams, D. (1972). Interpersonal attraction and social influence. *In* Tedeschi, J. T. (ed.), *The Social Influence Processes*, pp 197–238. Aldine Atherton, Chicago.

Walster, E., Aronson, E., and Abrahams, D. (1966). On increasing the persuasiveness of a low prestige communicator, *Journal of Experimental Social Psychology*, **2**, 325–342.

Ziller, R. C. and Behringer, R. D. (1960). Assimilation of the knowledge newcomer under conditions of group success and failure. *Journal of Abnormal and Social Psychology*, **60**, 288–291.

Zimbardo, P. G. (1960). Involvement and communication discrepancy as determinants of opinion conformity, *Journal of Abnormal and Social Psychology*, **60**, 86–94.

Author Index

Subject Index